CLASSIC ASIAN RICE

Lee Geok Boi

mc Marshall Cavendish
Cuisine

Editor: Lydia Leong
Designer: Bernard Go Kwang Meng
Photographer: Kiyoshi Yoshizawa, Jambu Studio

Copyright © 2010 Marshall Cavendish International (Asia) Private Limited

Published by Marshall Cavendish Cuisine
An imprint of Marshall Cavendish International
1 New Industrial Road, Singapore 536196

Other Marshall Cavendish Offices:

Marshall Cavendish International. PO Box 65829 London EC1P 1NY, UK
• Marshall Cavendish Corporation. 99 White Plains Road, Tarrytown
NY 10591-9001, USA • Marshall Cavendish International (Thailand) Co
Ltd. 253 Asoke, 12th Flr, Sukhumvit 21 Road, Klongtoey Nua, Wattana,
Bangkok 10110, Thailand • Marshall Cavendish (Malaysia) Sdn Bhd,
Times Subang, Lot 46, Subang Hi-Tech Industrial Park, Batu Tiga,
40000 Shah Alam, Selangor Darul Ehsan, Malaysia

Marshall Cavendish is a trademark of Times Publishing Limited

National Library Board, Singapore Cataloguing-in-Publication Data

Lee, Geok Boi.
Classic Asian rice /¬ Lee Geok Boi. – Singapore : Marshall Cavendish
Cuisine,¬ c2010.
p. cm.
Includes bibliographical references and indexes.
ISBN-13 : 978-981-4302-02-9

1. Cookery (Rice) 2. Cookery, Asian. I. Title.

TX809.R5
641.6318 -- dc22   OCN613267744

Printed in Malaysia by Times Offset (M) Sdn Bhd

DEDICATION

This cookbook would not be possible without the numerous cooks and foodie bloggers worldwide who delight in talking about their favourite dishes, sharing their recipes and passing on cooking tips to anyone who cares to listen, read their cookbooks, recipes and tips or watch them doing their thing on the Internet. Thank you for sharing.

This book is also dedicated to my friends who ate my experiments with relish on the whole, to my parents, Lee Thian Leong and Goh Eng Thye, who ate them unwittingly, as well as my daughters, Shakun who ate enthusiastically, and Savitri who ate cautiously; to my son-in-law Tom who found that some of the new flavours were actually quite good; and to my grandsons, Arjuna and Rama, in the hope that one day they will enjoy rice with more flavours than just plain boiled, coconut rice or chicken rice. May their rice bowls never be empty!

CONTENTS

RICE PORRIDGES AND RICE SOUPS 169

RICE DESSERTS AND RICE SNACKS 193

GLOSSARY 230

BIBLIOGRAPHY 240

INDEX BY COUNTRY 242

INDEX OF BASIC RECIPES 244

INTRODUCTION

In Asia, rice is synonymous with food and this is reflected in Asian languages and cultures. In China, a standard greeting amongst friends is "Have you eaten rice yet?" In Thailand and China, when you invite someone to sit down to a meal, you ask them to "eat rice". In several Asian languages, there are several words for rice from uncooked to various kinds of cooked rice and rice preparations. In Chinese, uncooked rice is called *mi* while cooked rice is *fan*. In Malay, cooked rice is *nasi* and uncooked milled rice is *beras* while unmilled rice is *padi*. In Hindi, *bhaat* means cooked rice and *chamal* is uncooked. Rice is central in almost all Asian cuisines, and in many parts of West Asia, rice makes up special meals. Imagine Indian curries without rice or Indonesian *rijstaffel* without rice. The Dutch word *rijstaffel* itself means "rice table". There are different words for different types of classic rice preparations. Words like pilaf, biryani, sushi and porridge conjure up specific expectations and specific preparations. Think "pilaf" or "biryani" and you have a vision of a platter of rice flavoured richly and cooked elaborately. There are famous Asian rice meals with special names and configurations of side dishes. *Nasi lemak* in Malay means "rich rice". In Malay and Straits Chinese cuisines, the rich rice is prepared with slightly different side dishes. Indonesian *nasi tumpeng* is a Javanese ritual meal prepared with different combinations of dishes for different occasions to be displayed round a mound of yellow rice that has been shaped into a cone (*tumpeng*). The choice of dishes and the number depend on the event that is being marked.

A signboard seen in many Singapore hawker centres and food courts is "Rice with Mixed Vegetables". The signboard announces that that food stall serves rice with assorted side dishes with the assortment always including meat and seafood and not just vegetables. The term "mixed vegetables" arose from the Chinese term for "side dishes eaten with rice" which can also mean "vegetables", hence its literal translation into English as "rice with mixed vegetables". *Nasi rames* or *nasi champur* (rice mix) is Indonesia's version of Singapore's "rice with mixed vegetables". Malaysia's *nasi kandar*, on the other hand, is an Indian Muslim rice meal with Indian Muslim-style curries and vegetables while Singapore's "banana leaf rice" is rice and Indian curries served on banana leaves, and Indonesian *nasi Padang* is rice served with curries and vegetables cooked in the style of Padang in Sumatra. Padang-style curries of meat, seafood and vegetables are rich in coconut milk and chilli. The name of the rice meal comes from the kind of side dishes served with the rice as well as the way it is prepared.

Such specific kinds of rice meals have interesting origins. Malaysia's *nasi kandar*, the common man's rice meal served in roadside food stalls and coffee shops, is said to have originated in Penang, Malaysia, where a large Indian Muslim community built up in the wake of 19th century British colonisation. The South Indian Muslims brought with them their ways of preparing meat, seafood and vegetables, ways that were naturally influenced to some extent by long years of association with Malay cuisine. In the north Malaysian state of Perlis, this Indian Muslim-style rice and curries meal is called *nasi ganja*, *ganja* being the Malay word for cannabis. However, there is no cannabis in *nasi ganja*. Perhaps it is a corruption of the word *kandar* which itself refers to the pole on which hawkers of old balanced two large containers of food hawking them from place to place. Traditionally, *nasi kandar* consists of a big plate of rice with assorted curries piled on top, giving a meal that varied in taste depending on the curries you ordered. This piling up of side dishes on top of plain boiled rice is seen in rice-eating cultures practically throughout Asia. In Iran, a number of classic stews are always served on top of boiled rice. In Nepal, there is *dhal bhaat*, *dhal* being the curried lentils that is always poured on rice (*bhaat*) no matter what other side dishes there may be.

Traditional Asian cuisines evolved as accompaniments to plain boiled rice. Scarce amounts of meat could be stretched further when eaten with plenty of rice and vegetables. In many parts of Asia, meat was (and still is) served only on special occasions and celebrations. Thus developed fragrant, tangy salads and spicy hot curries to be eaten with plain boiled rice. While such rice meals are everyday affairs, not so the pilafs first developed in Persia, a land of plenty with a wide range of tasty fruit, nuts, herbs and vegetables and grains like wheat and rice. With food security came civilisation, military power and political outreach. The Persian Empire was established by Cyrus the Great in 6th century BCE, an empire that stretched across eastern Iraq, Afghanistan and parts of Pakistan as well as the eastern half of Turkey. The spread of Islam and Arab influence from 537 CE gave rise to an Islamic civilisation that owed much to the adoption by the less sophisticated Arabs of the more developed Persian culture with its interest in food and wine. Spices and other exotic ingredients came from far afield. Trade between Persia, China and India go back many centuries. Persia was part of the ancient Silk Road. Medieval Arab cookbooks owe their inspiration to the Persian court practice of compiling luxurious and fashionable dishes into cookbooks. The wealthy commissioned cookbooks and organised cooking contests. Persian food culture has had a tremendous influence on the way rice is cooked and served to this day. In Persia, rice developed into a specialty for feasts and celebrations, a status that *polo* or pilaf still enjoys today.

The taste for firm grain and ways to produce it developed in the 12th century. The Persians came up with a way of cooking rice that got rid of all surface starch to get cooked rice grains that are tender yet firm and well-separated. The taste for this kind of high-quality rice remains to this day in Iran, the modern name for Persia. Cooking rice in this way, then boiling it with stock and spices, and layering and infusing the flavours to get pilafs was just another step towards getting tender, separated grains of rice. The wide variety of dried and fresh fruit, nuts, herbs and spices such as saffron, made the blending of these ingredients into the sweet-sour flavours in Persian rice dishes natural.

The 13th century Mongol invasion of Persia would take these pilafs to India. When the Persian-acculturated Mongols, now known as Mughals, swept into India in the 16th century and established Mughal rule, they brought with them the rich pilafs that so many of us think of as Indian. Although Indian biryanis have changed over time into spicier versions and with less of the fruit, one surviving Mughal India cookbook, *Nuskha-e-Shahjahani: Pulaos from the Royal Kitchen of Shah Jahan*, shows the Persian origins of Mughal pilafs with the liberal use of fruit and nuts with meat and intense sweet and sour flavours. (Shah Jehan was the Mughal emperor who built the Taj Mahal to immortalise his love for his queen, Mumtaz Mahal.) In South and West Asia and indeed many parts of Indianised Southeast Asia, the royal status of pilafs has remained to this day. It is still the quintessential rice dish prepared for special occasions and festive meals, the effort of preparing it being the best indication that the guests who feast on it are indeed honoured guests. The West, South and Southeast Asian taste for rich pilafs contrast interestingly with the Japanese culinary reverence for plain boiled rice, yet another facet of the island-nation's preference for basic and natural flavours seen in their passion for all kinds of raw and lightly dressed food. Unlike the West Asian taste for nicely separated grains, the Japanese like their rice sticky and white glutinous rice has an important place in festive meals, making its appearance as mochi in Japanese New Year celebrations and as *sekihan*, a preparation of glutinous rice and adzuki beans.

RICE, ITS ORIGINS AND ITS PLACE IN CULTURE

Even before the beginning of recorded history, rice has been eaten in Asia. However, its origins and where it was first domesticated remains in doubt. Archaeological work has uncovered both long-grain (*indica*) and short-grain (*japonica*) rice remains that go back thousands of years. Rice remains have been found in China, Thailand, the Philippines, as well as India. It is more than likely that there are discoveries still to be made buried in caves, lakes and fields wherever rice is still being eaten in large quantities. That wild grasses developed into Asian rice (*Oryza sativa*) is not in doubt; there was a parallel development with African rice (*Oryza glaberrima*). It is a fact that rice came to be cultivated as a grain in different areas at points in time that go back thousands of years. In Asia, this beltway where rice became domesticated stretches from India to southern China through mainland Southeast Asia, all areas where large quantities of rice are still consumed and grown today. Rice, being a plant that likes wet feet, is said to have spread along the course of rivers east and west of its original sites of development. Today, there are more than 12,000 varieties of rice according to the International Rice Research Institute (IRRI) website and rice cultivation has since spread all over the world. IRRI reports that rice is cultivated in six of the seven continents with the exception of Antarctica and in more than 100 countries. From as high as 3,000 m (9,842 ft) above sea level in the Himalaya to the temperate zones of Japan, Korea, US and the deserts of Australia and Egypt, rice is now grown. According to IRRI's Rice Almanac, it is the world's most important economic activity, feeding the largest number of people in the world, and eaten by more than half the world's population.

By virtue of its ability to sustain human beings and human civilisation, rice and the mystique surrounding its origins and continued ability to feed people have become entrenched in the cultures of numerous rice-eating cultures. The more important rice is to the economy and diet, the deeper its roots in the culture. Rice is often depicted as the sacred gift of a goddess to humans. Offerings of rice and rice cakes are made to the gods and goddesses in many rice-eating cultures. In Bali, regular offerings are made to Dewi Sri, the goddess who gave the Balinese rice. Thailand's rice goddess is known as Mae Posop, revered as the goddess of agricultural abundance. In parts of Thailand, the first grains of a new harvest are offered up to the temple. The Hindu goddess of wealth and prosperity, Lakshmi, is also the goddess of rice. South Indians call her Annalakshmi, "Anna" meaning food and "Lakshmi" wealth. Rice is the staple in South India with wheat breads being more usual in the north. Interestingly, northern Indians tend to prepare elaborate rich pilafs for celebratory meals, harking back to Mughal times. The South Indian harvest festival, Pongal, also known as Sankaranthi, is celebrated with the ritual cooking of rice that must overflow the pot to signify abundance. The deities honoured during Pongal are Indra, the God of Rains, Surya the Sun God, and the sacred cow. Rain, sun and draught animals for ploughing the paddy fields are key elements in successful rice cultivation.

In Japan, rice was once used as legal tender, with the worth of samurais measured in rice. Like many rice-growing countries, Japan still practises various annual rituals centring on rice. One is the annual spring rice-planting ritual which the emperor presides over at the imperial rice-field in the palace grounds in Tokyo. At harvest-time, he performs a thanksgiving ritual which features rice from all over Japan offered to the imperial household. The high status that traditional Japanese give to rice is best seen in its appearance at the end of a formal dinner as nothing more than a bowl of plain boiled rice accompanied by little more than some pickles and a light soup. The flavour of the pearly-white sticky rice is not to be diluted by oil or meat. In the past, rice was too precious to be eaten every day at every meal. Instead the daily fare consisted of mixed grains known as *gokoku* boiled into a porridge called *okayu*. Given the high status of plain boiled rice, many Japanese are willing to pay high prices for well-flavoured home-grown rice. A kilogramme of top-grade short-grain rice from a fancied region in Japan can cost more than S$10 compared to the couple of dollars for Australian or US short-grain. So particular are the Japanese about the quality of their cooked rice—and the way it must be served warm—that it is no wonder that they came up with the first rice cooker.

Most of the rice grown in the world today is grown in the flood-prone areas of Asia and much of the rice grown is consumed in Asia as well. More than half the world's population of some 6.8 billion people—or some 4.2 billion people—eat about 90 per cent of the world's crop of rice. How much does each Asian eat? In 1999, the annual consumption of rice in Iran was nearly 30 kg (66 lb) per person. Iran is West Asia's biggest consumer of rice followed by Iraq. Compare the Iranian statistic to Turkey's 7.2 kg or Thailand's 100.8 kg per person for the same period. Rice is eaten not just as a daily staple but also consumed in other forms such as rice crackers, rice cereals, puffed rice, rice flakes, rice wine, rice breads, rice snacks, and other rice-based or partially rice-based food products. Rice is easy to store, easy to cook and easy to digest. It takes less effort, time and fuel to boil a pot of rice than to prepare a loaf of bread. It is also filling, easily eaten and digested by young and old, the sick and the healthy. It is nutritious especially if left unmilled, although white rice is the most common form consumed by the majority of rice eaters. Unmilled or brown rice is, however, becoming increasingly popular, as indicated by the wider variety of brown rice available in supermarkets. Brown rice is high in complex carbohydrates, has a fair amount of protein with all eight amino acids as well as vitamins and minerals such as vitamin D, calcium, fibre, thiamin, niacin, iron and riboflavin. An increase in the popularity of brown rice can only improve the nutrition of billions of Asians who still form the bulk of the poor in the world and whose nutritional needs are not being supplied by milled rice. One interesting statistic that some analysts trot out is that rice is becoming increasingly popular in non-traditional rice-eating countries such as the United States, Europe and Australia. Even if rice is not eaten daily, it is often on the menu in one form or other, be it fried rice or rice pudding. Paradoxically, as many parts of Asia go up the developmental ladder, the place of rice in their diet becomes less important. Traditional rice-eating countries are eating less rice even as non-traditional rice-eating countries are eating more. This decline in rice consumption because of the availability of more food choices and a growing taste for other staples does not signal any significant decrease in demand for rice. Billions still depend on rice. Continuing population increases will keep the demand for rice ever upwards.

TYPES OF RICE AND COOKING CHARACTERISTICS

Asian rice in general goes by the botanical name of *Oryza sativa*. The basic types of *O. sativa* that concern cooks are short-grain rice (*Oryza sativa subsp japonica*), long-grain (*Oryza sativa subsp indica*), with an in-between medium-short-grain that taxonomists are inclined to refer to as *javanica*, and glutinous rice (*Oryza sativa var. glutinosa* or *Oryza glutinosa*), also known as sweet or sticky rice which is widely eaten in Southeast Asia in desserts and snacks as well as being a staple in Laos and northeast Thailand. Where the cook is concerned, the categorisation of rice has to do with its cooking characteristics: short-grain tends to be stickier than long-grain, and glutinous rice the stickiest of all. To add to the confusion, some short-grain types are labelled medium-grain. But it does not matter what it is called so long as the rice has a texture that you enjoy. You can even use short-grain to make a pilaf if that is what you like best—as Indian restaurants in Japan do because that is the way the Japanese like their rice. The most important thing is to know the cooking characteristics of your rice. There are also specialty rice that require special handling. Black medium-grain rice and black glutinous rice need not only pre-soaking but longer boiling as they are unmilled rice with their bran layer still on. Chinese black medium-grain is also known as forbidden rice presumably because only the emperor was allowed to eat this unusual rice according to legend. Black medium-grain rice and black glutinous rice are not the same although they look alike and can even smell alike when it is being cooked. Black medium-grain does not have the glossy look of black glutinous rice. When buying black medium-grain or black glutinous rice, look carefully at the labels as both types of black rice look identical. A quick troll on the Internet shows that there are a number of different types of black rice grown in different countries. Black rice whether medium-grain or glutinous is not actually jet-black but rather a dark black-purple-red colour. North American wild rice (*Zizania aquatica*) is not a rice at all despite its name, although in colour, if not appearance, it resembles black rice.

Rice can also be categorised by the stage of milling and treatment of the rice. Rough rice or paddy has the kernels still within the hull or husk. The hull must be removed by milling or pounding before the rice is packed or cooked. Brown rice is rice with only the hull removed, the bran layer remains. Brown rice may be cooked as it is or milled into white rice. The bran layer is especially rich in B-complex vitamins as well as in fibre and minerals. When the bran layer is milled till the rice is white, it becomes milled white rice or polished rice. The very popular Thai jasmine rice is noted for its silky polished grains. Parboiled rice is when rough rice or paddy is pressure-steamed with the husk on to yield a more firm and more separated grain when cooked. The pressure-steaming also drives vitamins and minerals into the kernels. Enriched rice is cleaned white rice with various nutrients added to it during packaging. This type of rice should be cooked straight out of the packet according to the instructions on its packaging. Lastly, there is pre-cooked or instant rice which can be either brown or white rice. Pre-cooked rice is completely cooked rice which has been dehydrated. Like enriched rice, instant rice, which is sometimes called converted rice, must not be rinsed but rehydrated according to the instructions on the packet. Enriched and instant

rice are rare in Asia, the majority of Asians cooking their rice from scratch.

Another way of categorising rice is by age: new or aged rice. New rice cooks differently from aged rice. Ageing rice is supposed to affect the texture. Newly harvested rice or "new rice" is more starchy and the cooked grains are more sticky. New rice is popularly used for making porridge where long-grain is the more usual daily fare. Bulk packs of Thai jasmine rice sold in the US are sometimes marked "new harvest" although I have found that even when they are not so-labelled, they are stickier than Thai jasmine rice bought in Singapore. The Thai jasmine label may be the same but the rice is clearly not the same. The premium aged rice is basmati which comes from the Punjab region of either India or Pakistan. It is aged for at least a year. Basmati keeps uncommonly well. I once kept a bag of basmati for close to five years and the rice still tasted great when I got round to cooking it. Basmati also cooks uncommonly well, yielding lovely separated grains of thin, long grains of rice, making it perfect for pilafs. Although this cannot be said of basmati, in general rice differs from bag to bag, with some needing more or less water to get your desired results. The only way to find out how that fresh bag of rice will cook is to prepare a small amount of the rice plain before using it to make a pilaf. Rice is a very forgiving grain and the amount of water is easily adjusted once you know what suits your taste.

One way of categorising rice is by aroma such as Thai jasmine or fragrant rice. Aromatic rice of which there are several varieties has an appetising fragrance obvious when the rice is being cooked and if the rice is served hot soon after cooking. The smell disappears when the rice turns cold. Some popular types of aromatic rice are Thai jasmine rice, basmati, texmati (US-grown basmati-type rice), Uncle Ben's Aromatic, Konriko and wild pecan rice. Black medium-grain rice and black glutinous are aromatic rice and can have a stronger fragrance than even Thai jasmine rice. In recent years, however, the black glutinous rice purchased in Singapore does not seem to be as fragrant as I remember it to be. Perhaps new types are entering the market. When I was young, its fragrance always told me to expect *pulot hitam* for dessert.

HOW A RICE MEAL IS EATEN

The dining space may be a large platter on the ground, a platter on a carpet, dishes on a low table with diners seated on the floor or a regular Western-style dining table with seating on chairs. The one common feature is that most Asian meals are eaten communal style with a set of shared dishes. West Asians even eat out of the same platter, the rice being heaped with meat and sauces and guests helping themselves to the same platter in unison. Before eating, the Arabic word "*Bismallah*" is said in praise of Allah and to give thanks for the food in the same way that many devout Christians give thanks before starting a meal. As long as the meal is not over, "*Bismallah*" may be said to bless the food. In general, from East to West Asia, the host always helps his guests to the choicest parts of the food. In West Asia, the host does not eat with his guests but rather spends his time seeing that his guests get the best bits and eat well. As eating with fingers is the usual West Asian way, the host would be unable to perform this duty of serving his guests if he were to soil his fingers by eating with them. Where chopsticks are used, food is taken from the communal dishes with a serving spoon. If the dining is formal, individual serving spoons are laid out that are to be used only for scooping from the communal dish, and each guest will have a side plate for placing his serving of food. Individual eating spoons are never dipped into the communal dish. Whether food is eaten with the fingers as in South Asia or with fork and spoon as in parts of Southeast Asia, food from the communal dish is always scooped out with the serving spoon and never taken with fingers or the individual eating spoon. In India, there is also another way of serving a meal that obviates the need for serving spoons or at least not individual ones. A wedding feast or a meal in a restaurant may be served on banana leaves whether eaten seated on the floor or at a table. In Singapore, "banana leaf rice" refers to restaurants that serve South Indian curries and rice on banana leaves. When you sit down for a meal at a "banana leaf" restaurant or at an Indian wedding feast, the first thing that is placed in front of you is a large banana leaf. In restaurants that offer a standard meal, there is no need to order. You get a generous helping of rice, a few pieces of poppadom and one or two chutneys. The servers come around with buckets of vegetable curries and you say yes or no to what is there. You can also ask for extra items such as *thyroo* (yoghurt) or *resam* (pepper water). The price would be the same whether or not you had the second or third helping of rice or curries. The signal to the servers that you are done is when you fold over your banana leaf. One possible reason for the original use of banana leaves was the avoidance of ritual contamination arising from Hinduism's caste system. The leaves are discarded after use and everyone gets a fresh leaf. Another reason was probably practical. Someone celebrating a wedding or a birth could feed friends and neighbours without having to invest in crockery or cutlery as the meal is eaten with fingers. In markets in India, you see huge piles of banana leaves for sale. Other leaves are substituted where banana leaves are less common. Once while on a trek in Nepal, I came across some women plucking very large green leaves and learnt that they were preparing for a wedding and the leaves were the dinner plates. So popular is eating from a banana leaf in Indian culture that there are now plates made in the shape of a banana leaf! As an aside, hot rice on a banana leaf always tastes special.

Communal-style eating in Asia has some implied courtesies. If food is eaten with just the fingers or if the palm is also used, only the right hand must be used as the left hand is assumed to be the hand used for cleaning after defaecation. There is also a Muslim belief that the left hand is the hand that Satan uses to eat and drink with. When eating from a common platter West Asian-style, guests eat the food nearest to them. It is considered rude to reach for choice bits at the top or in another corner of the platter. Hence the role of the host in seeing that the choice bits are put in front of his guests. To eat with fingers, the rice, meat and gravy are shaped into a small ball and the ball pushed into the mouth with the thumb without the fingers touching the lips. In chopsticks-wielding countries, the chopsticks do not enter the mouth either. The rice is pushed into the mouth by bringing the rice bowl close to the lips, if eaten Chinese-style. Bits of meat and vegetables are pushed in at the same time. The more delicate and formal way is to place a small mouthful of food in the individual spoon and the spoonful put into the mouth. If a sliver of meat is picked up with the chopsticks, the piece touched by the chopsticks should always be the piece taken up. The meat is consumed with minimal touching of the mouth. In the parts of Southeast Asia where fork and spoon are replacing fingers, the same courtesies as using the communal serving spoon to get food and not fishing in the communal dish with your own spoon are observed. If you eat with your fingers, the communal spoon is held with your left hand so that you do not dirty the communal spoon. Other observances include not licking your chopsticks or spoon or your fingers, no matter how finger-lickin' good the meal may have been.

In places where fingers are used, there is the ritual of washing hands before and after the meal. In Indian restaurants, there is always a tap nearby for washing hands. In a more posh restaurant or at more formal occasions, servers may go around with an ewer of warm water and a basin for cleaning the hand before the meal, with a second round of perfumed water at the end of the meal together with a fresh towel for drying the wet hand. Only the right hand is cleaned by dipping into the bowl of water or held over the basin while the server pours water over the fingers. The towel draped over his arm may be used for drying cleaned fingers. At its simplest, a bowl of clean water with or without a slice of lemon or cold tea is brought to the table before the meal begins for the hand to be washed and another at the end of the meal for the dirty fingers to be cleaned.

Traditional Asian hospitality dictates that there must always be food left over at the end of the meal or the host will feel he has treated his guests shabbily. Not only must guests be served plenty of food, but this must also be the best. Asian hospitality is measured by the quantity as well as the quality of the meal. Stories of Indian villagers going into debt to celebrate a wedding are legendary. West Asian hospitality arose from desert Arab traditions where a stranger outside your tent must always be given food and drink. The sharing of food with strangers can still be seen to this day in the city—especially when strangers are easily spotted. On a visit to Syria, Jordan and Lebanon in 2009, shopkeepers would hand out free samples if my friends and I showed any curiosity about the shop window display or stepped into the shop to ogle the food especially the sweets. The gifts ranged from kebabs, sweets, breads, cookies, cakes, vegetables and fruit to coffee and tea! In South Asia, making sure that guests leave with fragrance on their breath or sweetness in their mouth is de rigueur. A little dish filled with fennel or cumin seeds with or without small cubes of sugar or rolled in sugar is served at the end of the meal or placed at the counter near the cashier for you to help yourself. In West Asia, rose water is sprinkled on departing guests, the lingering fragrance serving as a reminder of a pleasant occasion. In South Korea, restaurants always offer guests a stick of chewing gum or a sweet primarily because there is so much garlic in Korean food and you do not want to be breathing out garlic fumes the rest of the day.

Rice as the Asian staple has led to the evolution of some very interesting ways to prepare, serve and eat food. When the rice is eaten with fingers, it is easier to eat in handfuls when moistened with a thick sauce to hold the grains together. Meat has to be boiled till tender so that it is easily torn into pieces for consumption with the rice or prepared in bite-size pieces. If the meat has to be boiled till tender, robust stews taste best. At the same time, such stews have rich, thick gravies that not only taste good with rice but also hold dry boiled rice together.

When the rice is eaten with chopsticks, the meat and vegetables have to be in bite-sizes rather than be chunky. Having food in small pieces means that quick cooking such as stir-fries is desirable and possible. At the same time, cutting meat into small pieces spreads a small amount further and a little feeds more. As can be seen in the recipes that follow, some of the hidden considerations for preparing the food in a certain way and serving the rice with certain kinds of side dishes are very much linked to the way food is served and eaten.

USING THE RECIPES

Many of the recipes in this book were prepared with one of the new super rice cookers that can cook all kinds of rice as well as steam and bake. However, you do not need a rice cooker, basic or super, to do any of the recipes and all the recipes can be prepared using traditional methods such as boiling or parboiling as well as whatever combination of old and new ways that you prefer or have the equipment for. Knowing your equipment and your rice are what counts because you can then adjust accordingly. There are tips on how to make adjustments as well as notes on what is the desired texture or consistency and sometimes on how to make substitutes.

Note also that the sections are not divided by type of rice although certain sections may give that impression because it seems to feature only one type of rice. The sections are divided by the way the rice is prepared and served. Flavoured Rice has all the biryani and pilaf recipes as well as Southeast Asian classics like *nasi lemak*. The Rice Porridges and Rice Soups section is self-explanatory but a closer look at the recipes shows that some recipes are for long-grain and some for short-grain while others combine not only long-grain with short-grain but also with glutinous rice. Rice Porridges and Rice Soups are all savoury while the section on Rice Desserts and Snacks has all the sweet rice recipes at the beginning and the savoury snacks in the second half. Rice Desserts and Snacks features all three main types of rice but white glutinous rice does predominate because it is the most common rice for many desserts, dumplings and rice cakes.

Although the recipes are almost all for white milled rice, brown rice can be used instead in many recipes provided some adjustments are made to the amount of liquid as well as method of cooking. Even with more liquid and a longer cooking time, expect to get a firmer and more chewy rice with brown rice than with white. Even substituting short-grain for long-grain or basmati when making a pilaf is possible provided you keep in mind the fact that the pilaf is not going to taste like one made with a long-grain rice.

One thing to note is that despite references to a certain dish having very ancient roots, my recipes are not period recipes and make no attempt to re-create any of the ancient period recipes with period ingredients. They are all modern recipes inspired by my interest in cooking experiments, re-creating at home the tasty food discoveries from my travel, from my reading and buying of numerous cookbooks over the years, as well as the pleasure I get from combining the same ingredients in very dissimilar ways or dissimilar ingredients in the same ways, all to come up with a dish that will be the focal point of one of my favourite activities which is preparing a meal for friends and family. They are also recipes configured mostly to my preferences and those of friends who have partaken of my experiments. With the growth of the Internet, a living source of inspiration for some of my kitchen experiments are the huge communities of foodie bloggers who love talking about their favourite dishes. Bloggers and websites not only inspired some of my experiments but I was also able to cull much information about rice and rice preparations in Asia. May their rice pots always be on the boil and every meal be blessed with huge platters of rice. "*Lai chi fan*" (Let's eat rice), the traditional Chinese invitation to a meal, or "*Mari makan nasi*" (Come eat rice) as a traditional Straits Chinese nyonya would say.

Lee Geok Boi

THE BASICS

There are some 12,000 varieties of rice today and quite a few variations in cultural preferences for this staple, so it is not surprising that turning out a perfect meal with rice is going to depend on various factors not least of which is the kind of rice. Fortunately for the cookbook writer, there are a number of basics that remain and which makes this section possible. Whether short-grain, long-grain, medium-grain, glutinous, mixed grain or brown, rice must be cooked with water, partially cooked and steamed with water, or soaked in water and steamed. Water can be substituted with stock for cooking the rice but no matter how fancy the final rice dish may be, it all starts with getting the rice and liquid ratio right. The major difficulty with getting this simple equation right is that rice varies in its ability to absorb water. Even a supposedly same type of rice need not absorb water the same way. Some need less than others. The first basic, therefore, is to know your rice and how it behaves when cooked. The second basic is that you must adjust the water or stock ratio to rice given in these recipes with the characteristics of your particular rice in mind. The rice I cook with normally and those recipes that specify long-grain is Thai fragrant long-grain bought in Singapore. What is marked Thai long-grain fragrant or jasmine rice does not always cook the same way if bought elsewhere. (I have been trying for some years now to get rice marked Thai jasmine long-grain bought in Asian stores in St Paul, MN, to behave like the supposedly similar rice bought in Singapore.) The short-grain I use is Australian short-grain.

Another basic is that the different types of rice can be cooked in identical ways although one particular way may be more common than another. White glutinous rice, for example, is usually steamed although you can boil it too. Long-grain rice can also be steamed but boiling is more usual. Tradition and personal preferences play a big part in how rice is cooked. If you like soft rice, then it does not matter to you that the rice is not firm, separated grains. On the other hand, if you were making a biryani or fried rice, you do want your rice to be firm and separated grains. Another basic is that plain boiled rice or rice porridge is always eaten with side dishes and while the type of rice consumed plays a part in ethnic definition, the side dishes play an even bigger role in defining the cuisine. After all, short-grain rice is short-grain rice but *bulgogi* is distinctly Korean and *shabu-shabu* definitely Japanese. Both form different meals even though eaten with the same type of rice. This section contains the basics of rice cooking such as the ways to cook rice. It also contains the basics such as spice mixes that make the rice dishes of one place different from another. At the same time, the basics that are common to more than one rice dish such as fried onions are also given here although some such basic steps are repeated in the recipes too.

ADJUSTING TO TASTE

Although the recipes do not always say that you have to adjust the seasoning to taste, this is presumed to be necessary because no two cooks ever season their food in exactly the same way and taste preferences vary greatly. Another reason to do taste tests is that similar ingredients do not all have the same tartness, saltiness or spiciness, and knowing your ingredients from previous experience will give you a dish more to your taste.

WEIGHTS AND MEASURES

All the measurements for rice, water and other ingredients are with the metric cup and this must not be confused with the smaller 160-ml (5$^1/_3$ fl oz) cup that comes with every rice cooker. Two rice cooker cups of rice equal 1$^1/_2$ metric cups of rice or 300 g (11 oz). Weight and volume may not always be the same. It depends on the moisture content. However, the difference is small and immaterial.

Part of the reason these recipes ask for 3 metric cups rice is that half that amount equals 2 rice cooker cups. This is a good amount for small families and those who do not eat a lot of rice, while preparing 3 metric cups gives you enough for a small party or a large family. It makes for less awkward divisions should you want to halve the recipes. In general, the side dishes have also been configured for between four and six adults. However, because leftovers of rice and side dishes are always enjoyed the day after, the quantities err on the side of more rather than not enough. Do not double any of the recipes because the quantities here will cook nicely in the average 5- or 6-cup rice cooker which is the size found in the average home.

1 metric cup rice = 200 g (7 oz)
1 rice cooker cup rice = 150–160 g (5$^1/_3$ –5$^3/_4$ oz)
1 small bunch spring onion/coriander leaves
  /Chinese celery/mint = 15 g ($^1/_2$ oz)
2 shallots = 25 g (1 oz)
2 cloves garlic = 10 g ($^1/_3$ oz)
1 small onion = 50 g (1$^2/_3$ oz)
1 medium onion = 75 g (2$^1/_2$ oz)
1 large onion = 100 g (3$^1/_2$ oz)
1 large tomato = 150 g (5 $^1/_3$ oz)
1 slice ginger or galangal is 0.2-cm ($^1/_{10}$-in) thick
1 thumb-size knob refers to the length rather than the width
  A thumb-size knob of ginger is about 5-cm (2-in) long.

LIQUID MEASURES
15 ml = 1 Tbsp
60 ml = 2 fl oz = $^1/_4$ cup (4 Tbsp)
75 ml = 2$^1/_2$ fl oz = $^1/_3$ cup
125 ml = 4 fl oz = $^1/_2$ cup
250 ml = 8 fl oz = 1 cup
500 ml = 16 fl oz = 2 cups
1 litre = 32 fl oz = 4 cups

CLEANING AND WASHING RICE

Although none of the recipes in this book includes a step for cleaning rice, it has to be cleaned before it is cooked unless you are cooking enriched or instant rice. The first step in cleaning rice is to pick through the rice you are going to cook to remove any foreign objects such as small stones or chaff, such padding being common when rice used to be sold by weight rather than standardised packages. In many parts of Asia, rice is still sold by weight and the sight of the woman of the house picking through rice to prepare the evening meal is still to be seen in rural Asia. Picking through rice is still done with white glutinous rice with the objective of removing any long-grain rice that always seem to be mixed up with glutinous rice. In Singapore and many parts of Asia, glutinous rice is sold loose by weight and some long-grain rice invariably fall into the sack of glutinous rice. Removing such long-grain rice will give cooked glutinous rice a very smooth mouth-feel free of gritty bits, especially when preparing certain desserts. Long-grain rice does not soften like white glutinous rice.

Rice also needs to be washed to get rid of any off odours. Basmati rice smells like it has been bagged in gunny or jute sacks for ageing even though it may be sold in plastic packaging. The smell of jute sacking is an odour I remember from my childhood when rice was delivered to the house in a jute sack. (My mother would then transfer the rice to the rice bin.) However, I find that the smell disappears with washing and during cooking. So how should rice be washed and how thoroughly? One common instruction seen in many cookbooks is that the rice should be rinsed till the water runs clear or nearly clear, the rationale being that if all the excess starch clinging to the rice is washed away, the rice will cook into fluffy, separated grains. I have even come across the instruction to rub the rice between your hands as you rinse to do a more thorough job of washing the rice! If you do that, what you could end up with is broken rice, which is regarded in rice-producing countries as the poorer and cheaper grade of rice. Do not do that to your expensive whole grain rice. As for washing till the water runs clear, this is a waste of water. How the rice will turn out depends less on how the rice is washed than on the age and type of rice, how it is cooked and the amount of water. There are even brands of long-grain rice that tell you to rinse no more than once with uniformly tasty results. Besides rice which requires minimal rinsing, there is also enriched rice and instant rice, both of which must not be rinsed before cooking. The only kind of rice that I found best to rinse till clear was some Indian parboiled rice. Here, longer rinsing got rid of much of the somewhat musty odours.

The easiest way to wash rice is to place the rice in a large sieve and hold it under a cold water tap. Swish the rice very lightly with your fingers or shake the sieve in circles under the running water. About 10 seconds of this should be enough to clean most export quality long-grain or short-grain rice. Basmati is a special case because of the jute sack odour. Increase the rinsing by another 10 seconds. Rinsing in a sieve serves several purposes. If the rice is to be soaked, it can be left to soak inside the sieve placed in a basin of cold water. If the rice is to be drained and cooked right off, getting accurate measurements of water or stock is easier if the washed rice has been strained first. If using a rice cooker, there are markings in the rice pot to indicate how much water for each rice cooker cup of rice. Note that 3 metric cups (600 g / 1 lb $5^1/_3$ oz) rice equal 4 rice cooker cups rice.

TO SOAK OR NOT; TO FRY OR NOT

Whether to soak the rice or not depends partly on the rice as well as how it is to be cooked and the equipment to be used. Long-grain that is to be boiled into plain rice does not need soaking at all. On the other hand, the same rice to be cooked with stock, coconut milk, milk or meat and oil may need soaking. Soaking for 30 minutes is more than sufficient to allow the liquid to penetrate the rice grains more evenly and not leave the rice slightly gritty. If you do not have the time to soak the rice, you can also avoid this grittiness by using a little more liquid. In general, a 30-minute soak is quite sufficient for a Thai long-grain, and 1 hour for basmati. On the other hand, black and white glutinous rice, including brown rice require longer soaking, in some instances overnight or 8 hours. Soaking long- or short-grain is also done if you want to speed up the cooking of rice porridge and want to limit the amount of fuel used. The rice should be rinsed clean first before soaking in cold water. Do not over soak rice unless you are making rice porridge.

Should you fry the washed or soaked rice before boiling it? Biryani recipes in old cookbooks often recommend this step. However, having made biryani and other flavoured rice with and without frying the rice, I have found that frying does not enhance the flavour of the biryani in any way. Apart from the nuisance of having to clean and dry the rice first before you can fry it, I found on occasion that too vigorous stirring broke up the soaked and drained rice and made my biryani look like it had been made with broken rice. The texture of the cooked rice also seems too dry and hard rather than fluffy. Rather than fry the rice, control the texture of the rice by controlling the amount of water added and also by soaking or not soaking the rice.

HOW MUCH WATER?

Apart from personal and cultural preferences for harder or softer rice, the amount of water depends on the type and age of the rice, the equipment used to cook the rice as well as what else you are doing with the rice. Some brands of rice have their own rice to water ratios but bulk-rice packs usually leave it up to the cook and personal preference. I experimented with my usual Singapore-bought premium Thai long-grain with ratio of rice to water that varied from 1:1 to 1:1.5 to 1:2. The first was "barely cooked", while the other two gave "very firm" to "firm" rice with fluffy, well-separated grains. This texture is good for eating with side dishes and for making pilaf and fried rice.

On the other hand, the 1:2 ratio for unsoaked basmati got me a rice that was just a tad too firm although it was not gritty. When I soaked the basmati for an hour and used the same 1:2 ratio, I got an excellent result. While in St Paul, MN, I used the same 1:2 ratio to cook a rice marked "Thai Jasmine Rice" and found that it cooked into a very sticky soft rice while the 1:1 ratio gave a slightly gritty but less sticky rice. My conclusion? It all depends on the rice you have. Although I have specified the amount of water and rice, do not be surprised if the rice comes out a tad too soft or a tad too dry. You will have to adjust the water or stock to your kind of rice. Note that the comments on the rice to water ratios apply to both long-grain and short-grain rice. The 1:2 ratio that I used for short-grain also gave me the kind of rice that I like in being firm but cooked through. The rice was just mildly sticky.

It is not just rice that needs water control. Porridges, rice soups, stews and curries need to be cooked in water too. The amounts of water for these dishes are also estimates because not everyone cooks the same way. The gravy, soup or stock you are left with depends on how high you have the heat or how low, whether your stew pot is covered, semi-covered or open. A small, slow fire will boil down the liquid more slowly, while higher heat will dry up the liquid more quickly. So rather than give the exact times to boil or stew something, I have tended to describe the state that the meat, gravy or food item should be at before you add something or stop cooking. In general, it is better to have too much liquid than not enough. Boiling down to reduce watery gravy to the right thickness is better than thinning a too-dry stew with more water to get some gravy.

HOW TO COOK RICE

Whether boiled rice is called *chelo* in Farsi, *gohan* in Japanese, *bhaat* in Hindi, *nasi* in Malay or *fan* in Chinese, preparing it is nothing more than combining rice and water and boiling the two. Some types of rice are fairly consistent in the way they behave when you do this. Short-grain comes out sticky and tender; white and black glutinous rice differ in both texture and amount of water needed to cook the rice but in general it will not differ from bag to bag. The one kind of rice with wider variations is long-grain rice whose cooked texture can range from sticky to fluffy and separated. The exception is basmati, a long-grain aromatic rice with fairly consistent results from bag to bag and country to country. All rice is cooked either by boiling, steaming or a combination of the two. One traditional way is to boil the rice with just enough water to plump up the grains with all the water absorbed into the rice. Another equally ancient method is parboiling where the rice is boiled in a large quantity of water which is poured out and the half-cooked rice is allowed to finish cooking in a covered pot over a low fire. The parboiling method can also be combined with steaming. Here the half-cooked rice is scooped into a steamer pot and the rice is steamed till fluffy.

Rice of all types can also be cooked by steaming alone but the rice must first be soaked for some four hours or more in cold water before the rice is steamed for about 10 minutes. While steaming of glutinous rice is common, it is much less common for long-grain or short-grain rice where the absorption method or parboiling is more usual. Steam-cooking long-grain rice gives fluffy and well-separated grains. Even short-grain rice is less sticky when steam-cooked as compared to boiling. Steam-cooking is practically fail-proof, and it is impossible to burn or undercook the rice if it has been pre-soaked well ahead of time. Even if the rice has not been soaked for long enough and the rice is still a little gritty, sprinkle a couple of spoonfuls of water on the rice after the initial 10 minutes of steaming and continue steaming to further cook the rice. Steamed rice rarely turns mushy. Steaming allows you to control the texture more easily because you can open the steamer to check on the progress and whether the rice is at the preferred texture. The negative to all these plus points is that very few busy people want to steam rice, this being a more involved process than plain boiling. If you already eat a lot of rice, it is best to get yourself a rice cooker. It takes the guesswork out of cooking rice. If you like rice crust, you can even get one that produces rice crust or *tah-deeg* as it is called in Farsi. The Iranians love *tah-deeg*, so rice cookers made for the Iranian market can make *tah-deeg*.

In the days when rice was cooked over a wood or coal fire—as it still is in the huge swathes of Asia that are still without electricity—rice crust formed at the bottom of the rice pot if the pot was left for too long over the fire. What was a necessary evil became something prized because the crust did not always form if the pot was taken off the fire early enough. Today, there are other rice-eating cultures besides the Iranians who appreciate rice crust. In the Philippines, the rice crust is called *tutong* while in Indonesia, the crust called *intip* can also be further dried and fried into rice crackers called *rengginang*. In Japan, rice crust is called *koge* and it is never wasted but scraped up, toasted and then served in a bowl of hot green tea or even just hot water. It can also be mixed with softer rice and made into rice balls seasoned with miso, seaweed and sesame salt. And if it is really too burnt, why you make rice tea with it!

BASIC RICE RECIPES

TRADITIONAL ABSORPTION METHOD (WITH OR WITHOUT CRUST)

To cook rice on the stove-top, the pot must never be more than one-third full of rice and water. This is to allow the rice to boil up without overflowing. Too large is better than too small (unless you are celebrating Pongal, the Malayalee harvest festival, and want the rice to overflow). Salt is optional depending on whether you are preparing West, South, Southeast Asian or East Asian-style boiled rice, with salted boiled rice being usual the further west you go. If you want to get rice crust, cook the rice with an additional 125 ml (4 fl oz / $^1/_2$ cup) water.

Long-grain rice 600 g (1 lb 5$^1/_3$ oz / 3 cups)

Water 1.5 litres (48 fl oz / 6 cups)

Salt (optional) 1$^1/_2$ tsp

WITH CRUST

Ghee/butter 60 ml (2 fl oz / $^1/_4$ cup), melted

1. Combine rice, water and salt in a large pot, cover and bring to the boil. It should take under 5 minutes. Once rice is boiling, uncover pot and stir rice well.

2. Cover pot again and turn heat down to low. Cook rice for another 5 minutes. If your pot is too small to boil vigorously with the cover on without spilling out, leave the cover off till the water level has gone down and won't overflow the pot, usually after another 5 minutes.

3. Stir rice, then turn down heat and cover pot. If using a pot with a glass cover, you can see when the water is almost gone and little holes appear on the surface of the rice. However, if not using a glass lid, do not open pot to check. Instead, check for steam. If the steam is in very small puffs or no longer coming out of the pot, turn off heat.

4. Rest rice for at least 10 minutes before serving.

TO MAKE RICE WITH CRUST (TAH-DEEG)

1. At step 3, when water is mostly gone, pour in melted ghee or butter, cover pot and keep over low heat for 30 minutes. A heat diffuser will give a more even-coloured *tah-deeg*. Plain boiled rice can also be kept heated in this way with some extra water to get a simple *tah-deeg*.

2. To ease crust off bottom of pot, sit rice pot in a container of cold water for 5–10 minutes. Use a straight-edged spatula to lift crust and rice out in large pieces.

3. If cooking rice with stock or water for making a pilaf, do not let the rice crust form just yet. The rice can even be half-cooked as infusing will cook the rice further and the *tah-deeg* formed at that point.

Persian-style Rice Crust (tah-deeg)

Cooking oil, egg or yoghurt can be added to the bottom of the pot to guarantee the formation of *tah-deeg*. An alternative to forming the crust over the stove-top is to bake the rice placed in a metal pot in a 160°C (325°F) oven for 20–30 minutes. *Tah-deeg* is given pride of place at the top of the rice platter served to guests. *Tah-deeg* made with any of these ingredients is easier if you parboil rice (page 23). Note that there are Japanese rice cookers that make *tah-deeg* for the Iranian market.

1) Ghee/Oil Tah-Deeg

Ghee/olive oil 60 ml (2 fl oz / ¼ cup)

1. Melt ghee or heat oil in a rice pot over low heat. Spread the fat a little up the sides of pot. Put cooked or parboiled rice into pot.
2. Cover pot and keep it on low-medium heat for 20–30 minutes.

2) Yoghurt Tah-Deeg

Yoghurt 60 ml (2 fl oz / ¼ cup)
Water 2 *Tbsp*
Salt ¼ *tsp*

1. Mix together yoghurt, water and salt and pour into a pot. Spread yoghurt mixture to cover bottom of pot and swirl it a little up the sides of pot. Pour parboiled rice into pot.
2. Cover pot and keep it on low-medium heat for 20–30 minutes.

3) Egg Tah-Deeg

Egg 1
Salt ½ *tsp*

1. Beat egg and salt together lightly. Do not get it frothy. Pour beaten egg into rice pot and swirl egg to cover bottom of pot and a little up the sides. Pour parboiled rice into pot.
2. Cover pot and keep it on low-medium heat for 20–30 minutes.

TRADITIONAL PARBOILING

There is some confusion in the term "parboiled rice". Parboiling can refer to a method of treating unmilled rice when the rice is pressure-cooked to drive nutrients into the rice kernels before milling. Such rice is sold labelled "Parboiled rice". India and the US are the main sources of parboiled rice, with Uncle Ben's being the best-known. However, "parboiling" can also refer to a particular method of cooking rice where the rice is boiled in plenty of water and the water drained off after 5–10 minutes of boiling. The half-cooked rice is then finished off on a low fire or by steaming. Because much of the starch on the surface of the grains is drained off with the water, rice cooked by parboiling usually comes out as nicely separated grains. In parts of India, China and where rice is cooked by parboiling, the rice water is never discarded but made into a cooling and nourishing drink. This rice water is considered to be very nutritious and fed to the very young and the old and infirm. (It is nutritious because of the water-soluble vitamins in it.) It is also added to dhal curries, stews or braised meat as it makes a good thickener, thus reclaiming the water-soluble nutrients from the rice. The Chinese use this rice water as treatment for anyone who has had diarrhoea or an upset stomach.

Long-grain rice 600 g (1 lb 5^1/$_3$ oz / 3 cups)

Water 2 litres (64 fl oz / 8 cups)

Salt 1^1/$_2$ tsp

1. Combine ingredients in a pot and bring to the boil over high heat. Uncover pot and continue boiling for 5–10 minutes depending on how soft you want the rice.

2. Turn off heat and pour out water.

3. Cover pot and return it to low heat for another 15–30 minutes, the longer if you want *tah-deeg*.

PERSIAN-STYLE PARBOILED RICE

1. In Iran, another way to ensure the prized fluffy separated grains is to boil the rice for 10 minutes and then rinse it in cold water.

2. Pour rice into a sieve and run cold tap water over rice. Return rice to the pot, cover and sit pot over low heat for 10–30 minutes, the longer time if you want *tah-deeg*. If desired, put *tah-deeg* ingredients (page 22) into pot before putting in rinsed half-cooked rice.

KATEH (PERSIAN RICE CAKE)

The crusty *tah-deeg* holds the rice together into a crunchy cake. The melted ghee flavours the rice and the salt is cooked into the rice. *Kateh* makes a convenient picnic food although in humid weather, the crust will not stay crunchy for long but will turn chewy. Cook the rice in a large pot so that the rice cake will be thinner and hold together better. If you have a flat-bottom wok, you could even do the last step in it. You need to have a wok with a lid.

Long-grain rice 400 g (14^1/$_3$ oz / 2 cups)

Salt 1^1/$_2$ tsp

Water 1.5 litres (48 fl oz / 6 cups)

Ghee 60 ml (2 fl oz / ^{1}/$_4$ cup), melted

1. Combine rice, salt and water in a covered pot and bring to the boil. Stir rice, then turn heat down to medium-low and continue boiling till water is almost all gone and surface of rice has little holes, or if the steam is in very small puffs or no longer coming out of the pot.

2. Turn down heat to low, uncover pot and pour melted ghee into rice. Cover top of pot with several layers of paper towels and put lid back on. If using a heat diffuser, keep covered pot on medium heat for another 20–30 minutes to form the crust.

3. Fill the kitchen sink with some cold water and sit pot in this cold water for 10 minutes to loosen crust from the bottom of pot.

4. To serve, either slide out whole rice cake and cut into wedges or lift rice cake out in pieces. The softer rice can also be scooped out into a serving plate, and rice crust scraped out in pieces and piled on top of rice.

STEAMING WHITE GLUTINOUS RICE/RICE

All glutinous rice desserts and snacks in this book can be prepared with steamed glutinous rice although some of the recipes give instructions for boiling the rice instead. If the white glutinous rice has been soaked, do not boil it or the rice will become too soft. Only unsoaked glutinous rice should be boiled and even then, a combination of boiling and steaming seems to give a better texture. Although the high-end rice cookers have a glutinous (sticky) rice setting, glutinous rice can actually be boiled in an ordinary rice cooker or even a pot on the stove if you are prepared to keep an eye on it all the time and have good control over the heat. Here are the generic instructions for steaming white glutinous rice specifically, but which can also be modified for steaming any long- or short-grain rice.

1. Soak the rice either overnight or for some hours in cold water. The length of the soak affects the steaming time. Long- or short-grain rice does not need such long soaking.

2. If your steamer tray has rather big holes, line the bottom with a piece of muslin or greaseproof paper that has been well punctured with small holes to allow the steam through but prevent the rice from dropping to the bottom.

3. Spread the rice thinly on the muslin or paper and steam for about 10 minutes. Start timing when the water is boiling but there is no need to be exact so long as there is water in the steamer.

4. Dissolve salt in some water or coconut cream and stir evenly into the rice. When doing this step, you can either scoop the rice out of the steamer tray and mix in the salt and liquid in a mixing bowl, or you just stir the liquid directly into the rice in the steamer tray. Turn off the heat before you do that to avoid scalding yourself.

5. Return the rice to the steamer tray and continue steaming for between 20 and 30 minutes depending on the preferred consistency. If it is still too firm, sprinkle a tablespoon or two of liquid (water or coconut milk) and continue steaming till it is the right texture. It should be a little softer than what you like because the rice will harden once it cools. Conversely, it can also be harder than you like if the rice is going to be further boiled, grilled or steamed once it has been made into a cake or dumpling.

6. Halfway through the steaming, the rice at the top should be turned over to the bottom so that it gets steamed properly too. This is especially important if your steamer is not large enough to allow the rice to be spread out as a thin layer. This turning over ensures even cooking of the rice.

7. If the rice is to be cooled first before wrapping, cool the rice in a covered container to prevent the rice from turning crusty.

BOILING-STEAMING GLUTINOUS RICE

If the glutinous rice is to be boiled first before steaming, there is no need to soak the rice beforehand unless it is black glutinous rice. Black glutinous rice is a whole grain rice, that is, unmilled, and so it takes twice as long to cook to tenderness compared to white glutinous rice and it needs more water as well. The boiling-steaming is method is good for black glutinous rice because of the tough bran on the rice grains. For white glutinous rice, the water ratio should be 1:1 or a little less if the rice is to be wrapped and steamed or boiled again. For both black and white glutinous rice, the rice is cooked using your preferred method till completely done or semi-cooked. The salt can be boiled with the rice but not the coconut cream or milk if used, to avoid an undesirable "cooked" taste.

1. Cook rice using your preferred method until rice is done or semi-done according to the recipe.

2. Stir the coconut cream or milk into the boiled rice and prepare the rice cake or wrap the dumplings before steaming.

3. When the rice cake or dumplings are ready for steaming, steam the rice to your preferred consistency by adjusting the steaming time.

PREPARING OTHER INGREDIENTS

Although there are no instructions for peeling and cleaning onions, garlic, potatoes, vegetables, herbs and whole spices, all onions and garlic are peeled first before being rinsed clean and sliced, cubed or pounded. Any root, e.g. ginger or vegetable that is usually skinned or peeled first should be prepared its usual way. For example, carrots are usually peeled while green beans are usually trimmed. All vegetables are rinsed cleaned first before they are cut up.

MEAT
Whatever the meat, it must be rinsed clean first before it is cut up or marinated depending on the recipe. Certain meats such as mutton, lamb or beef may need pre-cooking till tender before it is layered with rice. The length of time required depends very much on the meat, the amount of water or whether you need stock or want plenty of gravy. Meat that is to be sliced thinly should always be sliced across the grain. In some West and South Asian pilafs, the cooked meat is stripped from the bones before the meat and rice are layered and the flavours infused to complete making the pilaf. The bones can be further boiled with any existing appropriate stock to improve the flavour of the rice to be cooked in the stock.

DHALS, LENTILS AND DRIED BEANS
These should always be rinsed well before soaking or pre-cooking.

GINGER
Ginger is used whole, in slivers and slices, or ground to a paste. Sometimes, only the juice is used. If used whole, the piece of ginger is smashed to release the fragrance. The pale thin skin on the rhizome must first be scraped off with a small knife.

WHOLE SPICES
Spices such as cinnamon sticks and cardamoms are often used whole. They should be rinsed lightly in a sieve under running water and left to dry on a paper towel before use if the spices have been bought loose. Branded spices can be used straight out of the tin or bottle. Whole spices may be lightly fried in oil or simply cooked together with the rice or the meat.

SAFFRON
Saffron does not require any rinsing. This very expensive spice may be used as it is straight out of the box or soaked first in a little water or milk. It can also be crumbled into small pieces. To do this, first dry the required amount in its packaging, if paper, or wrap in a small piece of paper towel and place on the lid of a very hot pot for a few seconds. Do not overheat. Then crumble the crisp threads with your finger and thumb.

TOASTING NUTS
The nuts used in West and South Asian pilafs are actually fried in oil rather than dry-fried or toasted in an oven. Nuts fried in oil stay firmer when cooked with rice. Always keep aside some of the nuts for use as a garnish on top of the rice to be added just before serving.

EQUIPMENT

RICE COOKER

The rice cooker made its first appearance in Japan in 1955 and since then it has changed the way millions of Asians cook rice. It is practically idiot-proof if you follow the instructions and even if you use guesswork where water proportions are concerned, I have never found it to fail. Invented by the Japanese, the original rice cooker consists of an inner pot, usually made of aluminium, in which the rice and water are placed and an outer pot with heat sensors that cook the rice, switch the heat off and keep the cooked rice warm. Most models include a "keep warm" button partly because serving anyone cold rice is considered very rude in Japanese etiquette. Low-end models do not have this feature. Today's high-end rice cookers with fuzzy logic can do more than boil rice. The top-end models can cook long-grain, short-grain, mixed grain rice or brown rice, make rice porridge, cook glutinous rice, steam as well as bake a cake at the touch of a button. The different kinds of rice require different amounts of water and cooking time and some rice cookers can even add on soaking time, if appropriate. Japanese rice cookers made for the Iranian market can even make perfect *tah-deeg* (so say Internet bloggers who are interested in cooking Persian-style rice).

One standard feature is the non-stick coating which in some rice cookers are so thin that you are warned not to scratch the lining. Were it not for this lining wearing out and getting scratched—even when you do not scoop out rice with a metal spoon—rice cookers would have a longer life span. This thin lining also means that you will not be able to use the pot for frying onions and spices that are to be cooked with the rice. If you do it anyway, note that with some rice cookers, you have to cool the pot first before putting it into the rice cooker. With these rice cookers, a hot rice pot can throw the sensors out of whack and the "cook" button cannot be pushed down. One quick way to cool the pot is to sit it in a basin of cold water. Being made of aluminium, the rice pot does not retain heat well.

HEAT DIFFUSER

Cooking rice over a coal fire makes for a more even spread of heat than cooking on a gas stove which more often than not chars the parts of the rice that are directly over the gas burners even when you have the flames low. To avoid this, get a metal or aluminium plate for placing over the gas burners to even out the heat. More than a decade ago, I bought an expensive cast-iron plate from a William Sonoma store in the US but in 2009 I found an equally effective aluminium plate from an Ace hardware store for just US$3. In a kitchen shop in Aleppo, Syria, I also came across at least two kinds of heat diffusers also priced similarly. A heat diffuser is also useful when boiling porridge where the same problem of uneven heat distribution and rice sticking to the bottom occurs frequently. A heat diffuser eliminates the need to constantly stir the rice to prevent it from catching at the bottom. Essentially, the diffuser thickens the bottom of your pot and spreads out the heat better. It is perfect for the last stage of pilaf-making when you are infusing as well as for making Persian *tah-deeg*. It is also good for stewing meat and boiling beans. A substitute heat diffuser can be made out of an Indian *tawa* or chatty (the flat cast-iron pan used to make chapatti).

MEAT THERMOMETER

This is a very useful tool when making roasts. It takes the guesswork out of it. There are instant-read and digital thermometers, as well as pop-up thermometers that usually come packed together with frozen turkeys. Good thermometers will have a table for the appropriate temperatures that each type of meat should reach to be considered cooked.

STEAMER

A steamer pot is very useful when you want to do a lot of steaming and nothing beats the multi-layered Chinese bamboo steamer. This sits in a wok or any deep frying pan that just needs to be a little bigger than the steamer. As long as the steamer can sit inside the water-filled pan, the seal will be good enough to keep the steam flowing upwards through the layers. A multi-layered steamer is more useful than a wider steamer what with kitchen space being at such a premium. Instead of spreading the rice for steaming on just one level, the rice can be spread across two or three layers. The layers can be rotated for more even cooking.

GRILLING EQUIPMENT

Other than using a barbecue set or an oven with a grill feature, grilling in a kitchen equipped with just a gas stove is still possible if you look out for the appropriate grilling equipment. These can range from the simple wire grid placed over the gas jets to something more fancy like this kebab grill pot that I found in a kitchen shop in Aleppo, Syria. The shopkeeper indicated that it was for grilling kebabs. (I had just bought some metal skewers.) The grill pot consists of a pot with a large cut-out at the bottom for the gas flames. A thin bar sits across this cut-out with a pin protruding from the centre to suspend a metal fan that rotates to spread the heat as you grill. The skewers are suspended across the top of the pan or they rest on a metal grill placed on top. The bottom has a lip that can be filled with some water to keep the grilling kebabs moist. The grill pot works very well and does kebabs beautifully. However, you can also grill directly over gas jets on a wire rack of a suitable height placed above the flames although it gets messy. Because Japanese cuisine has a lot of grilling, there are also good Japanese-made grilling mats. I found one that has a ceramic base to spread heat with a wire rack positioned at a good height for grilling. If there is no way you can grill, the kebabs can be "grilled" directly on a just slightly oiled well-heated cast-iron *tawa* which has no sides so that the skewers of meat can sit on the hot metal. Another alternative is to fry the meat with minimum oil over high heat till cooked.

MORTAR AND PESTLE

There are some ingredients that need to be pounded either because it is a very small amount or it cannot be ground with water in a food processor because you don't want to dilute it. If you want to make mochi, you will of course need a deep one, not the dinky ones for pounding small pieces of spice. It is also useful for making sambal *belacan*. The proper mortar and pestle for making Japanese mochi is a large heavy block of wood with a depression carved out on top. The cooked rice is placed in this depression. The pestle is a large heavy wooden mallet. Because the block of wood is so heavy, the mortar does not move when the rice is being pounded. If you want to try making mochi the traditional way, improvise with a deep Thai-style mortar and pestle which is easily available in stores patronised by Southeast Asians.

SPICE MIXES

Spices perk up rice and side dishes no end, but putting together a spice blend is one of the more time-consuming aspects of cooking. If you keep a few little jars of ready-to-use spice mixes, it will speed up cooking whether the mixes are wet Southeast Asian blends or West Asian dry mixes. Having several blends of spice mixes gives variety to your cooking, hence the different blends of spices in this section. Originally, spice mixes were made from scratch with freshly toasted whole spices but the next best thing is to make the blends with ground spices rather than buy ready-to-use spice blends. At least with homemade blends, you know that the mix has not been padded with non-essential ingredients like flour. You also know how old your ground spices are and if they are very fresh, the spice blends will stay fragrant for a long time. I have kept spice blends for more than 3 years. Because spice oils are volatile, dry spice blends should be stored refrigerated in an airtight bottle while wet ones should be frozen. All the mixes here are made with commercially prepared ground spices.

• If you really want to start from scratch, the whole spices must first be rinsed clean, then dried in the sun, under a fan or in a 50°C (120°F) oven. The spices are then quickly pan-fried till fragrant before they are ground or pounded till fine in a mortar and pestle. The best modern appliance for grinding seed spices is a small coffee mill which should be used only for grinding spices. Note that some spice oils such as clove will discolour the plastic parts. Spices are easiest to grind or pound when they are still brittle and dry from pan-frying.

• To dry leafy herbs for adding to spice mixes such as *za'atar*, put the cleaned and patted-dry herb on two to three layers of dry paper towels, cover it with another two to three layers of paper towels and microwave on high for 30 seconds to 1 minute. The timing depends on the quantity. More herbs would require more time. Check if dry and crisp. If not, repeat in 5–10 second intervals till dry and crisp but not browned. The herb should still be green. Crumble it when cool enough to handle and store in a bottle in the refrigerator. Drying herbs is another way of storing a good crop for another day although fresh herbs are usually better than the dried variety. Some dried herbs such as parsley are nearly as good as the fresh ones when used in stews.

• To dry orange, lemon or lime peel, remove the zest from the skin and chop finely first before drying it placed on paper towels in the microwave oven. Dried lime or lemon peel is a substitute for *noomi Basra* as well as for kaffir lime leaves.

GARAM MASALA 1 Makes about ½ cup

I have never seen ground black cardamoms anywhere and what is sold as ground cardamom is green cardamom. The only way to get ground black cardamom is to make your own by peeling black cardamoms to get the seeds. Alternatively, just add a couple of black cardamoms in the cooking and omit it from the spice mix. Black cardamom seeds must be dried briefly in the microwave oven before pounding or grinding as they can sometimes be damp inside. The seeds do not need rinsing. However, Indian bay leaves must first be rinsed clean, wiped dry and dried further in a microwave oven for a minute or less to crisp the leaves for easier grinding or pounding. The ground spices should be mixed in a small glass jar and the jar refrigerated until needed to extend shelf life.

Ground cumin ½ Tbsp

Ground black pepper ½ Tbsp

Ground ginger ½ Tbsp

Ground coriander 2 tsp

Ground fennel 2 tsp

Ground cloves 1 tsp

Ground cinnamon 2 tsp

Ground nutmeg 2 tsp

Indian bay leaves 3

Ground cardamom 1 tsp

Black cardamom seeds 1 tsp,
    finely pounded

1. Combine spices and store in a jar in the refrigerator.

GARAM MASALA 2 Makes about ¼ cup

Ground fennel 1 Tbsp

Ground ginger 1 Tbsp

Ground cardamom 2 tsp

Ground cinnamon 2 tsp

Ground cloves 2 tsp

1. Combine spices and store in a jar in the refrigerator.

ADVIEH (PERSIAN SPICE MIX)

The word "advieh" means medicines in Farsi but whatever the medicinal value of spices, they give food distinctive flavours despite the small amounts used. The three spice blends increase in intensity and robustness with *Advieh 1* being the most delicate, *Advieh 2* the more expensive because of the saffron and *Advieh 3* the most robust and cheapest. Tiny dried fragrant roses and rose petals are fairly easy to find now that floral and herbal teas are fashionable. While raw pistachios are preferred nuts for *advieh*, substitute with ground roasted pistachios or ground almonds if not available. Look for dried roses in South Asian as well as West Asian stores. To crumble the saffron or rose petals for mixing, dry it well first (page 26).

ADVIEH 1   Makes about ¹/₂ cup

Ground cinnamon 2 *tsp*

Ground nutmeg 2 *tsp*

Ground rose petals 2 *tsp*

Ground green cardamom 2 *tsp*

Ground cumin *1 tsp*

Ground pistachios *1 Tbsp*

1.   Combine ingredients and store in a jar in the refrigerator.

ADVIEH 2 (WITH SAFFRON)   Makes about ¹/₂ cup

Ground cinnamon *1 Tbsp*

Ground green cardamom 2 *tsp*

Saffron threads 2 *tsp, finely chopped/ground*

Ground pistachios 2 *Tbsp*

Dried rose petals ¹/₄ *cup, finely ground*

1.   Combine ingredients and store in a jar in the refrigerator.

ADVIEH 3 (WITH TURMERIC)   Makes about ³/₄ cup

Ground turmeric 2 *Tbsp*

Ground coriander 2 *Tbsp*

Ground cumin *1 Tbsp*

Ground black pepper *1 Tbsp*

Ground green cardamom 2 *tsp*

Ground cloves 2 *tsp*

Ground cinnamon *1 tsp*

Ground fenugreek ¹/₂ *tsp*

1.   Combine spices and store in a jar in the refrigerator.

BAHARAT 1 (SYRIAN/IRAQI SPICE MIX 1) Makes about ⅓ cup

Allspice is a spice from Jamaica that gets its name from the way it smells of cinnamon, cloves and cardamoms albeit very mildly. It is a convenient combination of fragrances. If dried limes are not available, use dried lime peel. Many West Asian stews, in particular those made with strong-tasting meat such as mutton, are accented with dried limes known as *noomi Basra* to tone down the strong flavour. This spice mix is similar to Gulf Baharat in including chilli powder.

Ground allspice 1½ *Tbsp*

Ground paprika 2 *Tbsp*

Red chilli powder ½ *Tbsp*

Ground black pepper ½ *Tbsp*

Ground *noomi Basra 2 Tbsp*

1. Combine ingredients and store in a jar in the refrigerator.

BAHARAT 2 (LEBANESE/SYRIAN/IRAQI SPICE MIX 2) Makes about ½ cup

The ground cinnamon used in some West Asian spice mixes can also be Chinese cinnamon or cassia which has a slightly different fragrance from either Indonesian or Sri Lankan cinnamon. Spice shops in Syria and Lebanon can have all three kinds sitting side by side. I also found small pieces of cassia in a bag of sage for making Bedouin sage tea that I bought in Wadi Rum in Jordan. Chinese cassia in West Asian spice blends is not surprising given the centuries-old trade links between West and East Asia. Along with silks and porcelain from China, Arab traders also carried back spices for its trade with Europe in medieval times.

Ground paprika 100 g (3½ oz)

Ground black pepper 1½ *Tbsp*

Allspice 1 *Tbsp*

Ground cumin 2 *tsp*

Ground coriander 2 *tsp*

Ground cinnamon 1 *tsp*

Ground cloves 1 *tsp*

Ground nutmeg 1 *tsp*

1. Combine spices and store in a jar in the refrigerator.

BAHARAT 3 Makes about ½ cup

Ground paprika 3 *Tbsp*

Ground black pepper 2 *Tbsp*

Ground cumin 1 *tsp*

Ground coriander 1 *tsp*

Ground turmeric 1 *tsp*

Ground ginger 1 *tsp*

Ground cloves ½ *tsp*

Ground cardamom ½ *tsp*

Ground nutmeg ¼ *tsp*

1. Combine spices and store in a jar in the refrigerator.

BAHARAT 4 Makes about ½ cup

Ground black pepper 2 Tbsp
Allspice 1 Tbsp
Ground paprika 1 Tbsp
Ground cinnamon 1 tsp
Ground nutmeg ½ tsp

1. Combine spices and store in a jar in the refrigerator.

GULF BAHARAT Makes about ½ cup

Of all the *baharat* mixes, this is the spiciest because Gulf Arabs like their food on the spicy side. Another essential in the mixture is *noomi Basra*. If this is unavailable, dry chopped lime zest in the microwave oven and add to the spice mixture. Besides the dried limes giving a fruity flavour, they also moderate the strong flavour of mutton and lime. Lime peel may be substituted with sumac although its tang is different from lime. To grind *noomi Basra*, first wipe with a damp cloth and dry in the sun or in a 120°C (250°F) oven till very dry. Pound with a mortar and pestle till fine or as preferred.

Red chilli powder 3 Tbsp
Ground cumin ½ Tbsp
Ground cinnamon ½ Tbsp
Ground coriander ½ Tbsp
Ground cloves 1 tsp
Ground black pepper 1 tsp
Ground cardamom ½ tsp
Ground nutmeg ¼ tsp
Ground *noomi Basra* 2 Tbsp

1. Combine ingredients and store in a jar in the refrigerator.

BHAR (LEBANESE SPICE MIX) Makes about ¼ cup

The Lebanese are rather fond of ginger if what I saw in Lebanese spice shops and grocery stores in the *souks* (Arabic markets) is any guide: there was always a tub of fresh ginger on sale.

Ground allspice 1 tsp
Ground black pepper 1 tsp
Ground white pepper 1 tsp
Ground cinnamon 1 tsp
Ground cloves 1 tsp
Ground nutmeg 1 tsp
Ground fenugreek 1 tsp
Ground ginger 2 tsp

1. Combine ingredients and store in a jar in the refrigerator.

Za'atar (west asian herbal spice mix)

Za'atar originally referred to a type of wild thyme which once grew freely in the more verdant parts of West Asia such as Israel, Lebanon and Syria. However, it has become so endangered that picking it has been banned. This wild thyme has been said to combine the flavours of oregano and marjoram with European thyme. Hence za'atar mixtures often include marjoram and oregano. Today, za'atar refers to a blend of herbs and spices of which thyme is one of the ingredients. Regional variations may include fennel, sumac, cumin and other seed spices together with the dried herbs. One of the chief uses for za'atar is as a seasoning for bread with the za'atar baked into rolls and croissants, sprinkled on bread and toasted on mini pita breads. Eaten as a dip, dry za'atar is mixed with olive oil first. Spoonfuls of za'atar may also be sprinkled into meat marinades, stews as well as vegetables as a seasoning. The herb and spice combinations vary depending on what the za'atar is to be used for. Za'atar for cooking is meant for meat and vegetables while za'atar for bread is meant to be eaten with bread or as a dip when mixed with olive oil. Lebanese parents make za'atar sandwiches or za'atar pizza on the eve of examinations as za'atar is believed to boost brain power! Both za'atar 1 and 2 can be used for cooking but you might prefer za'atar 2 as a dip.

Za'atar 1   Makes about ¹/₄ cup

Dried thyme 1 Tbsp

Sumac 2 Tbsp

Ground marjoram ¹/₂ Tbsp

Ground oregano ¹/₂ Tbsp

Ground cumin 1 tsp

White sesame seeds 1 Tbsp,
   toasted and pounded

1. Combine ingredients and store in a jar in the refrigerator.

Za'atar 2   Makes about ¹/₄ cup

White sesame seeds 2 Tbsp,
   toasted and pounded

Ground thyme 1 Tbsp

Sumac 2–3 Tbsp

Ground cumin ¹/₂ tsp

Salt 2 tsp

1. Combine ingredients and store in a jar in the refrigerator.

Japanese Sesame Salt (gomashio) or Korean Sesame Salt

Japanese sesame salt or gomashio and Korean sesame salt are the same. It is basically toasted sesame seeds, usually white with or without some black sesame seeds added for colour.

White sesame seeds 40 g (1¹/₃ oz
   / ¹/₄ cup)

Black sesame seeds (optional)
   ¹/₂ Tbsp

Salt 1 tsp

1. Pan-fry white sesame seeds in a dry frying pan for 2 minutes or till a few seeds start to brown and the smell is fragrant. Turn off heat and stir in black sesame seeds.

2. Cool seeds and pound briefly to break up seeds and release oils. Mix with salt and store in a glass jar in the fridge.

3. Use to garnish plain rice as well as other East Asian rice dishes.

STRAITS CHINESE MEAT CURRY POWDER   Makes 250 g (9 oz)

Curry powders for meat and curry powders for seafood have different compositions and the former should not be used for seafood. This mild curry powder is in fact a generic curry powder for any meat although it is more commonly used for making chicken curry. The flavour of the curry powder can be changed by varying the first three ingredients.

Ground coriander 125 g (4¹/₂ oz)

Ground cumin 25 g (1 oz)

Ground fennel 25 g (1 oz)

Ground dried red chillies 75 g (2¹/₂ oz)

Ground turmeric 1 Tbsp

Ground white pepper ¹/₂ Tbsp

Ground cardamom ¹/₂ tsp

Ground cinnamon ¹/₂ tsp

Ground cloves 1 tsp

1. The curry powder can be toasted and mixed together at the same time by dry-frying the mixture in a wok over low heat for 2 minutes. Stir-fry continuously, taking care not to scorch the spices.

2. If the curry powder is not to be dry-fried, mix the ground spices together in a plastic bag. Hold the mouth shut and shake well.

3. Bottle the curry powder and refrigerate to extend its shelf life.

GHEE

Called samn in Arabic but known to those familiar with South Asian cooking as ghee or ghiu, this oil is clarified butter. It is the West Asian substitute for alya, the fat extracted from the tail of fat-tailed sheep, and which was once widely used for festive cooking in medieval times. More expensive than ordinary oils, ghee is always used for making West Asian pilafs which are usually festive dishes, and less so for ordinary home-cooking. Ghee, on the other hand, has long been used in South Asian cooking, sometimes in very small amounts to flavour cheap dhal dishes. India exports several brands of tinned ghee. There is also Australian tinned ghee. If you can't find tinned ghee in the supermarket, make it from butter. Homemade ghee is delicious if somewhat expensive.

Butter 250 g (9 oz)

1. Melt butter in a pot over low heat. Simmer till butter stops frothing, oil becomes clear and milk solids sink to the bottom of pot. However, take care not to over brown the milk solids.

2. Carefully spoon oil or ghee out, leaving the solids at the bottom. Store ghee in a bottle or tin in the fridge. It solidifies in the cold.

3. Use residue in the pot to butter toast or fry rice.

FRIED ONIONS AND NUTS

This is a common ingredient in so many West and South Asian pilafs that keeping a jar of fried onions in the fridge will speed up the making of a pilaf on the run. You can do the same with nuts such as pine nuts, almonds and cashews that so often garnish any pilaf. Although the nuts are usually referred to as "toasted", they are actually more often than not fried in oil. Any leftover oil can be refrigerated and used when making your next pilaf. When frying pine nuts, take care not to over-brown them. They turn brown fairly quickly. Almonds should be split or slivered thickly before frying. Cashew nuts may be halved to make a little go a longer way.

Ghee/cooking oil 125 ml (4 fl oz / ¹/₂ cup)

Onions 250 g (9 oz), peeled and thinly sliced, or nuts (pine nuts, almonds, cashews)

1. Heat ghee or oil in a wok over low heat and when the oil is hot, stir in sliced onions or nuts. Stir-fry till onions/nuts begin to brown. At this point, stir and keep a close eye on onions/nuts. As soon as onions/nuts are a pale gold but less brown than you would prefer, turn off heat and keep stirring. The residual heat will brown the onions/nuts further. If the onions/nuts are still a little pale, turn on the heat for another 30 seconds.

2. Scoop onions/nuts out of the hot oil and drain on paper towels.

3. The oil used for frying onions can be bottled and used with your next Asian stew.

Onion Juice

Onion juice and ginger juice are sometimes used for marinating and flavouring meats where the pulp is not wanted. To prevent the juice from squirting all over while you pound, use a spoon and scoop out the juice as you pound. The juice can also be pressed out from the pulp through a sieve and the pulp returned to the mortar for further pounding.

Chopped onion 150 g (5^1/$_3$ oz)

1. Pound chopped onion in a mortar and pestle. Extract juice and keep bottled in the refrigerator.
2. The onion pulp can be used as part of a ground spice paste. It will not be so fragrant but will give bulk to your curry or stew.

Ginger Juice

Skinned old ginger 1 thumb-size knob

1. Pound ginger in a mortar and pestle. Extract juice and keep bottled in the refrigerator.

Ginger Paste

Ginger paste and garlic paste are essential in many South Asian recipes whether for rice, meat or vegetables. If you plan to make South Asian food often, make plenty of the pastes and freeze for later use. The steps are the same whether making garlic or ginger paste although garlic is naturally less juicy than ginger. Slice the ginger thinly before pounding to cut up the fine fibres.

Thinly sliced and chopped skinned old ginger 150 g (5^1/$_3$ oz)

1. Pound chopped ginger in a mortar and pestle. To prevent the juice from squirting all over while you pound, use a large spoon and scoop out the juice as you pound. Pound till ginger is a fine paste.
2. Mix juice with the paste. Store in a bottle and refrigerate or freeze until needed.

Garlic Paste

Garlic 150 g (5^1/$_3$ oz), peeled

1. Pound garlic in a mortar and pestle to a fine paste. Store in a bottle and refrigerate or freeze until needed.

Garlic-flavoured Olive Oil

This oil can be used as a quick dressing for salads as well as to dress plain boiled rice or brushed on kebabs and grilled meat for instant flavour.

Olive oil 125 ml (4 fl oz / ^{1}/$_2$ cup)

Garlic 4 cloves, peeled and mashed

1. Mix oil and mashed garlic together. Leave to stand overnight before using.

FRIED GARLIC AND GARLIC OIL

Garlic oil and fried garlic are common garnishing for rice porridges and rice soups in particular in Southeast Asia and China. It is a useful condiment to have in the fridge if you make rice porridge or rice soups often.

Garlic 150 g (5¹/₃ oz), peeled

Cooking oil 250 ml (8 fl oz / 1 cup)

1. Chop garlic in a food processor till fairly fine but not mushy. If food processor does not chop without any liquid or turns everything into mush, hand-chop garlic.

2. Heat oil in a wok and add chopped garlic.

3. Stir constantly till garlic begins to turn a nice shade of yellow. Turn down heat if garlic is browning unevenly.

4. About 1 minute before colour is ideal, turn off heat but continue stirring till garlic is a golden brown.

5. Scoop garlic onto a plate lined with paper towels. When cool, bottle fried garlic. Refrigerate to extend shelf life.

6. Pour cooled oil into a bottle with a screw-top and store in the fridge to extend shelf life.

FRIED SHALLOTS AND SHALLOT OIL

When sliced shallots are fried in oil, the browned shallots are used as a garnish or cooked with rice. The fragrant oil and the fried shallots are also used to flavour rice porridge and rice soups.

Cooking oil 250 ml (8 fl oz / 1 cup)

Shallots 150 g (5¹/₃ oz), peeled and thinly sliced

1. Heat oil in a wok and add shallots when oil is hot. Do not use high heat.

2. Stirring constantly, fry till shallots are a golden colour.

3. Turn down heat if bits of shallot start to brown too quickly while the rest is still wet and soft.

4. To get a nice golden brown, watch the heat and the colour carefully. When shallots are a pale yellow, turn heat off but continue stirring till colour deepens. If shallots are still too pale, turn heat on briefly and keep stirring. Just a minute before the colour becomes ideal, turn heat off and continue stirring till shallots stop changing colour.

5. Scoop shallots out onto a large platter lined with a few paper towels. When cool, bottle fried shallots and refrigerate to extend shelf life.

6. Pour cooled oil into a bottle with a screw-top and store in the fridge to extend shelf life.

SIDE DISHES

Many Asian dishes, if not most, taste best when eaten with rice, just as rice becomes special when eaten with these dishes. Although the label "Side Dishes" may imply that they are secondary to the star which is rice, like any good movie, the star shines even more brightly when there is a great supporting cast and that is the role of side dishes in most Asian cuisines. Meats, seafood, vegetables and sauces all add something extra to rice whether plain or flavoured just as many iconic Asian dishes cannot be really enjoyed without rice. What is biryani without some pickles or chutney to act as a foil and bring out its flavours? And what is curry without rice? At the same time, there are some side dishes that are essential to the character of certain meals such as Straits Chinese fried fish and Straits Chinese *nasi lemak* sambal to give you Nasi Lemak. The kind of side dish changes a plate of boiled rice from being a West Asian meal to one from South or Southeast Asia, just as the kind of rice changes the cuisine from West to East Asia. While some side dishes are iconic to a particular region, many are almost generic and equally tasty with rice preparations of several regions.

If you take a look at a map of Asia, it is easy to see how the foods of different parts of Asia fuse with those of the neighbours or are influenced by the terrain. For example, it is no surprise that lamb is the essential meat in West Asia given that sheep thrive better in the more arid landscape or that seafood predominate in countries such as Indonesia and Japan with their long coast lines. These side dishes are almost all prepared ahead of time with quite a few improving from a long rest to let the flavours meld. Some such as pickles and chutneys must in fact be made several days if not weeks ahead.

An interesting point to note is that many of these side dishes can cross cultures. West Asian kebabs and stews taste equally good with South Asian flavoured rice and even with certain Southeast Asian ones. Southeast Asian fried fish or prawns will go with flavoured rice from almost anywhere. Indian dhal curries and yoghurt-flavoured dishes would go very well with practically all the West Asian rice dishes. Knowing what to mix and match, what tastes good with which side dish comes with trial and error. In general, the more strongly flavoured dishes go better with more strongly flavoured rice. Experiment and find your own combinations.

STRAITS CHINESE FRIED FISH IN FOUR FLAVOURS

Although called Straits Chinese because these were some of the ways fish was prepared in my Straits Chinese home when I was growing up, these are actually generic Southeast Asian dishes and likely to be found in many homes all over the region. One reason for their popularity is that the basic ingredients are easy to use and easily available. Both whole and fish steaks can be seasoned in any of the four ways given here, plain salt being one of the four ways.

Firm-fleshed white fish 800 g–1 kg
  (1³/₄ lb–2 lb 3 oz)
Cooking oil for frying

PLAIN SALTED FISH

Salt 1½ tsp

ASSAM FISH

Salt 1½ tsp
Tamarind pulp 50 g (1²/₃ oz)

TURMERIC FISH

Salt 1¹/₂ tsp
Ground turmeric ¹/₂ Tbsp

CANDLENUT AND TURMERIC

Salt 1¹/₂ tsp
Candlenuts 4 whole nuts, finely
  pounded
Turmeric 1 thumb-size knob,
  peeled and finely pounded

1. Rub fish with salt and if preferred, season with chosen flavour. Marinate for at least 2 hours or overnight in the fridge before frying.

2. If fish is seasoned with tamarind pulp, discard tamarind pulp, rinse marinated fish clean and wipe dry before frying. If tamarind is not rinsed off, the fish will blacken very quickly before it is cooked through.

3. If fish is seasoned with candlenut and turmeric, the oil has to be hot enough to cook the fish well, but not so hot that the seasoning is burnt before the fish is cooked. To achieve this, turn down heat once a crust has formed around fish and cover frying pan.

4. Serve fish preferably hot.

Note:

Always pat fish dry with paper towels including inside the stomach before putting it into the hot oil to avoid excessive splattering. One way to reduce oil splatter is to cover the wok or frying pan with a glass lid. Using a paper towel, wipe the underside of this lid periodically to stop the moisture from dripping into the hot oil. The lid will also help cook the fish more quickly besides reducing the mess.

The oil should be heated till it is about to start smoking before the fish is put into the oil. This gets a crust to form quickly on the fish. Turn the fish only when a crust has formed. If turned too early, the fish will stick and break up especially if it is a tender fish.

ASSAM PRAWNS (TAMARIND PRAWNS)

This is another generic Southeast Asian way of preparing prawns. Some cooks fry the prawns in their shells with or without the heads with some tamarind pulp. Some split the prawns in their shells down the middle to extract the dirt track and season the prawns with tamarind and salt before frying. To enhance the tamarind flavour although it is a little more work, I prefer to shell the prawns but keep the tails and heads on. If the head is kept, the whiskers and sharp tips on the head have to be trimmed with scissors. (The heads can be chewed and sucked for the tasty juices.) The prawns also need to be slit down the middle to remove the dirt track. Marinating overnight also strengthens the tamarind flavour.

Medium-large prawns in their shell
  1 kg (2 lb 3 oz)
Tamarind pulp 80 g (3 oz / ¹/₄ cup)
Water 2 Tbsp
Salt 1 tsp
Cooking oil 60 ml (2 fl oz / ¹/₄ cup)

1. Prepare prawns according to preference (see headnote.) Marinate prawns with tamarind pulp and salt. Mix tamarind with water if it is very dry. Marinate for at least 2 hours or overnight in the fridge.

2. If prawns are shelled, rinse, then squeeze out as much water as you can. Pat dry with paper towels before frying. If prawns were marinated in their shells, skip step.

3. Heat oil in a wok till very hot. Put in prawns, with tamarind pulp for prawns in shells, and fry, stirring constantly.

4. If prawns have been fried with tamarind pulp, remove seeds and pulp before serving. Serve hot or at room temperature.

Note:

If using frozen prawns, they will weep when fried. To dry the prawns out, take them out of the wok when they turn pink and boil off the excess juices. Return the prawns to the wok, turn up heat and brown the prawns.

Peanuts and Anchovies

The combination of dried salted anchovies and fried peanuts is another generic Southeast Asian dish that can be eaten with rice and rice porridge as well as with special rice preparations like *nasi lemak*. Dried anchovies or *ikan bilis* comes either whole or gutted. Smaller anchovies crisp more easily but are more fiddly to gut. Do not use Japanese dried anchovies as these are usually too large, besides being very expensive.

Dried anchovies (*ikan bilis*) 100 g
  (3¹/₂ oz)
Peanuts 200 g (7 oz)
Cooking oil 60 ml (2 fl oz / ¹/₄ cup)
Dark soy sauce ¹/₂ tsp
Fine sugar 1 Tbsp
Red chilli powder (optional) 2 tsp

1. Rinse dried anchovies clean, pat dry with paper towels, then dry them by spreading out on paper towels in the sun or under the fan or baking in a low oven.
2. Roast peanuts with or without skins till they no longer taste raw.
3. Heat oil in a wok till hot, then add dried anchovies and stir-fry, turning constantly. Turn down heat after 1–2 minutes, especially if anchovies are browning too quickly but are still not crisp.
4. When anchovies are starting to crisp, sprinkle soy sauce, sugar and chilli powder, if using, over anchovies and mix well. Adjust seasoning to taste. Add roasted peanuts and continue frying for another 10 minutes or more to cook chilli powder, brown peanuts and crisp fish.
5. Dish out onto paper towels to drain. Cool, then bottle until needed.

Straits Chinese Nasi Lemak Chilli Sambal

This chilli sambal to go with Nasi Lemak freezes well and I am never without a box of it in the fridge. While some like their chilli sambal sweetish, I prefer it more tart to act as a foil for the rich rice. Adjust the seasoning to taste. This sambal can also be fried with cleaned dried anchovies and sliced onions to make an extra side dish to go with many rice dishes.

Water 250 ml (8 fl oz / 1 cup)
Tamarind pulp 50 g (1²/₃ oz)
Shallots 125 g (4¹/₂ oz), peeled
Dried red chillies 30 g (1 oz),
  seeded and soaked
Salt 1 tsp
Sugar 2 Tbsp
Cooking oil 60 ml (2 fl oz / ¹/₄ cup)

1. Mix water with tamarind pulp and strain away solids.
2. Blend tamarind juice with shallots and softened dried chillies.
3. Put all ingredients together in a microwave-safe dish, cover and cook in the microwave oven for about 20 minutes, stirring occasionally. Cook to a thick, moist and shiny consistency. Add a little more water if necessary to get the right consistency. Overcooking is better than undercooking.

Sambal Belacan

This mix of red chillies and dried prawn paste pounded together must not be confused with *belacan* which is just plain prawn paste. Although sambal *belacan* tastes best pounded in a mortar and pestle rather than all blended together in a food processor, you can reduce pounding time by first chopping the chillies coarsely in a food chopper. Sambal *belacan* keeps well in the fridge for up to a month. It can also be frozen in serving sizes. Use firm Malaysian-style prawn paste that comes in a block that is firm enough to cut and roast, not the liquidised *belacan* from Hong Kong.

Red chillies 150 g (5¹/₃ oz), seeded
Dried prawn (shrimp) paste 45 g
  (1¹/₂ oz / 3 Tbsp)
Kaffir lime leaves (optional) 2

1. Chop chillies coarsely in a food processor.
2. If toasting prawn paste on a grill or in an oven-toaster, press it into a thin, flat piece, then toast both sides till lightly brown. Do not burn it or the sambal will taste bitter. Alternatively, "toast" by dry-frying crumbled pieces in a wok till lightly brown, stirring constantly.
3. Pound chopped chillies and toasted prawn paste in a mortar and pestle to a paste.
4. If varying the flavour with kaffir lime leaves, chop leaves finely and stir into pounded sambal *belacan*.
5. Store in a glass bottle in the fridge.

CHICKEN CURRY

The word "curry" is believed to come from the Tamil word "*kari*" meaning "sauce", and for centuries, "curry" has been used to refer to a way of preparing meat, seafood and vegetables with spices and root herbs into a soup, stew or thick mixture to be eaten with a grain such as rice or bread. This mixture can be enriched with milk, coconut milk or yoghurt or soured with tamarind, vinegar and other souring ingredients. Curries are eaten all over South and Southeast Asia but with enormous variations in flavour and heat depending on the spice mixes and root herbs used. One common way to prepare a curry is to use a curry powder made up of various ground spices. The mixes for meat and seafood are different and packets of curry powder are usually marked for "meat" or "fish" curry.

STRAITS CHINESE CHICKEN CURRY

Water 500 ml (16 fl oz / 2 cups)

Grated coconut 500 g (1 lb 1½ oz)

Tamarind pulp 50 g (1 2/3 oz)

Cooking oil 60 ml (2 fl oz / ¼ cup)

Cinnamon stick 1, about 6-cm (2½-in)

Cloves 2

Cardamom 2 pods

Chicken 1 kg (2 lb 3 oz), chopped into pieces

Salt 1½ tsp

SPICE PASTE

Shallots 200 g (7 oz), peeled

Garlic 75 g (2½ oz), peeled

Water 125 ml (4 fl oz / ½ cup)

Straits Chinese meat curry powder (page 35) ¾ cup

1. Prepare spice paste. Blend shallots and garlic in a food processor with a little of the water till fine. Mix the remainder of the water with curry powder.

2. To get coconut milk, mix 400 ml (13⅓ fl oz / 1⅔ cups) of the water with the grated coconut. Using a clean muslin cloth bag, squeeze out coconut milk and set aside.

3. Mix the remainder of the water with tamarind pulp, strain away solids and set aside tamarind juice.

4. Heat oil in a pot and stir-fry shallot and garlic paste with cinnamon, cloves and cardamoms for 1 minute. Add curry powder paste and fry till oil surfaces.

5. Add chicken and salt and mix well. Fry for a few minutes, then stir in tamarind juice and bring to the boil.

6. Add coconut milk and bring to the boil. Turn down heat and simmer till chicken is cooked.

7. Turn off heat and stand curry for several hours to develop flavours before serving.

INDIAN-STYLE MEATBALLS IN YOGHURT SAUCE

This yoghurt sauce is uncooked and flavoured with mint while the meatballs are fried. However, if you prefer a warm dish, the sauce can be heated. If heating the sauce, however, turn off the heat when bubbles start to appear. Do not allow the sauce to boil as yoghurt separates when boiled. (See West Asian cooked yoghurt sauce, page 47.)

Yoghurt 500 ml (16 fl oz / 2 cups)

Red chilli powder 1 tsp

Salt 2 tsp

Mint ½ cup, chopped

Minced lamb/mutton 500 g (1 lb 1½ oz)

Ginger 8 slices, peeled and finely chopped

Onion 50 g (1 2/3 oz), peeled and finely chopped

Garlic 2 cloves, peeled and finely chopped

Ground cumin ½ tsp

Ground cinnamon ¼ tsp

Ground black pepper ½ tsp

Cooking oil for frying

1. If making uncooked yoghurt sauce, beat yoghurt with chilli powder and 1 tsp salt. Stir in chopped mint. If making cooked yoghurt sauce, heat sauce, then stir in chopped mint.

2. Mix minced meat with remaining 1 tsp salt and the remainder of the ingredients. Divide into 16 portions and form into patties.

3. Heat oil in a frying pan and fry patties till meat is cooked.

4. To serve, pour yoghurt sauce over hot patties.

NORTH INDIAN CHICKEN CURRY

Ghee/cooking oil 60 ml (2 fl oz / 1/4 cup)

Black cardamom 3 pods

Cinnamon stick 1, about 6-cm (2 1/2-in)

Tomatoes 100 g (3 1/2 oz), cubed

Green chillies 2, seeded

Chicken 1 kg (2 lb 3 oz), chopped into pieces

Salt 1 1/2 tsp

Water 500 ml (16 fl oz / 2 cups)

Yoghurt 125 ml (4 fl oz / 1/2 cup)

SPICE PASTE

Onion 100 g (3 1/2 oz), peeled and ground to paste

Garlic 4 cloves, peeled and ground to paste

Ginger 1 thumb-size knob, peeled

Water 125 ml (4 fl oz / 1/2 cup)

Ground coriander 1 1/2 Tbsp

Ground fennel 2 tsp

Ground cumin 2 tsp

Red chilli powder 1–2 Tbsp

Ground turmeric 1 tsp

1. Prepare spice paste. In a food processor, grind onion, garlic and ginger to a fine paste with 2 Tbsp of the water. Mix powdered spices with the remainder of the water to a paste.

2. Heat ghee/oil in a saucepan and sauté ground onion, garlic and ginger paste together with cardamoms and cinnamon till fragrant. Add paste of powdered spices and fry till oil surfaces.

3. Add tomatoes, green chillies, chicken, salt and enough water to cover chicken. Bring to the boil, then turn down heat and simmer gently till chicken is cooked. The time required depends on the size of the pieces.

4. Stir in yoghurt, adjust seasoning to taste and return to the boil. Turn off heat and rest for several hours to let flavours develop before serving curry.

DHAL CURRY

This is a basic dhal curry that goes with most kinds of flavoured rice from South Asia and can be served as part of Nepali dhal *bhaat* (rice with dhal). Instead of flavouring with garam masala at the end of the cooking, stir in 1/2 cup chopped coriander leaves. Although mung or masoor dhal cooks and softens in 30 minutes or less, if the dhal is very aged—as sometimes happens with me—it will take longer.

Ghee 3 Tbsp

Cumin seeds/mustard seeds/ fenugreek 1 tsp

Ginger 5 thin slices, finely shredded

Mung/masoor dhal 120 g (4 1/2 oz / 1 cup), soaked 30 minutes

Water 1 litre (32 fl oz / 4 cups)

Ground turmeric 1/2 tsp

Salt 1 1/2 tsp

Garlic 4 cloves, peeled

Potatoes 100 g (3 1/2 oz), peeled and cubed

Fresh/dried red chillies 2, seeded and chopped

Coriander leaves 1 small bunch, chopped

Any garam masala (page 30) 1/2 tsp

1. Heat ghee in a pot and fry cumin, mustard or fenugreek till fragrant. If using mustard seeds, fry until they start popping.

2. Add ginger, dhal and water and bring to the boil. Skim off the scum that rises to the top.

3. Add ground turmeric, salt, garlic and potatoes and simmer till dhal and potato cubes are tender. The dhal curry should be the consistency of a thick soup.

4. Add chillies and coriander leaves and simmer for a couple of minutes to cook chillies. Sprinkle garam masala on dhal and serve hot with rice.

Note:

If serving Nepali dhal bhaat, the dhal curry is always poured over the rice.

DHAL CHAR (SOUTH INDIAN DHAL STEW)

Dhal char is an essential part of many South Indian meals and it is eaten with anything dry such as rice or *roti prata*. It is also an excellent side dish with biryani, its slight tartness lifting jaded palates. A thick dhal and vegetable stew, the curry is enriched by the addition of some mutton and mutton bones. However, it is easily made into a vegetarian dish if the meat is left out. If so, increase the tomatoes to give a more meaty flavour to the stew.

Tamarind pulp 75 g (2 1/2 oz / 1/3 cup)

Water 2 litres (64 fl oz / 8 cups)

Cooking oil 3 Tbsp

Fenugreek seeds 1/2 tsp

Mutton 300 g (11 oz), cubed

Mung/masoor dhal 60 g (2 oz / 1/2 cup), soaked 30 minutes

Tomatoes 200 g (7 oz), cut into wedges

Potatoes 250 g (9 oz), cubed

Aubergines (eggplants) 400 g (14 1/3 oz), cubed

Salt 1 1/2 tsp

Green chillies 3, seeded and split

SPICE PASTE

Dried red chillies 30 g (1 oz), seeded and softened in water

Water 3 Tbsp

Ground coriander 1 Tbsp

Ground cumin 1 Tbsp

Ground fennel 1/2 Tbsp

Ground turmeric 1/2 tsp

Ginger paste (page 36) 1/2 Tbsp

Garlic paste (page 36) 2 tsp

1. Mix tamarind pulp and water. Strain and discard solids.

2. Prepare spice paste. Grind softened dried red chillies with the 3 Tbsp water. Stir other ground ingredients together into chilli paste.

3. Heat oil in a pot and fry fenugreek seeds for 1 minute, then add spice paste. Fry till fragrant and oil surfaces.

4. Stir in mutton and half the tamarind water and bring to the boil. Turn down heat and simmer till mutton is nearly tender. Add more tamarind water if needed.

5. Add dhal and half the tomato wedges and continue to simmer till dhal begins to break up. Add potatoes.

6. When potatoes begin to get soft, stir in aubergines and salt. Add more tamarind water if needed.

7. Simmer till aubergines are soft, adding more tamarind water if mixture gets too thick. There should be at least 3 cups of gravy in it. Add green chillies last and turn off heat when chillies change colour.

8. Rest for several hours before serving with a biryani. Dhal char keeps well.

LAMB/CHICKEN KEBABS   Makes 16–20 skewers

Skewers of freshly grilled meat are such standard fare in West Asia that butcher shops and kebab shops are typically found side by side. In fact, some butcher shops double as kebab shops in small towns. Perhaps such kebabs were the origins of Malay-Indonesian satay? Satay is, however, eaten with a special sauce, unlike kebabs. In West Asia, meat always means lamb, while chicken or beef is always so-called. West Asia has some of the tastiest lamb I have ever eaten, perhaps because the meat is still basically organic. Flocks of sheep can be seen wandering even in the most arid landscape. When making cubed lamb kebabs, cook lightly to keep the lamb tender. Marinating the meat in yoghurt or lemon juice also helps to tenderise it, as does adding 1/4 tsp bicarbonate of soda to the marinade, although more sensitive taste buds can sometimes detect its presence. (It tastes vaguely soapy.) Another way to tenderise tough meat is to beat it with a meat hammer or back of the cleaver the old-fashioned way before seasoning.

Onion juice (page 36) 2 Tbsp

Lamb/boneless chicken 1 kg (2 lb 3 oz), cut into cubes

Any *baharat* or *advieh* (pages 31–33) 2 tsp

Salt 1 tsp

Yoghurt 125 ml (4 fl oz / 1/2 cup)

Olive oil 1 Tbsp + more for basting

1. Prepare meat a day ahead or at least 2 hours before grilling. Mix onion juice into meat, then *baharat* or *advieh* and salt, followed by yoghurt and olive oil. Place in a covered container in the refrigerator and leave overnight or for at least 2 hours before grilling.

2. Oil skewers before threading meat. Grill or barbecue for 6–8 minutes depending on meat and size of cubes. Chicken will cook faster while lamb will take a little longer.

3. Remove meat from skewers and serve with rice or bread.

GROUND MEAT KEBABS Makes 16 skewers

Metal skewers, whether the broad flat Turkish-style ones or the narrow square-sided kind, are the best for making kebabs. With metal skewers, heat is carried from the outside through to the inside to cook the meat more quickly. The bevelled sides also allow you to turn and rest the skewer on each of its sides to cook the kebab more evenly. Rounded bamboo skewers tend to roll and rest on the heavier side and the exposed bamboo burn as well. To make more kebabs with less ground meat, mix in a small handful of softened fine-grained bulgur. This mixture will give you a more spongy kebab than one made purely of meat. For added flavour, soften the bulgur with lemon juice rather than water. An alternative to bulgur is corn flour. Unlike cubed meat kebabs, ground meat kebabs must be grilled resting on a wire base.

Ground lamb/chicken/beef 750 g (1 lb 11 oz)

Any *baharat* (pages 32–33) 1 tsp

Salt 1 tsp

Olive oil 2 tsp

Onion 50 g (1²/₃ oz), peeled and chopped

Flat-leaf parsley/coriander leaves ¹/₄ cup, chopped finely

Corn flour (optional) 2 tsp

Lemon wedges

1. Mix minced meat with *baharat*, salt, olive oil, chopped onion and herb of choice. Divide into 16 portions and shape meat around the middle of an oiled skewer. The kebabs can be formed as one even-sized tube on the skewer itself or the meat shaped into long ovals or several small ovals or small round balls that are skewered for grilling.

2. Grill or barbecue kebabs for 5–7 minutes depending on the size of kebabs as well as the kind of meat. Lamb and beef can be just cooked, but chicken should be cooked a little longer. The meat should still be juicy.

3. Serve with squeezes of lemon juice. Enjoy with rice or bread.

KAFTA ANTAKYA (ANTIOCH-STYLE MEATBALLS) Makes about 16 skewers

On the way to the well-preserved St Simeon Church ruins some distance from Aleppo, Syria, I came across this delicious ground meat kebab. I was later told that this was an Antioch-style kebab. (However, I am quite sure that just as there is no such dish as Singapore Noodles in Singapore, there is no *kafta Antakya* in Antioch!)

Minced lamb 750 g (1 lb 11 oz)

Salt 1 tsp

Any *baharat* (pages 32–33) ¹/₂ tsp

Flat-leaf parsley ¹/₄ cup, chopped

Garlic 2 cloves, peeled and finely chopped

Lemon juice 1 tsp

Olive oil 2 tsp

1. Mix together all the ingredients and form mixture into 15 g (¹/₂ oz) patties. Shape round or oval.

2. Thread about 4 patties on each oiled skewer, keeping them round, oval or shaping into a tube.

3. Grill for 5–7 minutes depending on thickness of meat. Serve with rice or pita bread.

SHISH TA'UK (LEBANESE CHICKEN SKEWERS)

Although *shish ta'uk* is said to be Lebanese, I have also seen these grilled chicken cubes in Syria and Jordan and I am sure there are grilled chicken cubes elsewhere in West Asia, just as there is also freshly grilled whole chicken almost everywhere which, like *shish ta'uk*, is sold wrapped in pita bread and comes with a bag of some sort of garlic mayonnaise. The flavour of any kebab, grilled or roasted chicken can be varied by using a different spice mix, but use a spice mix that does not have *noomi Basra* in it because there is already lemon juice in the marinade.

Chicken meat 1 kg (2 lb 3 oz), cut into 2.5-cm (1-in) cubes

Salt 1 tsp

Any *baharat*, *advieh* or *bhar* (pages 31–33) 1¹/₂ tsp

Lemon juice ¹/₂ Tbsp

Olive oil 2 tsp

1. Mix chicken with rest of ingredients. Place in a covered container and stand overnight in the refrigerator.

2. Thread 4–5 chicken cubes onto each oiled skewer.

3. Grill for 6–8 minutes till cooked through. Serve with rice or pita bread.

Roasted Broccoli or Cauliflower

This is not only easy but also tasty and the roasted broccoli or cauliflower goes so well with many rice dishes especially the flavoured ones. The long, slow roasting gives the vegetables a chewy texture as well as a smoky flavour. The florets should be large because they shrink considerably after roasting.

Olive oil for brushing pan and
   vegetables
Salt (optional) 1 tsp
Broccoli/cauliflower 2 kg
   (4 lb 6 oz), cut into large florets

DRESSING
Lemon juice or yoghurt sauce
   (page 47)

1. Preheat oven to 150°C (300°F).
2. Brush a baking pan with olive oil. Rub some olive oil and salt, if used, into florets. Spread florets on pan and bake for 45 minutes to 1 hour or till florets shrink and there are some nicely browned bits.
3. Dress with lemon juice or yoghurt sauce and serve with any South or West Asian pilaf or rice.

Vegetable Kebabs

Instead of threading meat with vegetables and cooking them together which can cause the meat to be overcooked (as some vegetables can take longer to soften than meat to cook), why not grill the vegetables separately?

Any or all of the following:
Red/green/yellow capsicums
   (bell peppers), seeded and cut
   into large squares
Onion, peeled and cut into
   wedges
Broccoli, cut into large florets
Cauliflower, cut into large florets
Courgette (zucchini), cut into
   large cubes
Aubergine (eggplant), cut into
   large cubes
Fresh button mushrooms
Whole tomatoes
Olive oil for brushing on
   vegetables

1. Thread vegetables together on metal skewers and brush lightly with olive oil.
2. Grill till vegetables soften and are partially browned.
3. Serve with meat kebabs and rice.

West Asian Cooked Yoghurt Sauce

I ate at the famous Al-Kawali restaurant in Old Damascus in 2009. The tart and salty yoghurt sauce in which the lamb I ordered was served, was especially tasty with buttered rice. (I have since found that it is delicious with plain rice too.) Interestingly, I had come across a similar yoghurt sauce in Jerash, Jordan, in a dish of baked lamb kofta (ground meat). This is my take on that yoghurt sauce. Yoghurt separates when boiled. One way to prevent this is to thicken the sauce with egg, corn flour or rice flour to prevent it from separating. Another way which is my preferred method is to turn the heat off once bubbles appear to avoid boiling the yoghurt. If the yoghurt is very thick, like Greek-style yoghurt which is thickened with cream, it has to be thinned with milk. The sauce must be stirred or whisked continuously once it has been added to the hot ghee to get a smooth sauce.

Greek-style yoghurt *500 ml (16 fl oz / 2 cups)*

Milk *250 ml (8 fl oz / 1 cup)*

Corn flour (optional) *1 Tbsp*

Garlic *2 cloves, peeled and finely chopped/mashed*

Salt *1 tsp*

Ghee *1 Tbsp*

HERBS (CHOPPED)
- Dill
- Coriander leaves
- Spring onion
- Mint leaves
- Flat-leaf parsley

1. Using a small wire whisk, mix together yoghurt, milk, corn flour if using, chopped garlic and salt till smooth.

2. Melt ghee in a saucepan till hot, then stir in yoghurt mixture and continue stirring or whisking till bubbles appear on the sauce and it begins to boil. Turn off heat.

3. Use sauce as a dressing for kebabs, roasted meat, vegetables and rice.

West/South Asian Uncooked Yoghurt Sauce

This basic sauce tastes great with any West or South Asian pilaf whether or not the rice dish has any sauce or other flavours. The tartness of the yoghurt contrasts well with rich flavours. Because food is usually eaten with fingers in these regions, rice is easier to handle when there is a sauce to hold the grains more or less together. The common West Asian cultural practice of guests eating out of one large communal platter makes a sauce almost essential when eating rice. The yoghurt sauce also makes an excellent dressing for cucumber, grilled meats and vegetables. If the sauce is flavoured with spices or herbs, resting it for at least an hour improves the flavour especially if the flavour is garlic.

Yoghurt *750 ml (24 fl oz / 3 cups)*

Salt *1 tsp*

Milk (optional) *as needed*

ALTERNATIVE FLAVOURS
- Garlic *3 cloves, peeled and finely mashed*
- Ground cumin *1/2 tsp*
- Mint *1 cup, finely chopped*
- Coriander leaves *1 cup, finely chopped*
- Onion juice (page 36) and chopped onions *1/2 cup*

1. Mix yoghurt and salt together. If yoghurt is very thick and you want a pouring sauce, stir in enough milk to thin the yoghurt. Adjust seasoning to taste. Add any alternative flavours if desired.

2. Place in a covered container in the refrigerator overnight before serving. Serve as a sauce with rice or as a dressing with grilled meat or vegetables.

Lamb in Yoghurt Sauce

This is an approximation of that delicious lamb in yoghurt sauce that I ate at Al-Kawali in Damascus. Naturally, the flavour will also depend on the quality of the lamb. If the lamb is a very tender fillet, the meat can be simply grilled and the sauce poured over the grilled meat.

West Asian cooked yoghurt sauce (page 47) 1 quantity

Cooked chickpeas/broad beans (optional) 1 cup

LAMB

Bone-in lamb 1 kg (2 lb 3 oz)

Water 1 litre (32 fl oz / 4 cups)

Onion 150 g (5^1/$_3$ oz), peeled and quartered

Any baharat, advieh or bhar (pages 31–33) 1 tsp

Salt 1^1/$_2$ tsp

1. Bone lamb, trim fat and remove as much silver skin as you can. Cut meat into cubes, chunks or thick slices.

2. Put meat, bones and water into a pot and bring to the boil. Skim off the scum before adding the rest of the ingredients. Return to the boil. Turn down heat and simmer till lamb is tender.

3. Remove meat and onion if desired. Discard bones and freeze any remaining gravy for cooking with rice another day.

4. Add cooked yoghurt sauce, lamb and cooked chickpeas/broad beans if using. Add salt to taste and return to the boil. Do not overboil sauce.

Baked Kofta in Yoghurt Sauce, Jerash-style

This is my take on the baked lamb kofta in yoghurt sauce that I ate at a tourist restaurant in Jerash, Jordan.

Corn flour 1 Tbsp

Milk 125 ml (4 fl oz / ^{1}/$_2$ cup)

Yoghurt 250 ml (8 fl oz / 1 cup)

Minced lamb 400 g (14^1/$_3$ oz)

Salt 1 tsp

Ground black pepper ^{1}/$_2$ tsp

Parsley a handful, chopped

Chopped garlic ^{1}/$_2$ Tbsp

1. Preheat oven to 160°C (325°F).

2. In a baking dish, mix corn flour into milk and stir in yoghurt.

3. Mix meat, salt, pepper, parsley and garlic and form into a large meatball. Place meatball into baking dish with yoghurt sauce and bake for 20–30 minutes or till meat is cooked.

Note:

An alternative to baking kofta is to cook it in the microwave oven. Cover the baking dish and cook in the microwave oven for 5–7 minutes on High. The time depends on the wattage of the microwave oven as well as how thin or thick the meat patty is. Reduce the time if the meat is spread out over a wider surface.

WEST ASIAN AUBERGINE STEW

One of the preparatory steps seen in many aubergine recipes is salting the aubergine to "draw out the bitterness". However, the only aubergines I have found to be bitter are the tiny, round, green Indo-Chinese aubergines, never the bigger, long or round purple or green variety. Aubergine that is fried or browned before being stewed will taste very different from sliced aubergine added straight into the stew. Having seen the huge amounts of oil that frying aubergine absorbs, I no longer fry aubergine in oil but prefer to brown them on a lightly greased cast-iron frying pan or Indian chatty pan (the flat cast-iron pan used for making chapatti or *roti prata* also called a *tawa*).

Aubergines (eggplants) *1 kg (2 lb 3 oz)*

Olive oil *60 ml (2 fl oz / 1/4 cup)*

Onions *100 g (3 1/2 oz), peeled and thickly sliced*

Garlic *3 cloves, peeled and chopped*

Lamb/mutton *300 g (11 oz), cubed*

Any *baharat, bhar or advieh* (pages 31–33) *3 tsp*

Tomatoes *250 g (9 oz), chopped*

Salt *1 1/2 tsp*

Water *750 ml (24 fl oz / 3 cups)*

Flat-leaf parsley/coriander leaves *1 cup, chopped*

1. Halve aubergines lengthwise and if they are very long, cut them in half. Discard stems.

2. Brush some oil on cut side of aubergines and place cut side down on a hot cast-iron pan or *tawa*. Brown both flesh and skin.

3. Heat olive oil in a saucepan and fry onions till they begin to brown. Add garlic and fry till fragrant. Add lamb/mutton and fry till meat changes colour.

4. Stir in chosen spice mix, tomatoes, salt and water. The amount of water added depends on the type of meat. Add more water if needed as aubergines absorb liquid. Bring to the boil, turn down heat and simmer till meat is tender. It will take at least an hour.

5. Add aubergines and parsley/coriander leaves and continue simmering till aubergines are tender but still whole. There should be at least 2 cups of gravy left in pan.

6. Serve stew ladled over plain boiled rice.

WEST ASIAN BEAN STEW

If you discount the time for softening the beans, this is an easy everyday dish to serve with rice or flatbread. Any kind of dried beans can be cooked this way although certain ones such as chickpeas may need pre-boiling. As boiled beans such as broad beans or chickpeas freeze well, boil a large pot and freeze some for another day. One of the easiest ways to cook beans is to boil them in a slow cooker overnight.

Olive oil *60 ml (2 fl oz / 1/4 cup)*

Onions *200 g (7 oz), peeled and chopped*

Garlic *3 cloves, peeled and chopped*

Dried beans (white, chickpeas, pinto, lentils) *400 g (14 1/3 oz / 2 cups), soaked overnight*

Lamb/mutton/chicken *200 g (7 oz), cubed or coarsely chopped*

Tomatoes *250 g (9 oz), chopped*

Salt *1 1/2 tsp*

Water *750 ml (24 fl oz / 3 cups)*

Any *advieh, baharat or za'atar* (pages 31, 33, 34) *2 tsp*

1. Heat olive oil in a saucepan and fry onions and garlic till garlic starts to brown. Add meat, mixed spices, salt, tomatoes, beans and water and bring to the boil. The amount of water needed will depend on the state of the beans and the type of meat being cooked.

2. Turn down heat and simmer till meat and beans are tender. There should be at least 2 cups gravy left in pan.

3. Serve stew ladled over plain boiled rice.

Note:

If combining chicken and beans, make sure the beans are tender by pre-cooking before starting on the stew. If making the stew with mutton, this tough meat can be cooked together with tough beans like chickpeas.

Margat Bamia (Iraqi ladies' finger stew)

Ladies' finger (okra) secretes a mucus that gives this vegetable its distinctive and somewhat slimy mouth-feel that some dislike. To get rid of this mucus, my mother would soak the cut vegetable in several changes of water, as the mucus does not break down with long cooking. I never bother doing this as I rather like the mouth-feel of ladies' fingers. While West Asian ladies' finger comes in tiny finger-lengths, Southeast Asian ladies' finger is usually at least double that and will need to be cut into slices or halved. When buying ladies' finger, pick the tender ones as mature ladies' finger can be rather stringy. To check for tenderness, bend the small narrow tip. If it breaks, it is tender. When preparing ladies' finger, trim off and discard the tough stem as well as the tips.

Baharat 1 (page 32) 3 tsp

Salt 1 1/2 tsp

Lamb ribs/cubes 500 g
    (1 lb 1 1/2 oz)

Olive oil 60 ml (2 fl oz / 1/4 cup)

Garlic 2 cloves, peeled and
    chopped

Water 1 litre (32 fl oz / 4 cups)

Tomatoes 300 g (11 oz)

Noomi Basra 2

Ladies' fingers (okra) 500 g
    (1 lb 1 1/2 oz), cut into 3-cm (1-in)
    pieces

Lime juice to taste

1. Rub baharat and 1/2 tsp salt into meat and set aside.

2. Heat olive oil in a saucepan and brown lamb. Add garlic when lamb is seared.

3. Add water, tomatoes, remaining salt and dried limes and bring to the boil. Turn down heat and simmer till meat begins to get tender.

4. Stir in ladies' fingers and continue simmering till vegetable and lamb are tender.

5. Adjust seasoning to taste with lime juice. There should also be at least 2–3 cups of gravy left in pan.

6. Serve stew ladled over plain boiled rice.

Fakhitiyya (Syrian stewed lamb with sumac and walnuts)

The inspiration for this stewed lamb came from Lilia Zaouali's *Medieval Cuisine of the Islamic World*. Yoghurt, sumac and ground walnuts are ancient West Asian flavourings while tomatoes, a South American native, are today grown all over the more verdant parts of West Asia in plastic hot houses.

Olive oil 3 Tbsp

Onion 100 g (3 1/2 oz), peeled and
    chopped

Garlic 2 cloves, peeled and
    chopped

Lamb cubes 750 g (1 lb 11 oz)

Ground walnuts 100 g (3 1/2 oz /
    1 cup)

Tomatoes 150 g (5 1/3 oz), skinned
    and chopped

Sumac 3 Tbsp

Salt 1 1/2 tsp

Water 1 litre (32 fl oz / 4 cups)

Yoghurt 125 ml (4 fl oz / 1/2 cup)

1. Heat oil in a saucepan and fry onion till translucent. Add garlic and fry till fragrant.

2. Add lamb and walnuts and fry till oil surfaces. Add tomatoes, sumac, salt and water and stew till meat is tender and gravy is rich and thick. If necessary, add more water for stewing.

3. Stir in yoghurt and return to the boil. Turn off heat once bubbles appear to prevent yoghurt from separating. Dish out and serve.

KIMCHI FRIED WITH MEAT

This Korean dish is excellent with rice porridge as well as plain boiled rice whether short-grain or long-grain. Tart *kimchi* combines well not only with meat but also seafood such as prawns, squid or firm-fleshed fish.

Pork/chicken/ beef 250 g (9 oz), *cut into strips*

Sesame oil 2 *Tbsp*

Light soy sauce 1 *Tbsp*

Dark soy sauce *a few drops*

Cooking oil 1 *Tbsp*

Onion 50 g (1²/₃ oz), *peeled and cubed*

Green chillies 2, *seeded and sliced into strips*

Red chillies 2, *seeded and sliced into strips*

Kimchi 2 *cups, squeezed dry and sliced into strips*

Salt ¹/₂ *tsp*

Chopped garlic 2 *tsp*

Spring onions 2, *cut into finger lengths*

Coriander leaves 1 *large bunch, coarsely chopped*

1. Season meat with 1 Tbsp sesame oil and light and dark soy sauce. Leave to marinate while preparing other ingredients.

2. Heat remaining 1 Tbsp sesame oil with 1 Tbsp oil in a pan and fry onion for 2 minutes. The onion should still be firm.

3. Stir in meat and fry till cooked before adding green and red chillies and *kimchi*. Fry till *kimchi* is heated through and green chillies change colour.

4. Lastly, add salt, garlic, spring onions and coriander leaves and mix well.

CHICKEN CABBAGE SOUP

This simple soup can be served with almost all of the rice dishes in this book, even though it has a somewhat Chinese flavour because of the fried garlic. An alternative to fried garlic is fried shallots which is added and boiled with the cabbage, the way some chicken rice stalls in Singapore prepare their cabbage soup.

Cooking oil ¹/₂ *Tbsp*

Chopped garlic 1 *tsp*

Rich chicken stock (page 80) 1 litre (32 fl oz / 4 cups)

Salt 1 *tsp*

Cabbage 2 *large leaves, shredded*

Chopped spring onion

1. Heat oil in a saucepan and brown garlic. Add chicken stock, salt and cabbage and bring to the boil. Simmer till cabbage is soft.

2. Garnish with chopped spring onions.

STEAMED CHICKEN, SINGAPORE-STYLE

Steamed chicken rice is one of the most popular dishes enjoyed in Singapore. The "steamed" chicken is actually not steamed, but cooked in a special way in very hot water that leaves the meat tender and moist and still a little red at the thigh bone. Some foreigners are horrified by this, but the many Singaporeans who eat such meat daily are none the worse for it. Perhaps the garlic-ginger-and chilli sauce (recipe below) that goes with chicken rice eliminates the hazard! (The food and agriculture department in Singapore once tested just such a mixture as a pesticide.) If it bothers you, get a meat thermometer to check the internal temperature to be certain the meat is cooked through.

Salt 2 tsp

Ginger 1 large thumb-size knob, peeled and smashed

Chicken 1 kg (2 lb 3 oz)

CONDIMENTS AND GARNISHING

Sliced cucumbers

Sliced tomatoes

Sesame oil 2 Tbsp or more to taste

Light soy sauce 1 Tbsp or more to taste

Chopped coriander leaves

Chopped spring onion

1. Place salt and ginger into a large pot of water and bring to the boil. Immerse whole chicken into boiling water and return to the boil. Keep water on the boil for 5 minutes. Turn off heat, cover pot and let bird sit in hot water for 30 minutes.

2. After 30 minutes, return water to the boil, turn off heat, cover pot and let bird sit in hot water for another 30 minutes.

3. Repeat step 2 one more time. This should be enough to cook a 1-kg (2 lb 3 oz) chicken. After the last 30 minutes is up, remove chicken and immerse it in a basin of cold water for about 30 minutes to stop the cooking. Drain well.

4. Cut chicken up and arrange on a serving plate on a large bed of sliced cucumbers and tomatoes. Drizzle generously with sesame oil mixed with light soy sauce. Garnish with chopped coriander and spring onion.

Note:

The water used for cooking the chicken can be turned into stock for making the chicken rice if more chicken bones are boiled in it.

If undercooked chicken bothers you, use a meat thermometer to check the internal temperature of the chicken. Insert the tip into the thickest part of the chicken (the area between the inner thigh and breast), and ensure that the internal temperature has reached 82°C (180°F). If you don't have a meat thermometer, keep the water on the boil for 5 minutes (each time you return it to the boil) before turning off the heat and leaving the bird to sit.

SINGAPORE CHICKEN RICE CONDIMENTS

The condiments consist of three parts, with chilli and ginger being essential, and the dark soy sauce optional especially if the chicken is a roast chicken. The chillies and ginger are ground separately and you help yourself to more of whatever you like better. Some cooks combine the ginger and chillies and grind them together.

GROUND CHILLIES

Red chillies 150 g (5¹/₃ oz), seeded

Rice vinegar 1 Tbsp

Water 1 Tbsp

Salt ¹/₂ tsp

Sugar 1 tsp

1. To make ground chillies, blend all ingredients together till fine in a food processor. Add more water if mixture is too stiff to blend well.

GROUND GINGER

Ginger 150 (5¹/₃ oz), peeled and thinly sliced

Rice vinegar 2 tsp

Salt ¹/₂ tsp

Water 1 Tbsp

Sesame oil 3 tsp

1. To make ground ginger, blend all ingredients except for the sesame oil, into a fine paste in a food processor. Stir in sesame oil last.

CHINESE ROAST CHICKEN

Chinese "roast" chicken is actually deep-fried whole chicken, but deep-frying a whole chicken takes lots of oil, requires a large wok and is hard to do at home. Instead, roasting the chicken or chicken parts in an oven is far easier and just as tasty. You can also chop the chicken into pieces, season and fry them. Needless to say, fried chicken is not for the figure-conscious, so try the alternative cooking methods offered here. Whether whole or in parts, chicken seasoned in any of the three basic ways below can be fried, roasted or grilled. Basic roast chicken and garlic and soy sauce chicken are delicious with practically all of the more plain flavoured rice dishes such as tomato rice, while five-spice roast chicken would be better with the more Southeast Asian ones such as Singapore chicken rice.

BASIC ROAST CHICKEN

Salt 2¹/₂ tsp

Ground white pepper 1 tsp

Chicken (whole or parts) 1.5 kg
    (3 lb 4¹/₂ oz)

GARLIC AND SOY SAUCE CHICKEN

Garlic 8 cloves, peeled and finely
    mashed

Dark soy sauce ¹/₂ Tbsp

Light soy sauce 1 Tbsp

Salt 1 tsp

Ground white pepper 1 tsp

Chicken (whole or parts) 1.5 kg
    (3 lb 4¹/₂ oz)

FIVE-SPICE ROAST CHICKEN

Chinese five-spice powder 2 tsp

Dark soy sauce 2 tsp

Light soy sauce 3 Tbsp

Salt 1 tsp

Sugar 1 Tbsp

Ground white pepper ¹/₂ tsp

Chicken (whole or parts) 1.5 kg
    (3 lb 4¹/₂ oz)

1. To marinate a basic roast chicken, rub salt and pepper into chicken. Cover and leave to marinate for at least 2 hours or overnight in the fridge.

   To marinate a garlic and soy sauce chicken, mix together seasoning ingredients and rub all over and inside chicken if using whole chicken. Cover and leave to marinate for at least an hour or overnight in the fridge.

   To marinate a five-spice roast chicken, rub seasoning all over and inside chicken if using whole chicken. Cover and leave to marinate for at least an hour or overnight in the fridge.

TO ROAST CHICKEN

2. Place marinated chicken on a rack in a roasting pan, breast side facing down if using a whole chicken.

3. Preheat oven to 160°C (325°F) and roast back of chicken for 30–45 minutes or till it is browning nicely. Turn chicken over to roast breast for another hour or till internal temperature at the thickest part in the inner thigh next to the breast reaches 82°C (180°F).

4. If some gravy is desired, when the dripping at the bottom of the roasting pan turn a dark brown, pour in a cup of chicken stock. The stock prevents the dripping from drying out so that you get enough dripping for gravy. It also keeps the chicken moist during roasting.

5. Rest roast for 20–30 minutes before carving or chopping up.

TO DEEP-FRY CHICKEN

2. When frying chicken and other food, select an oil with a high burning temperature. Peanut oil is best. Never use oils like olive or corn which break down quickly.

3. Heat oil well before starting. To check if the temperature is hot enough, dip a pair of wooden chopsticks into the oil near the bottom of the pan. If bubbles appear from the ends, the oil is hot enough.

4. Add a few pieces of chicken at a time and never so many that the temperature of the oil drops drastically. You can tell by the fact that the chicken has stopped sizzling in the oil.

5. When the temperature is right, the fried chicken will look dry rather than oily, be a lovely brown colour and be cooked through.

6. Drain well before serving.

Salt-baked Chicken

I was inspired to try salt-baking chicken when I spotted these 5-kg (11-lb) bags of coarse salt from Thailand. This is sufficient for burying 1 kg (2 lb 3 oz) of chicken. Although this dish is not hard to do, be warned that you could wreck a pot doing it on the stove top. I packed a large pot with coarse salt and heated the salt for 30 minutes before burying the chicken in the hot salt. The heating salt made alarming cracking noises and the inside of the pot turned black, but the chicken did get salt-baked. It is far easier to bake the chicken in the oven if you have a large roasting pan that you can fill with salt. Chicken parts are easier to bury in salt and cook more quickly than a whole chicken.

Ginger juice (page 36) *1 Tbsp*

Chinese rice wine *1 Tbsp*

Salt *1 tsp*

Light soy sauce *1/2 tsp*

Chicken parts *1 kg (2 lb 3 oz)*

Greaseproof paper *3 sheets*

Coarse salt *5 kg (11 lb)*

CONDIMENTS AND GARNISHING

Cucumbers *2, sliced*

Tomatoes *3–4, sliced*

Sesame oil *2 Tbsp or more to taste*

Light soy sauce *1 Tbsp or more to taste*

Coriander leaves

Spring onion

1. Mix ginger juice with rice wine, salt and soy sauce. Rub seasoning into chicken, cover and leave to marinate in the refrigerator overnight.

2. The following day, place coarse salt in a large roasting pan and heat in an oven at 180°C (350°F) for 1 hour.

3. Before baking, wrap chicken in 2 sheets of greaseproof paper, then wrap the bundle in another sheet of greaseproof paper. The chicken parts should be spread out into a flat bundle for even baking.

4. Wearing oven gloves and using a ladle, bury wrapped bundle of chicken in the hot salt. Bake for 1 hour or until chicken is done. An alternative to baking is to cook the wrapped chicken buried in hot salt in the microwave oven for 20–25 minutes depending on your oven.

5. Unwrap and chop chicken. Arrange on a serving plate on a large bed of sliced cucumbers and tomatoes. Drizzle generously with sesame oil mixed with light soy sauce. Garnish with chopped coriander and spring onion.

Steamed Minced Pork with Salted Egg

Steamed minced pork with salted egg or salted vegetables are comfort foods in many Chinese-Singaporean homes. When someone is under the weather, he is usually served rice porridge with one or two of these side dishes. The saltiness of the salted eggs can be reduced by discarding one of the salted egg whites and substituting with an unsalted egg. The salted mustard greens should be soaked in cold water for about 10 minutes to reduce the saltiness but do not over soak. Chop the vegetable before mixing with the minced pork. Substitute the pork with chicken if preferred but the classic combination is with pork.

Salted egg yolks *2, chopped*

Minced pork *200 g (7 oz)*

Egg *1*

Water *60 ml (2 fl oz / 1/4 cup)*

Ground white pepper *1/4 tsp*

1. Mix all ingredients together in a microwaveable dish with a cover. Ensure that salted egg is spread out.

2. Cook on High in a microwave oven for about 7 minutes or till meat is cooked. The time depends on the wattage of your microwave oven. Alternatively, place dish without cover in a steamer and steam till meat shrinks away from sides of dish.

3. Serve hot.

Steamed Minced Pork with Salted Mustard Greens

Salted mustard greens *150 g (5 1/3 oz)*

Minced pork *150 g (5 1/3 oz)*

Water *60 ml (2 fl oz / 1/4 cup)*

Ground white pepper *1/4 tsp*

1. Soak salted mustard greens for 10 minutes before chopping up.

2. Mix all ingredients together in a microwaveable dish with a cover. Cook on High in a microwave oven for 7 minutes or till meat is cooked. The time depends on the wattage of your microwave oven. Alternatively, place dish without cover in a steamer and steam till meat shrinks away from sides of dish.

3. Serve hot.

Onion and Chilli Omelette

This very South and Southeast Asian omelette must surely be prepared daily in millions of homes all over Asia wherever chillies, onions and eggs are found. However, there are subtle differences. Many Indians in Singapore like to spice their onion omelette with green chillies and a few curry leaves. In India, some add chopped tomato and green chillies. In my Straits Chinese home, we spice it with sliced red chillies, while my Malay neighbour makes her onion omelette with pounded red chillies. The Thais add a dash of fish sauce to their omelette in place of salt. And in rural areas where duck eggs are aplenty, the omelette may be made with duck eggs instead.

Eggs 3

Salt or fish sauce to taste

Red/green chillies 1, seeded, sliced or pounded

Cooking oil for frying

Onion 100 g (3 1/2 oz), peeled and sliced to preferred thickness

1. Beat eggs and stir in salt or fish sauce and chillies.
2. Heat 1 Tbsp oil in a frying pan till very hot, then fry onion till edges begin to brown. Scoop out and stir into beaten eggs.
3. Reheat pan with 1 Tbsp oil till very hot. Pour half the egg mixture into hot pan, halving onion and chillies as well.
4. When one side of omelette has browned, fold or turn over, depending on whether you like your omelette soft in the centre or firm. Fold if soft is preferred. Turning over is more Asian and some cooks will chop up the omelette in the pan into large well-fried pieces. If the omelette is kept as a large round piece, fold over as soon as it is out of the pan and slice before serving.

Salted Radish Omelette

This omelette is not only delicious with rice porridge but also cheap and easily recreated. It is a standard menu item at rice porridge stalls in coffee shops and food courts, as well as fancy Taiwan porridge restaurants.

Salted radish 100 g (3 1/2 oz), chopped

Eggs 3

Ground white pepper 1/4 tsp

Chopped garlic (optional) 1 tsp

Water 1 Tbsp

Cooking oil for frying

1. Soak chopped radish for 10 minutes in cold water to reduce saltiness, but do not over soak. Err on the side of salty if doing the taste test. Squeeze dry.
2. Beat eggs with pepper, garlic if using, and water.
3. Heat 2 Tbsp oil in a frying pan and fry salted radish for 5 minutes. Scoop out and stir into beaten eggs.
4. Add a little more oil to the pan if necessary and heat pan till hot. Pour half the egg mixture into frying pan, making sure that salted radish is roughly halved.
5. Fold omelette over if you like it soft or flip it over if you like it cooked through.
6. Dish out and serve.

Stir-fried Romaine Lettuce

Many East and Southeast Asian rice dishes need an accompanying side dish of vegetables be it a simple stir-fry or a vegetable soup. Romaine (cos) lettuce makes a good stir-fry especially the baby ones common in Singapore wet markets. The romaine can also be substituted with iceberg lettuce, another common vegetable worldwide. Both need nothing more than rinsing and tearing into bite-size pieces. Other leafy vegetables such as kale or spinach can be prepared the same way.

Cooking oil 2 Tbsp

Garlic 2 cloves, peeled and chopped

Oyster sauce 2 Tbsp

Romaine (cos) lettuce 500 g (1 lb 1 1/2 oz), torn into pieces

1. Heat oil in a wok and sauté garlic till it begins to brown. Stir in oyster sauce, fry for 1 minute, then add lettuce. Stir-fry continuously till lettuce goes limp and changes colour. Turn off heat.
2. Dish out and serve immediately.

Seeni Sambol (sri lankan onion sambal)

One reason this is a Sinhalese festive favourite is that it can be prepared ahead of time as the flavour improves when rested. The difficulty with making this sambal, however, is getting hold of Maldive fish even in Singapore, where there is a fairly large Sinhalese community. After a fruitless afternoon checking numerous grocery stores in Little India asking and looking for this wood-like dried bonito, I learnt from Sinhalese friends that there was just one shop in Little India that sold it and that it was called "*masi*" in Tamil. Note that Maldive fish can be substituted with Japanese *katsuobushi*, one of the basic ingredients in Japanese dashi. *Katsuobushi* is dried, smoked and mould-cured bonito that looks like a piece of wood.

Water 250 ml (8 fl oz / 1 cup)

Tamarind pulp 50 g (1²/₃ oz)

Cooking oil 60 ml (2 fl oz / ¹/₄ cup)

Onions 200 g (7 oz), finely sliced

Maldive fish/katsuobushi 200 g (7 oz), thinly shaved and pounded, or dried bonito flakes, pounded

Sugar 2 Tbsp

Salt 1 tsp

SPICE PASTE

Shallots 50 g (1²/₃ oz), peeled

Garlic 1 clove, peeled

Dried red chillies 30 g (1 oz), seeded and softened

Ginger 2 slices

Water 2 Tbsp

1. Prepare spice paste. Blend shallots, garlic, chillies and ginger with water in a food processor till finely ground.

2. Mix water with tamarind pulp and strain away solids. Set aside tamarind juice.

3. Heat oil in a pan and fry sliced onions till they begin to brown. Add spice paste and fry till oil surfaces. Add fish, tamarind juice, sugar and salt and simmer over low heat, stirring constantly to prevent sambal from sticking to the bottom of pan. It should be just slightly moist.

4. Dish out and leave to cool before bottling. Store in the fridge for up to a few weeks. Reheat serving portions as needed.

Quickie Daikon Pickle with Garlic

If you want a quick pickle to serve with flavoured rice or need a tangy side dish rather than a rich one, this pickle is the one to make. It can also be called a salad because it can be eaten as soon as it is mixed but it also keeps very well in the refrigerator. This is a generic pickle found all over East and Southeast Asia made in much the same way. Instead of daikon, fresh beans, cored cucumber and sliced onions can also be dressed the same way.

Daikon 250 g (9 oz)

Salt 1¹/₄ tsp

Red chilli 1, seeded and chopped

Garlic 2 cloves, peeled and chopped

Sugar 1 Tbsp

White rice vinegar 2¹/₂ Tbsp

1. Peel daikon and slice thinly or shred. Alternatively, cut daikon into bite-size pieces.

2. Rub daikon with salt and leave to stand for 30 minutes.

3. Squeeze out water from daikon.

4. Mix together chilli, garlic, sugar and vinegar and add daikon. If preferred, stand for 30 minutes before serving, or bottle and keep refrigerated until needed.

QUICK PICKLES SOUTH INDIAN-STYLE

This is a generic South Indian-style pickle that invariably appears when you order a plate of *nasi* biryani (biryani rice) at any Indian Muslim restaurant or food stall in Malaysia and Singapore. Make a batch for the next time that you make a flavoured rice. The pickles can also be served with any West Asian rice dish. Substitute mustard oil with any cooking oil if a more generic flavour is preferred.

Cucumber 400 g (14^1/$_3$ oz), cored and cut into finger-lengths

Salt ^{1}/$_2$ tsp

Carrots 200 g (7 oz), julienned

Red chillies 6, seeded and sliced coarsely

Garlic 4 cloves, peeled and thinly sliced

PICKLING MIX

Water ^{1}/$_2$ Tbsp

Ground turmeric 1 tsp

Red chilli powder 1 tsp

Mustard oil/cooking oil 60 ml (2 fl oz / ^{1}/$_4$ cup)

Mustard seeds 1 tsp

Ginger 1 thumb-size knob, peeled and thinly shredded

White vinegar 60 ml (2 fl oz / ^{1}/$_4$ cup)

Sugar 2 Tbsp

Salt ^{1}/$_2$ tsp

1. Rub cucumber with ^{1}/$_2$ tsp salt and stand for 30 minutes. Squeeze out the water.

2. Prepare pickling mix. Stir ^{1}/$_2$ Tbsp water with ground turmeric and chilli powder to get a thick paste.

3. Heat oil in a wok and fry mustard seeds till they pop. Add ginger shreds, then turmeric-chilli paste and fry till fragrant.

4. Add vinegar, sugar and salt and bring to the boil. Stir in cucumbers, carrots, chillies and garlic and fry for 2 minutes. Do not overcook.

5. Turn off heat and leave pickles to cool in wok. Bottle and leave to stand overnight before serving.

LAMOUN MAKBOUSS (WEST ASIAN LEMONS PICKLED IN OLIVE OIL)

These pickled lemons are so West Asian and taste divine considering the minimal effort involved. The lemon can be eaten like a chutney or used in stews, soups and salads. Try it with any West Asian rice with or without meat. Do not discard the olive oil when the lemons are gone. Use it as a salad dressing.

Lemons/large green limes 500 g (1 lb 1^1/$_2$ oz)

Salt 1 Tbsp

Olive oil to cover lemons well

1. Slice lemons/limes about 1-cm (^{1}/$_2$-in) thick. Spread slices out on a large plate or colander.

2. Sprinkle salt over lemon/lime slices and stand for 1 hour to let some of the juice drain away.

3. Fill a large glass jar half-full with olive oil, then put lemon/lime slices into the bottle. Top up with more olive oil. Be sure that the lemon is totally submerged. Hold the slices down with bamboo skewers if necessary.

4. Stand pickle for at least a month before serving. No refrigeration is required.

5. Serve as a relish with West and South Asian rice dishes. It can also be added to salads.

West Asian Pickled Onions

Pick small onions or alternatively, use shallots which also pickle well. Use a narrow jar so that you need less olive oil. Pickled onions keep well without refrigeration.

Water *1 litre (32 fl oz / 4 cups)*

Small onions / shallots *1 kg (2 lb 3 oz), peeled*

Cabbage (optional) *2 large leaves*

Red radish *200 g (7 oz)*

PICKLING MIX

Salt *2 tsp*

White vinegar *500 ml (16 fl oz / 2 cups)*

Garlic *6 cloves, peeled and thickly sliced*

Dill/bay leaves/ground cumin/dill seeds *2 tsp*

Olive oil *250 ml (8 fl oz / 1 cup)*

1. In a stainless steel pot, bring the litre of water to the boil. Blanch peeled onions/shallots for 10 seconds, and leaves of cabbage for 5 seconds. Do not blanch radish. Cool blanched ingredients in a colander.

2. Trim both tips of radish, then cut quarter slits at one end of the radish without quartering it unless the radish is rather large.

3. In a large glass jar, stir together pickling mix, then add cooled onions/shallots and red radish.

4. To keep onions/shallots submerged, cover top with the two blanched leaves of cabbage and hold down with bamboo skewers. If the jar is narrow enough, the bamboo skewers may be enough to hold the onions down.

5. Leave to stand for at least a week if pickling shallots, and at least a month if pickling larger onions. No refrigeration is required.

West Asian Mushroom Pickles

This easy pickle should be done ahead of time. The same marinade can be used to pickle lightly blanched vegetables such as mangetout (snow peas), French beans or slices of carrots. Such pickles are excellent with biryanis and pilafs.

Fresh button mushrooms *500 g (1 lb 1 1/2 oz), thickly sliced*

Onion *100 g (3 1/2 oz), peeled and cubed*

Olive oil *125 ml (4 fl oz / 1/2 cup)*

Lemon juice *2 Tbsp*

Salt *1/4 tsp*

Parsley *1 Tbsp, chopped*

Dill *1 Tbsp, chopped*

1. Mix all ingredients together in a glass jar and marinate overnight before serving.

Salad with Pomegranate Molasses

Look for pomegranate molasses in West Asian grocery stores. It makes an easy salad dressing as all you have to do is pour it out of the bottle. You may not even want the olive oil or salt if you are watching your oil or salt intakes. If you don't have pomegranate molasses, substitute with lemon juice. All kinds of vegetables both fresh and blanched can be dressed this way.

Romaine (cos) lettuce *500 g (1 lb 1 1/2 oz), torn into pieces*

Onions *100 g (3 1/2 oz), peeled and cut into small wedges*

Tomatoes *100 g (3 1/2 oz), cut into small wedges*

DRESSING

Pomegranate molasses or lemon juice *2 Tbsp*

Olive oil *1 Tbsp*

Salt *1/2 tsp*

1. Mix together ingredients for dressing. Adjust molasses/lemon juice and salt to the amount of vegetables .

2. Put salad ingredients into a salad bowl and stir in dressing.

NORTH INDIAN RAITA

Yoghurt-dressed salads known as raita are typically North Indian salads, but the popularity of yoghurt as food goes back thousands of years to when milk-producing animals were first domesticated in West Asia. This probably explains why raitas go well with West Asian rice dishes too. Although the best known raita is cucumber raita, this basic yoghurt dressing can be used with other vegetables and even with a mix of vegetables. Ring changes with different fresh herbs.

VEGETABLES FOR RAITA
- Carrots
- Onions
- Cucumber
- Blanched green or long beans
- Celery

DRESSING
Yoghurt *125 ml (4 fl oz / $^1/_2$ cup)*

Salt *$^1/_2$ tsp*

Any garam masala (page 30) or
  ground cumin *$^1/_4$ tsp*

Ground black/white pepper
  1 pinch

Mint/coriander leaves *$^1/_2$ cup,
  chopped*

1. Mix ingredients for dressing well together and pour over chopped or sliced vegetables, blanched or raw.

INDIAN TOMATO CHUTNEY

Mustard oil is the preferred oil for making Indian chutneys. If not available, substitute with any bland oil, like corn or soy oil.

Ripe tomatoes *500 g (1 lb 1$^1/_2$ oz)*

Mustard oil *125 ml (4 fl oz / $^1/_2$ cup)*

Mustard seeds *1 tsp*

Onions *150 g (5$^1/_3$ oz),
  peeled and chopped*

Ginger *1 small thumb-size knob,
  peeled and cut into strips*

Chilli powder *2 tsp*

Sugar *100 g (3$^1/_2$ oz)*

Salt *1$^1/_2$ tsp*

Vinegar *125 ml (4 fl oz / $^1/_2$ cup)*

Asafoetida or garam masala
  (page 30) *$^1/_4$ tsp*

1. Put tomatoes in a pot of water and bring to the boil. Simmer for 5 minutes, then discard the hot water and cover tomatoes with cold water. Peel skins and chop tomatoes coarsely.

2. In a stainless steel pot, heat oil and add mustard seeds. Fry until seeds start to pop. Press seeds with a spoon to break them.

3. Add chopped onions and ginger strips and fry until onions are soft. Add tomatoes, chilli powder, sugar, salt and vinegar. Bring to the boil.

4. When mixture boils, turn down heat and simmer until chutney is thick and glossy, like jam. Stir in asafoetida or garam masala.

5. Leave to cool before bottling.

Cooks from ancient times have made much of the bland nature of rice and combined it with fragrant spices, oils, vegetables and meat to get the most fabulous one-dish rice meals. The best known of flavoured rice dishes and the most time-consuming to prepare are biryanis which are also called pilafs, *polos*, *pulaos*, *polov*, among other names in the West, Central and South Asian regions where they always take pride of place at any special event. Then there are the spice- and vegetable-flavoured rice dishes such as Indian *jeera bhaat* (cumin rice), Indonesian clove rice and the various tomato-flavoured rice dishes of a number of countries. Flavoured rice dishes range in complexity from the simple addition of butter or ghee to the rice to complicated spice mixes, meat and vegetables. However complicated, the starting point of these flavoured rice dishes is almost always a long-grain rice, with basmati rice being considered the best rice for such dishes. One reason is that basmati is an aged rice which cooks into long, separated, fluffy grains. Basmati comes from the Punjab region of northern India once ruled by the Mughals who came from Islamised Persia. Even before Islamisation, Persia, now called Iran, already had a rich food culture that featured rice, dried fruit and nuts, still seen today in Indian biryanis and Iranian cuisine. Persian long-grain rice is said to resemble basmati in flavour and texture.

BIRYANIS, PILAFS AND OTHER FLAVOURED RICE

Flavoured rice is cooked in several ways that sometimes combine stove-top cooking with cooking in the rice cooker. Even the most complicated flavoured rice can be prepared in a rice cooker. The rice is boiled in the rice cooker usually with salt, oil, spices and other flavouring ingredients. The liquid may be water, stock or milk. If the meat is to be combined with rice, it may be cooked separately or together with the rice depending on the meat. Chicken or fish lends itself to this but ingredients like lamb, mutton or chickpeas need boiling till tender before being layered with the cooked rice. The rice can also be partially cooked for the purpose of melding the flavours of meat and rice, such as the process called *dum* which requires heat to be applied to the rice and meat, and this last stage will finish cooking the rice as well. In days of old, Mughal cooks placed their pot of biryani on a small fire and heaped a layer of burning coals on top of the covered pot. Today, the *dum* process or infusion of flavours may be done by baking the biryani in the oven, steaming in a steamer or cooking in the microwave oven. Not all flavoured rice dishes are so complicated. Some such as Singapore chicken rice requires minimum effort but achieves maximum flavour. The same goes for *nasi lemak* (Malay/Straits Chinese coconut rice) with its array of side dishes. Here are the three main steps in preparing biryanis, often regarded as the most difficult of flavoured rice dishes. The first step, that of making a spiced stock or *yakhni*, is not always necessary. As you will see, the whole process of producing a tasty biryani isn't so tough, although it requires time. Here are the most complicated steps simplified.

• Layering the Pilaf

The usual way to layer rice with meat and other ingredients is to line the bottom of the dish or pot with half the rice, spread the meat and other ingredients in the middle, and cover that with the remainder of the rice. Always spread some of the gravy over the meat and rice. The moisture is needed if you are using parboiled rice and even if you are not, it is essential in the infusion process. However, the rice should not be soaking in gravy. The number of layers can be doubled if your dish or pot is large enough and there is a lot of rice and meat. Thinner layers of rice will absorb flavours more easily from the meat and gravy. If your pot or dish is not large enough for a 3-cup biryani, divide the rice and other ingredients into two containers.

The biryani must be layered in a pot or dish with a cover. The cover keeps the flavours in and prevents drying out. A traditional way of sealing in the flavours was to make a thick dough with flour and water and seal the pot edge with it. The traditional alternative to a dough seal is to wrap the pot lid or dish cover with a clean, thick dishcloth first before putting the lid on the dish or pot. The easier modern way is to cover the top of the pot or dish with a layer of several sheets of paper towels and put the lid on top of the paper towels. The dishcloth or paper towels not only tightens the seal on the pot or dish, but also absorbs drops of steam that can turn the rice a little soggy. The amount of steam generated by infusing depends on how much gravy there is in the meat and the amount of gravy you want with the rice will depend to some extent on how cooked through the rice is and whether it is still gritty. If the rice is still gritty, more moisture during the infusing will finish cooking the rice at the same time as the flavours are infused. In fact, some cooks like doing it this way. If the rice is already cooked through, then the meat can be just moist.

• Infusing Flavours aka *Dum*

This is a key step in preparing biryanis, a process that Indian cooks refer to as *dum* which means "breath". All over India, you see references to *dum* biryani in menus and restaurant sign boards. It means that the biryani has been put through a process in which the cooked rice is layered with cooked meat, oil, spices and other ingredients and heated gently together to meld the flavours. One traditional way to "*dum*" was to put the pot of rice and meat over a very low wood fire and cover the lid of the pot (which would be flat) with a few live coals. (Even today, Indian pots have flat lids.) In ancient times, this slow infusing took hours and attention was paid to maintaining the fire at a constant level. Whether the infusing process is done on a wood fire or stove top, it is not uncommon for the bottom of the biryani to turn crusty and burn because of the oil that drips down to the bottom. This blackening gives the biryani a pleasant smoky flavour although not everyone likes it. The bitter blackened crust is discarded or fed to livestock. If the crust is not too black, it is enjoyed by many rice-eating cultures.

Today, infusing can be done in several ways depending on personal preference as well as the kind of equipment you have and are using. The tightly covered and layered rice can be baked, steamed, cooked in the microwave oven or on a stove-top or in a rice cooker. Timing is very important in some cases, not so in others; and the results differ. Baking tends to develop a crust around the edges of the covered dish. If baking, do it at 160°C (325°F) for 20 minutes. The microwave oven can harden the rice if overdone or overexposed parts may harden. If you cook using the microwave oven, reduce the setting to "low" and do not cook for more than 5 minutes. Steaming Chinese-style—placing the covered dish of layered rice in a steamer filled with water—yields a more tender, if vaguely moist pilaf and there is no crust formation. Timing is not critical when the pilaf is wet-steamed. This is not the traditional way but neither is microwaving.

On the other hand, timing is important if the pot of layered rice is infused on a slow gas ring or electric plate. A crust usually develops at the bottom and this crust is prized in some rice-eating cultures. If infused for too long, this crust will blacken. Charring of the bottom of the rice also happens in a rice cooker with this being more pronounced in the part of the rice pot in closest contact with the heating element. To use the rice cooker for infusing, half the cooked rice has to be scooped out into a large bowl, the meat and other ingredients put in the middle and the rest of the rice put on top. The rice cooker is then switched on to the "keep warm" setting if possible, or to "cook" if there is no "keep warm" setting. When using the "cook" setting in this way, the rice cooker should be turned off after 15 minutes and the rice left to rest for another 10–15 minutes before serving.

How the biryani is infused affects the way it is served. If the pilaf is layered and infused in an ovenproof dish or Dutch oven, it can be served as it is with the garnishing sprinkled on top. If it is layered in a saucepan and infused over the stove-top, dishing the pilaf into a large serving platter will allow you to show off the rice crust if it is desired and if it has not turned black.

• Smoky Flavours aka *Dhunghar*
For those who like smoky flavours, note that medieval Arab cooks would smoke their earthenware pot before making a pilaf, thus giving their rice a smoky fragrance. In Mughal India, Shah Jehan's cooks sometimes smoked stewed meat with live coals to get smoky flavours, a process called *dhunghar*. Live coals in a container would be placed at the centre of the pot of stewed meat and oil and spices put on the live coals to create smoke. The pot of meat would then be tightly covered to let the resulting smoke permeate the meat, after which the meat would be layered and infused with rice. Although the burning oil smells unpleasant, the resulting smoky flavour is rather delicious, It is, however, complicated to do in a modern kitchen without live coals. (See page 116 for detailed steps.)

BIRYANIS, PILAFS AND OTHER FLAVOURED RICE

STRAITS CHINESE NASI KUNYIT (YELLOW RICE)

Yellow rice is a festive favourite among the Straits Chinese, Malays and Indonesians, and can be made using white glutinous rice or long-grain rice. In the Straits Chinese communities in Malaysia and Singapore, *nasi kunyit* was once traditional at the feast to celebrate a child's first month. Once upon a time, the birth was celebrated only if it was a boy and boxes of *nasi kunyit* with the obligatory red eggs were brought round to relatives to herald his arrival. The Indonesians make yellow rice for *nasi tumpeng* where the rice is formed into a cone or *tumpeng* and displayed with various special dishes depending on the celebration. *Nasi kunyit* made with glutinous rice makes a nice change from eating plain long-grain rice with curry.

White glutinous rice 600 g
(1 lb 5^1/$_2$ oz / 3 cups)

Ground turmeric 2 tsp

Salt 1 tsp

Coconut cream 125 ml (4 fl oz /
^{1}/$_2$ cup)

1. Rinse rice clean, then soak rice in some water mixed with ground turmeric. Leave overnight.

2. The following day, drain rice, then steam for 10 minutes.

3. Mix together salt and coconut cream and stir it into the half-cooked rice. Mix well.

4. Continue steaming rice for another 20 minutes, turning rice over after 10 minutes so that the grains at the top are cooked properly. Continue steaming rice to your preferred texture. It should be cooked through but still al dente.

5. Serve with a chicken curry (page 42) or *assam* prawns (page 40).

YELLOW RICE

In many parts of Asia, particularly East and Southeast Asia, yellow is the colour of royalty, of gold and holy monks. Rice cooked with coconut milk, ground turmeric and salt, and flavoured with various spices appear in celebratory and ritual meals. Unlike saffron rice, yellow rice made with ground turmeric is much cheaper to prepare in the large quantities needed for communal celebrations. This yellow rice is found all over Southeast Asia on special occasions, but is so easy to prepare that you don't need a special occasion to cook it.

Long-grain rice 600 g (1 lb 5^1/$_3$ oz /
3 cups), soaked 30 minutes

Coconut milk 1.5 litres (48 fl oz /
6 cups)

Ground turmeric ^{1}/$_2$ tsp

Salt 2 tsp

Cinnamon stick/cloves/
cardamom 6-cm (2^1/$_2$-in) stick/
6 cloves/6 pods

1. Combine ingredients and cook rice using your preferred method until tender. Fluff up rice and rest for 10 minutes before serving.

2. Serve with chicken curry (page 42), fried fish (page 40), fried chicken (page 53) and pickles.

HOKKIEN OIL RICE

Like *nasi kunyit* for the Straits Chinese community, oil rice was a traditional dish served on special occasions such as the month-old baby celebrations in Hokkien families. Portions of the oil rice would be given away to announce the birth of a baby boy. As the name of the dish indicates, it is very oily. When lard was the oil of choice, the rice had an even more fantastic mouth-feel than with just vegetable oil. A traditional way to cook this rice was to stir-fry the rice in a large wok with half cups of water added progressively until the rice swelled up to an al dente texture. Although a good way to prepare large quantities, it is very tiring on the arm.

Dried shiitake mushrooms *20 g (²/₃ oz), soaked to soften; water reserved*

Dried prawns *1 Tbsp, soaked to soften and cleaned*

Cooking oil *60 ml (2 fl oz / ¹/₄ cup)*

Shallots *50 g (1²/₃ oz / ¹/₂ cup), thinly sliced*

Boiled belly pork *300 g (11 oz), thinly sliced*

Dark soy sauce *1 tsp*

Ground white pepper *¹/₂ tsp*

White glutinous rice *600 g (1 lb 5¹/₃ oz / 3 cups), soaked 1 hour*

Salt *2 tsp*

Water *750 ml (24 fl oz / 3 cups)*

Chopped spring onion

Hard-boiled eggs *1 per person*

1. Set aside water used for soaking mushrooms to cook rice. Slice mushrooms or leave them whole as preferred. Discard hard stems.

2. Pick through softened dried prawns for any bits of shell and discard. Chop prawns coarsely.

3. In a wok, heat oil and fry sliced shallots till golden brown. Scoop out shallots and set aside.

4. In the same oil, fry dried prawns till fragrant, then add mushrooms, belly pork, dark soy sauce and ground pepper. Fry for another 5 minutes.

5. Mix contents of wok with glutinous rice, salt and 625 ml (20 fl oz / 2¹/₂ cups) water and cook rice using your preferred method. The rice can be steamed in a casserole till it is tender or in a rice cooker with a glutinous rice setting. When rice is done, mix in fried shallots, reserving a little for garnishing.

6. To serve, press rice into a large bowl or individual serving bowls and unmould onto a serving plate. Garnish with spring onion and fried shallots before serving.

7. Serve oil rice with hard-boiled eggs and plenty of hot Chinese tea.

KAHA BHAAT (SRI LANKAN YELLOW RICE)

This is a festive rice prepared for celebrations such as the Sri Lankan New Year. Yellow is considered an auspicious colour in predominantly Buddhist Sri Lanka, yellow or saffron being associated with the robes of its many Buddhist monks. The tropical island abounds in coconut trees and its cinnamon is world-renowned. Naturally, this flavoured rice has both coconut milk and cinnamon.

Ghee *1 Tbsp*

Onion *100 g (3¹/₂ oz), peeled and finely sliced*

Long-grain rice *600 g (1 lb 5¹/₃ oz / 3 cups), soaked 30 minutes*

Coconut milk *1.5 litres (48 fl oz / 6 cups)*

Ground turmeric *¹/₂ tsp*

Salt *2 tsp*

WHOLE SPICES

Cloves *6*

Cinnamon stick *6-cm (2¹/₂-in)*

Cardamom *6 pods*

Curry leaves *1 sprig*

1. Heat ghee in a large saucepan. Add onion and fry until it begins to turn golden brown. Add whole spices and fry for 1 minute.

2. Combine fried spices with rice, coconut milk, turmeric and salt. Cook rice using your preferred method until rice is tender. When rice is done, fluff it up. Cover and rest rice for 10 minutes before serving.

3. Serve yellow rice with *seeni sambol* (page 56), curries and pickles.

STRAITS CHINESE NASI LEMAK

Nasi lemak means "rich rice" in Malay and although this recipe has been labelled "Straits Chinese", rich rice cooked with coconut milk is found all over South and Southeast Asia wherever there are coconut palms aplenty. *Nasi lemak* is both a festive favourite in many Southeast Asian homes as well as a standard breakfast dish in Singapore and Malaysia and is even eaten as a snack throughout the day. The side dishes eaten with *nasi lemak* defines the regional or ethnic character of a coconut rice meal. The Straits Chinese *nasi lemak* I grew up with was always eaten with fried seafood spiced with a special chilli sambal while Malay *nasi lemak* is commonly served with fried chicken (page 53).

Long-grain rice 600 g (1 lb 5^1/$_3$ oz / 3 cups), soaked 30 minutes

Coconut milk 1.5 litres (48 fl oz / 6 cups)

Salt 2 tsp

Screwpine (*pandan*) leaves 6, rinsed and knotted

1. Combine rice, coconut milk, salt and screwpine leaves and cook rice using your preferred method until rice is tender.

2. Serve *nasi lemak* with Straits Chinese *nasi lemak* chilli sambal, fried fish, *assam* prawns, peanuts and anchovies (pages 40–41) and sliced cucumber.

3. For Malay-style *nasi lemak*, add fried chicken (page 53) to the mix of side dishes.

KHEERI BHAAT (SRI LANKAN MILK RICE)

Kheeri bhaat means "milk rice" and the milk here refers to coconut milk. *Kheeri bhaat* is a festive rice served on special occasions such as the Sri Lankan New Year either as a sweet rice with jaggery (palm sugar) or as a savoury coconut rice eaten with one of Sri Lanka's many delicious and spicy sambals, with *seeni sambol* being the festive favourite.

Long-grain rice 600 g (1 lb 5^1/$_3$ oz / 3 cups), soaked 30 minutes

Salt 2 tsp

Coconut milk 1.5 litres (48 fl oz / 6 cups)

Cinnamon stick 6-cm (2^1/$_2$-in)

1. Combine all ingredients and cook rice using your preferred method until rice is tender.

2. Serve rice with a pickle and *seeni sambol* (page 56).

BURMESE COCONUT RICE

Because of the addition of ground turmeric, Burmese coconut rice looks like *nasi kunyit* (page 64). This dish is cooked with more ingredients than Straits Chinese or Malay *nasi lemak*, and the spices and fried onions give this coconut rice a taste similar to an Indian pilaf, which is not surprising, considering that the two countries share borders as well as with Bangladesh.

Cooking oil 2 Tbsp

Onion 100 g (3^1/$_2$ oz), coarsely chopped

Cloves 4

Cinnamon stick 6-cm (2^1/$_2$-in)

Long-grain rice 600 g (1 lb 5^1/$_3$ oz / 3 cups), soaked 30 minutes

Salt 2 tsp

Coconut milk 1.5 litres (48 fl oz / 6 cups)

Ground turmeric ^{1}/$_4$ tsp

1. In a frying pan, heat oil and fry onion till it begins to brown. Add cloves and cinnamon and fry for 1 minute taking care not to over-brown onions.

2. Combine rice with fried onion and remaining ingredients and cook rice using your preferred method until rice is tender. When rice is done, fluff it and stir down the ingredients. Let rice rest for 10 minutes before serving.

3. Serve coconut rice with chicken curry (page 42), fried fish (page 40), fried or roast chicken (page 53) and Burmese onion chutney (page 130).

INDONESIAN CLOVE RICE

In Indonesia, thousands of tonnes of cloves go up in smoke—such is the popularity of *kretek*, the quintessential Indonesian-style cigarette flavoured with ground cloves. Taking in secondary smoke when near a *kretek* smoker is a fragrant, even if potentially lethal, experience. Less fraught with danger is enjoying clove rice which is rice flavoured with coconut milk and cloves.

Long-grain rice 600 g (1 lb 5¹/₃ oz / 3 cups), soaked 30 minutes

Salt 2 tsp

Cloves 12

Coconut milk 1.5 litres (48 fl oz / 6 cups)

1. Combine rice, salt, cloves and coconut milk and cook rice using your preferred method until rice is tender.
2. Serve rice with chicken curry (page 42), fried fish (page 40) and pickles.

PANDAN RICE

The pandan leaves can also be simply knotted together and cooled with the coconut milk. This is *nasi lemak*. Turning the rice green with pandan juice makes it pandan rice!

Pandan (screwpine) leaves 6

Water 250 ml (8 fl oz / 1 cup)

Long-grain rice 600 g (1 lb 5¹/₃ oz / 3 cups), soaked 30 minutes

Salt 2 tsp

Coconut milk 1.25 litres (40 fl oz / 5 cups)

1. To make pandan leaf juice, blend pandan leaves with water. Squeeze mixture through a muslin bag and measure to get 250 ml (8 fl oz / 1 cup) juice, topping it up with more water if necessary.
2. Cook rice with salt, pandan juice and coconut milk using your preferred method until rice is tender.
3. Serve rice with chicken curry (page 42), fried fish (page 40) and pickles.

INDIAN GHEE RICE

This is a flavourful yet easily prepared festive rice. The spices, nuts and dried fruit can be varied according to what you have in the larder. Although everything can be cooked together, I much prefer to use the nuts as a garnish to keep them crunchy.

Ghee 6 Tbsp

Onion 100 g (3¹/₂ oz), peeled and thinly sliced

Cashew nuts/almonds 50 g (1²/₃ oz / ¹/₂ cup)

Long-grain rice 600 g (1 lb 5¹/₃ oz / 3 cups)

Salt 2 tsp

Water 1.5 litres (48 fl oz / 6 cups)

Dried fruit (e.g. raisins) 30 g (1 oz / ¹/₄ cup)

Garam masala 1 (page 30) 1 tsp

WHOLE SPICES

Cinnamon stick 6-cm (2¹/₂-in)

Cardamom 4 pods

Cloves 4

1. Heat ghee in a frying pan and fry onion till golden brown. Do not over brown. Scoop out and set aside.
2. In the same pan, reheat ghee and fry cashew nuts/almonds till golden brown. Scoop out and set aside with browned onion.
3. Reheat pan again and fry whole spices for 1 minute.
4. Combine rice, salt, water, contents of pan, dried fruit and half the fried onions and cook rice using your preferred method. When rice is cooked, fluff it up and stir in garam masala. Cover and rest rice for 10 minutes before serving.
5. Just before serving, garnish with fried nuts and remaining fried onions.
6. Serve rice hot with meatballs in yoghurt sauce (page 42) or dhal curry (page 43) and a pickle or chutney (page 59).

Nasi Uduk (indonesian coconut rice)

Also called *nasi gurih*, Indonesian coconut rice can be cooked with just coconut milk and a few cloves making it clove rice, or it can be cooked with more ingredients to make it more fanciful, as with the recipe below. This dish is very tasty, making it a great dish for celebrations. I love the kaffir lime leaf flavour. The rice is so tasty that it can be eaten on its own.

Long-grain rice 600 g (1 lb 5¹/₃ oz / 3 cups), soaked 30 minutes

Coconut milk 1.5 litres (48 fl oz / 6 cups)

Salt 2 tsp

Kaffir lime leaves 3, bruised

SPICE PASTE

Onion 100 g (3¹/₂ oz)

Garlic 3 cloves

Ground turmeric ¹/₂ tsp

Ground cumin ¹/₂ tsp

Ground coriander ¹/₂ tsp

Dried prawn (shrimp) paste (belacan) ¹/₂ tsp

Kencur 1 small knob, skinned

Water 250 ml (8 fl oz / 1 cup)

1. Blend spice paste ingredients in a food processor till fine. Put spice paste into a small pot and bring to the boil. Turn down heat and simmer till spice paste is fragrant and thick.

2. Spoon spice paste into a measuring cup and top up with coconut milk to get 1.5 litres (48 fl oz / 6 cups).

3. Combine rice with coconut milk and spice paste, salt and bruised kaffir lime leaves and cook rice using your preferred method until rice is tender. When rice is done, fluff it up. Cover and rest rice for 10 minutes before serving.

4. Serve with fried fish, assam prawns (page 40) or chicken curry (page 42) and pickles.

West Asian Rice with Ghee

This West Asian rice is even easier to make than Indian ghee rice (page 69). The basic recipe can be tweaked in a number of ways to give different flavours.

Ghee 75 ml (2¹/₂ fl oz / ¹/₃ cup)

Cloves 4

Cinnamon stick 6-cm (2¹/₂-in)

Basmati rice 600 g (1 lb 5¹/₃ oz / 3 cups), soaked 1 hour

Salt 2 tsp

Water 1.5 litres (48 fl oz / 6 cups)

1. Heat ghee in a frying pan and fry cloves and cinnamon for 1 minute or till fragrant.

2. Combine contents of pan with rice, salt and water and cook rice using your preferred method until rice is tender. When rice is done, fluff it up.

3. Serve rice with any West Asian stew (page 49) or kebabs or meatballs (pages 44–46, 48) and yoghurt sauce (page 47).

ADDITIONAL FLAVOURS

- Soak ¹/₂ tsp saffron in 1 Tbsp water. When rice is cooked, fluff it up and stir in saffron water at the same time.

- Rose water, fragrant dried rose petals or orange flower water can be stirred into the cooked rice when fluffing it up. This will give the rice a flower-scented flavour. Do not cook the flower water with the rice as the smell will evaporate.

Sabzi Polo (persian herb rice)

This is a traditional New Year dish that showcases the Iranian taste for fresh herbs and rice. The green colour of the dish connotes good luck—green being the colour long associated with Islam. It can be served with a meat stew, fish, salads and pickles. Stir the herbs into the rice only when the rice is done and not long before the rice is served so that the herbs stay green. Serve with a salad of fresh herbs.

Basmati rice 600 g (1 lb 5¹/₃ oz / 3 cups), soaked 1 hour

Salt 2 tsp

Leeks 300 g (11 oz), thinly sliced

Water 1.5 litres (48 fl oz / 6 cups)

Ghee 60 ml (2 fl oz / ¹/₄ cup)

Fresh herbs (e.g. dill, mint, coriander leaves, chives, spring onions, thyme, parsley, fenugreek leaves) 4 cups, chopped

1. Cook rice with salt, leeks and water using your preferred method until rice is tender.

2. When rice is done, fluff it up and stir ghee and chopped herbs into rice. You can also make a ghee *tah-deeg* at this point, if desired (page 22).

3. Serve herb rice with a Persian-style stew (pages 149–150), kebabs or any grilled meat (pages 44–45, 48), pickles (page 58) and yoghurt sauce (page 47).

Naranji Pulao (kashmiri orange pilaf)

This Kashmiri pilaf dates back to the days of the Mughal dynasties in the 16th and 17th centuries. The Mughals who ruled large swathes of the Indian subcontinent before the coming of the British in the 18th century came originally from Persia. They brought with them the Persian taste for fruit and nuts in their rice dishes, a preference still to be seen in Muslim Kashmiri food as well as in iconic Mughlai-style pilafs. Orange-flavoured pilaf is still cooked in Iran today. The pilaf will be tart or not, depending on the sweetness of the orange juice.

Ghee 60 ml (2 fl oz / ¹/₄ cup)

Cashew nuts a handful

Onion 100 g (3¹/₂ oz), peeled and thinly sliced

Raisins 30 g (1 oz / ¹/₄ cup)

Basmati rice 600 g (1 lb 5¹/₃ oz / 3 cups), soaked 1 hour

Salt 2 tsp

Water 1 litre (32 fl oz / 4 cups)

Oranges grated for 1 tsp zest and extracted for 500 ml (16 fl oz / 2 cups) juice

Orange flower water (optional) 1 Tbsp

WHOLE SPICES

Cinnamon stick 6-cm (2¹/₂-in)

Cloves 6

Black cardamom (see Glossary) 4 pods

1. In a frying pan, melt ghee and brown cashew nuts. Scoop out and set nuts aside for garnishing. Add onion and fry till it begins to brown. Add whole spices and raisins and fry for 2 minutes.

2. Combine contents of pan with rice, salt, water, orange zest and juice, and cook rice using your preferred method until rice is tender. When rice is done, fluff it up. Cover and rest rice for 10 minutes before serving. Just before serving, stir in orange flower water if using.

3. Garnish with cashew nuts and serve with a raita (page 59), meat curry or Persian-style stew (pages 149–150) and yoghurt sauce (page 47).

JEERA BHAAT (INDIAN CUMIN RICE)

The Nepali and Indian cooks who manned the kitchen tent on my Himalayan treks prepared this rice for an occasional treat and as my final parting meal to celebrate the conclusion of a great trek.

Ghee 75 ml (2¹/₂ fl oz / ¹/₃ cup)

Cumin seeds 1 Tbsp

Long-grain rice 600 g (1 lb 5¹/₃ oz / 3 cups)

Water 1.5 litres (48 fl oz / 6 cups)

Salt 2 tsp

Ground cumin ¹/₄ tsp

1. Heat ghee in a frying pan and fry cumin seeds for 1 minute. Be careful not to burn them.

2. Combine contents of pan, rice, water, salt and ground cumin and cook rice using your preferred method until rice is tender. When rice is done, fluff it up.

3. Serve with meatballs in yoghurt sauce (page 42), meat or dhal curry (page 43) or dhal char (page 44) and pickles (page 57).

ADA POLO (PERSIAN RICE AND LENTILS)

The dhal or lentils should be pre-cooked till tender but it should preferably not be the kind that breaks down easily into mush which mung and masoor dhal tend to do. Brown lentils, black dhal, green or yellow split pea or chickpeas keep their shape well. Any dried bean is best soaked in cold water for at least 1 hour before boiling till nearly tender. The minced meat can be lamb, chicken or beef.

Lentils/dhal 300 g (11 oz / 1¹/₂ cups)

Ghee/oil 3 Tbsp

Onion 100 g (3¹/₂ oz), peeled and chopped

Minced meat (lamb/beef/chicken) 300 g (11 oz)

Advieh 1, 2, or 3 (page 31) 1 tsp

Salt 2¹/₂ tsp

Water 1.75 litres (56 fl oz / 7 cups)

Basmati rice 600 g (1 lb 5¹/₃ oz / 3 cups), soaked 1 hour

West Asian dates 100 g (3¹/₂ oz), pitted and sliced

Raisins 100 g (3¹/₂ oz / ³/₄ cup)

GARNISHING

Lemon wedges

Coriander leaves/parsley

1. Boil lentils/dhal till it just softens. Drain and set aside.

2. Heat ghee/oil in a frying pan and fry sliced onion till it begins to brown. Add minced meat, advieh and ¹/₂ tsp salt. Continue frying for about 2 minutes. Add 250 ml (8 fl oz / 1 cup) water and bring to the boil. Turn down heat and simmer till meat is tender and there is still about 4 Tbsp gravy left.

3. Combine rice with cooked lentils/dhal, dates, raisins, remaining 2 tsp salt and remaining 1.5 litres (48 fl oz / 6 cups) water and cook rice using your preferred method until rice is tender. When rice is done, stir meat and gravy into rice. Cover and rest rice for 10 minutes before serving.

4. Garnish pilaf with lemon wedges and chopped coriander/parsley. Serve with a West Asian pickle (page 58) and yoghurt sauce (page 47).

BLACK DHAL BIRYANI

This biryani can be entirely vegetarian, in which case cook the rice with a vegetable stock. If mutton *yakhni* is too strong, use a chicken *yakhni*. For something less rich, make the biryani with plain rice flavoured with onions fried in ghee. It can also be made cheaper by substituting saffron with ground turmeric sprinkled directly into the hot rice or stirred into 1 Tbsp water before adding. Another cheap substitute for saffron is safflower.

Basmati rice 600 g (1 lb 5¹/₃ oz / 3 cups), soaked 1 hour

Yakhni (page 114) 1.5 litres (48 fl oz / 6 cups)

Salt 2 tsp

Garam masala 2 (page 30) ¹/₂ tsp

Saffron (optional) ¹/₂ tsp, soaked in 1 Tbsp water

Tomatoes 50 g (1²/₃ oz), skinned and thinly sliced

Green chillies 3, seeded and chopped

Coriander leaves ¹/₂ cup, chopped

Mint ¹/₂ cup, chopped

DHAL LAYER

Ghee 5 Tbsp

Onion 50 g (1²/₃ oz), peeled and thinly sliced

Black dhal 300 g (11 oz / 1¹/₂ cups), soaked overnight

Water 1.5 litres (48 fl oz / 6 cups)

Salt 1 tsp

Potatoes 250 g (9 oz), peeled and cubed

Tomatoes 100 g (3¹/₂ oz), chopped

Green chillies 3, seeded and chopped

Yoghurt 125 ml (4 fl oz / ¹/₂ cup)

SPICE PASTE FOR DHAL LAYER

Ginger paste (page 36) 2 Tbsp

Garlic paste (page 36) 1 Tbsp

Ground turmeric ¹/₂ tsp

Red chilli powder 1 tsp

1. Prepare dhal layer first. Mix together ingredients for spice paste. Melt ghee in a saucepan and fry sliced onion till golden brown. Scoop out and set aside.

2. Fry spice paste in hot oil till fragrant, then add dhal, water and salt and bring to the boil. Turn down heat and simmer till dhal is tender. Takes about 1 hour.

3. Add potatoes, tomatoes and chillies, and simmer till potatoes are done. The dhal curry should be thick, not watery. If there is too much liquid, boil some of it off. Stir in yoghurt and bring to the boil. Turn off heat.

4. Combine rice, *yakhni* and salt and cook rice using your preferred method until rice is tender. When rice is cooked, fluff it up and stir in garam masala, followed by soaked saffron with its soaking liquid if using and half the fried onion.

5. Layer rice with dhal curry, tomato slices, rest of fried onions and two-thirds of chopped green chillies, mint and coriander leaves, leaving some chilli and herbs for garnishing.

6. Cover layered rice and infuse biryani using your preferred method (page 62).

7. Stir remaining herbs and green chillies into biryani before serving with pickles (page 57) and a raita (page 59) or an uncooked yoghurt sauce (page 47).

TIMMAN Z'AFFARAN (IRAQI SAFFRON RICE)

This rice smells heavenly when it is being cooked because of the rose water. However, this smell evaporates and you have to sprinkle more rose water into the rice just before serving. The minced meat, whether mutton or lamb, should be simmered till tender.

Rose water 2 Tbsp

Saffron 1 tsp

Ghee 4 Tbsp

Almonds 10, halved

Onion 100 g (3^1/$_2$ oz), peeled and thinly sliced

Minced lamb/mutton/chicken cubes 250 g (9 oz)

Salt 2^1/$_2$ tsp

Baharat 1 (page 32) 2 tsp

Water/chicken stock (page 80) 1.75 litres (56 fl oz / 7 cups

Golden raisins 30 g (1 oz / ^{1}/$_4$ cup)

Fresh peas 100 g (3^1/$_2$ oz)

Basmati rice 600 g (1 lb 5^1/$_3$ oz / 3 cups), rinsed and drained well

Parsley 1 cup, chopped

1. Mix rose water with saffron threads and set aside.

2. Heat 2 Tbsp ghee in a wok and brown almonds. Remove and set aside for garnishing.

3. Reheat wok and stir in onion. Fry onion till soft and transparent, then stir in minced meat or chicken cubes, ^{1}/$_2$ tsp salt and baharat. Fry till meat changes colour. Add 250 ml (8 fl oz / 1 cup) water/chicken stock and simmer till meat is tender and just moist. Add raisins and peas and cook for another 2 minutes.

4. Combine rice with remaining 1.5 litres (48 fl oz / 6 cups) water/chicken stock, remaining 2 tsp salt and half the rose water-saffron mixture and cook rice using your preferred method until rice is tender. When rice is done, fluff it up and stir meat and chopped parsley into rice. Cover and rest rice for 10 minutes before serving.

5. To serve rice, dish out into a large serving plate. Sprinkle remaining rose water saffron mixture on rice and garnish with browned almonds.

6. Alternatively, the cooked meat can be spread at the bottom of a large bowl and the cooked rice pressed on top. Turn the rice over onto a serving platter. If doing this step, the rose-saffron water should be sprinkled into the rice before it is pressed on top of the meat. Garnish with almonds.

7. Serve with kebabs (page 44–46), pickles (pages 57–58) or salad and a yoghurt sauce (page 47).

PERSIAN-STYLE CHICKEN PILAF WITH APRICOTS

Look for sour dried apricots from say Turkey rather than the heavily-sweetened Californian dried apricots for this dish, even though Turkish apricots can also be rather sweet. If only sweetened dried apricots are available, add enough lemon juice to get a sweet-sour gravy. Alternatively, substitute with a sour fruit such as belimbing or frozen cranberries. If the fruit is very sour, sweeten with some sugar to taste.

Basmati rice 600 g (1 lb 5¹/₃ oz / 3 cups)

Salt 2 tsp

CHICKEN STEW

Ghee/oil 60 ml (2 fl oz / ¹/₄ cup)

Onions 200 g (7 oz), peeled and finely chopped

Raisins 100 g (3¹/₂ oz / ³/₄ cup)

Sour dried apricots 200 g (7 oz), thinly sliced

Ground cinnamon ¹/₂ tsp

Ground black pepper 2 tsp

Ground turmeric ¹/₄ tsp

Za'atar 1 (page 34) 1 tsp

Salt 1 tsp

Chicken 1 kg (2 lb 3 oz), cut into 6 pieces

Water 2 litres (64 fl oz / 8 cups)

Lemon juice to taste

Sugar to taste

1. Prepare chicken first so bones can be further boiled into stock for cooking rice. Heat ghee/oil in a pot and brown chopped onions. Stir in raisins and apricots, spices, salt and chicken. Fry for 2 minutes.

2. Add water and bring to the boil. Turn down heat and simmer till chicken is just cooked. Remove chicken and ladle out bulk of plain gravy into another pot, leaving about 500 ml (16 fl oz / 2 cups) gravy with fruit and spices.

3. When chicken is cool enough to handle, bone chicken and return meat to pot with fruit and spices. Adjust sweetness and sourness of gravy with lemon juice and sugar to taste. Bring to the boil, then turn off heat.

4. Put chicken bones into other pot with plain gravy and bring to the boil. Turn down heat and simmer for 20 minutes to get a richer chicken stock. Strain away solids and measure out 1.5 litres (48 fl oz / 6 cups) stock. Top up with water if necessary. Any leftover stock can be added to the chicken and fruit gravy.

5. Combine rice with 1.5 litres (48 fl oz / 6 cups) stock and salt and cook rice using your preferred method until rice is tender. When rice is done, fluff it up.

6. Layer rice, chicken and fruit, ending with a layer of rice. Infuse pilaf for 20 minutes using your preferred method (page 62). Save gravy for serving with pilaf. Reheat before pouring it over rice if it is served as a large communal platter or pass it around in a sauce boat if serving individual servings.

7. Serve pilaf with a salad and pickles (pages 57–58).

NASI AYAM (INDONESIAN CHICKEN RICE)

More than 40 years ago on a road trip through Java to Bali, a young Indonesian driver took my friends and I to a restaurant somewhere outside Jogjakarta where I had my most delicious meal of the trip. The nasi ayam was a large piece of chicken cooked in a tasty sauce and served on top of a heaping plate of white rice. This chicken curry is an approximation of that meal but cooking the rice with some of the gravy is my idea, an inspiration from cooking nasi uduk (page 70).

Cooking oil 3 Tbsp

Chicken 1 kg (2 lb 3 oz), cut into 6 pieces

Coconut cream 250 ml (8 fl oz / 1 cup)

Daun salam (Indonesian bay leaf) 4 leaves

Salt 3 tsp

Water 2 litres (64 fl oz / 8 cups)

Long-grain rice 600 g (1 lb 5^1/$_3$ oz / 3 cups)

Fried shallots (page 37) 2 Tbsp

SPICE PASTE

Shallots 150 g (5^1/$_3$ oz)

Garlic 6 cloves, peeled

Dried prawn (shrimp) paste (belacan) ^{1}/$_2$ tsp

Ground coriander 1 Tbsp

Kencur 2 small knobs

Lemon grass 1 large stalk

Candlenuts 5

Dried red chillies 4, seeded

Water 2 Tbsp

1. Blend all ingredients for spice paste in a food processor into a fine paste.

2. Heat oil in a pot and fry spice paste till oil surfaces. Add chicken, coconut cream, daun salam, 1 tsp salt and 1 litre (32 fl oz / 4 cups) water and bring to the boil. Turn down heat and simmer till chicken is cooked.

3. Ladle out 500 ml (16 fl oz / 2 cups) gravy and mix it with remaining 1 litre (32 fl oz / 4 cups) water and 2 tsp salt. Combine with rice and cook rice using your preferred method until rice is tender.

4. Serve rice on individual serving plates or using a communal platter. To serve, scoop out rice onto a plate and top with pieces of chicken. Garnish with fried shallots.

5. Serve with some pickles (page 56) or a stir-fried vegetable (page 55) and the rest of chicken gravy as a sauce. Sambal belacan (page 41) is another good side dish.

Singapore Chicken Rice

The original Singapore chicken rice was nothing more than rice cooked with chicken stock flavoured with ginger and mashed garlic, and the chicken nothing more than "steamed" chicken. Over time, variations have been made to the rice and "roasted" chicken is now also offered by these stalls that sell chicken rice. Years ago, I came across a chicken rice stall in a coffee shop in Serangoon Gardens that served the rice with salt-baked chicken. What makes Singapore chicken rice the fantastic dish it is are the condiments. This chilli sauce has now been bottled, but you can make your own if you can't find the bottled version. By the way, if the chicken rice you cook at home does not seem to taste like the one you get from the stall, it could be that the stall has added monosodium glutamate (MSG) to the rice. MSG gives food a moreish quality which explains why snack food often has MSG in it. Cook the rice with rich chicken stock—stock that has plenty of chicken fat and flavour to it—and you won't need the MSG.

1) Basic Chicken Rice

Long-grain rice 600 g (1 lb 5^1/$_3$ oz / 3 cups), soaked 30 minutes

Salt 2 tsp

Ginger 1 large thumb-size knob, peeled and smashed

Garlic 6 cloves, peeled, smashed

RICH CHICKEN STOCK

Fresh chicken bones, skin and fat 2 kg (4 lb 6 oz)

Water 3 litres (96 fl oz / 12 cups)

CHICKEN CHOICES

- Steamed chicken Singapore-style (page 52)
- Chinese roast chicken (page 53)
- Salt-baked chicken (page 54)

SIDE DISH AND CONDIMENTS

Chicken cabbage soup (page 51)

Singapore chicken rice condiments (page 52)

Thick dark soy sauce

1. Prepare rich chicken stock. Place chicken bones, skin and fat and water in a stock pot and bring to the boil. Turn down heat and simmer for 2 hours.

2. Strain chicken stock. Measure out 1.5 litres (48 fl oz / 6 cups) stock. Freeze the remainder for use in other recipes.

3. Combine stock with other ingredients and cook rice using your preferred method until rice is tender.

4. When rice is done, fluff it up. Cover and rest rice for 10 minutes before serving with your choice of chicken and chicken cabbage soup, Singapore chicken rice condiments and thick dark soy sauce.

Note:

Although the recipe for rich chicken stock is for making Singapore chicken rice, it can also be used for many of the flavoured rice dishes as well as rice porridges and rice soups. It can also be used to flavour many of the rice dishes where you want added flavour, and be lightly boiled with spices to make a quick spiced chicken stock known as yakhni for some of the biryanis. To make the stock rich, the skin and chicken fat are used, but the fat can be separated so that you use it only when you want to make chicken rice. Chicken fat can also be rendered to extract the oil more quickly than by boiling. To render fat, cut up large pieces of fat and put the lot into a small pot kept on a small fire till the oil comes out and you are left with pieces of brown crackling. This stock freezes well.

2) GINGER RICE

Long-grain rice 600 g (1 lb 5¹/₃ oz /
   3 cups), soaked 30 minutes
Old ginger 1 large thumb-size
   knob, peeled and smashed
Garlic 1 clove, peeled and
   smashed
Salt 2 tsp
Rich chicken stock (page 80)
   1.5 litres (48 fl oz / 6 cups)

1. Combine all ingredients and cook rice using your preferred method
   until rice is tender.

2. When rice is done, fluff it up. Cover and rest rice for 10 minutes before
   serving with your choice of chicken.

3) GARLIC RICE

Chicken fat/oil 3 Tbsp
Chopped garlic 4 Tbsp
Long-grain rice 600 g (1 lb 5¹/₃ oz /
   3 cups), soaked 30 minutes
Rich chicken stock (page 80)
   1.5 litres (48 fl oz / 6 cups)
Salt 2 tsp

1. Heat chicken fat/oil in a frying pan and fry garlic till golden brown.
   Do not over-brown.

2. Combine contents of pan with rest of ingredients and cook rice using
   your preferred method until rice is tender.

3. When rice is done, fluff it up and stir down garlic. Cover and rest rice
   for 10 minutes before serving.

4) CHICKEN RICE WITH PANDAN

Pandan (screwpine) leaves 6
Long-grain rice 600 g (1 lb 5¹/₃ oz /
   3 cups), soaked 30 minutes
Rich chicken stock (page 80)
   1.5 litres (48 fl oz / 6 cups)
Salt 2 tsp
Ginger 1 large thumb-size knob,
   peeled and smashed

1. Knot pandan leaves together.

2. Combine all ingredients and cook rice using your preferred method
   until rice is tender.

3. When rice is done, fluff it up. Cover and rest rice for 10 minutes before
   serving.

QUICK SOUTH ASIAN-STYLE CHICKEN BIRYANI

This biryani is quick in that the rice and chicken are boiled together instead of separately, the way biryani is more usually cooked in many parts of South Asia. This particular preparation is more appreciated when your kitchen equipment is limited to a rice cooker or a large cooking pot. Although the rice will still be damp and maybe still a little gritty in the centre, infusing takes care of the problem. This is a good biryani to attempt infusing the old-fashioned way with hot coals placed on the lid of the rice pot. If you make this biryani with mutton, the meat must be cooked with plenty of water till tender before you add the rice to the meat. Although it is best made with basmati rice which is a very firm rice, I have eaten Nepali biryani made by this method that used other long-grain rice. Do not soak the rice to reduce the chance of the rice becoming mushy if the water proportions are a little off.

Chicken 1 kg (2 lb 3 oz), cut into large pieces
Ghee 3 Tbsp
Onion 150 g (5^1/$_3$ oz), chopped
Green chillies 2, seeded and chopped
Tomatoes 150 g (5^1/$_3$ oz), chopped
Garam masala 1 (page 30) 2 tsp
Red chilli powder 2 tsp
Chicken stock (page 80)/water 1.25 litres (40 fl oz / 5 cups)
Basmati rice 600 g (1 lb 5^1/$_3$ oz / 3 cups)
Salt 2 tsp
Coriander leaves ^{1}/$_2$ cup, chopped
Hard-boiled eggs 6, shelled

MEAT MARINADE
Yoghurt 250 ml (8 fl oz / 1 cup)
Garlic paste (page 36) 2 tsp
Ginger paste (page 36) 1 Tbsp
Salt 1 tsp

1. Prepare meat marinade. Mix yoghurt with garlic and ginger pastes and salt. Rub over chicken, cover and leave to marinate for an hour or overnight in the fridge.

2. To cook chicken, heat ghee in a large saucepan and fry onion till translucent. Stir in green chillies, tomatoes, garam masala, chilli powder, chicken and marinade. Fry for 2 minutes or until oil surfaces. Add stock/water and bring to the boil. Turn down heat, cover pot and simmer chicken for 20 minutes.

3. Add rice and salt. Turn up heat and return to the boil. Turn down heat to medium, cover pot and cook till gravy has been absorbed into rice. It does not matter if rice is still a little gritty.

4. Preheat oven to 160°C (325°F). Scoop out chicken and rice into an ovenproof dish, adding chopped coriander and shelled hard-boiled eggs into rice at the same time. Cover dish with a layer of several sheets of paper towels, put lid on and bake biryani in the oven for 20 minutes.

5. Serve biryani with pickles (pages 56–58) or chutney (page 59).

PERSIAN CHERRY RICE

In the medieval Islamic world, cherries were once known as the "fruit of the king" and a pilaf like this would be prepared for a feast. This particular fruit-flavoured pilaf actually calls for fresh sour cherries rather than dried. I have a large bag of dried Syrian cherries and so I made the dish with these. While fresh cherries are found in many countries, some are really too sweet for this rice dish. If using fresh sweet cherries, omit the sugar and add more lemon juice for a more tangy taste. Dried sour cherries can also substitute for fresh ones, but check that the dried fruit has not been artificially sweetened. Unsweetened dried fruit can be found in the organic foods section of supermarkets or stores specialising in organic foods. A good substitute for fresh sour cherries is frozen cranberries.

Ground turmeric $^1/_2$ tsp

Salt 3 tsp

Ground black pepper $^1/_2$ tsp

Chicken 1 kg (2 lb 3 oz), skinned and chopped into 6 pieces

Sour dried cherries 200 g (7 oz)

Water 2 litres (64 fl oz / 8 cups)

Ghee 3 Tbsp

Onion 50 g (1$^2/_3$ oz), peeled and finely chopped

Garlic 2 cloves, peeled and chopped

Tomato 50 g (1$^2/_3$ oz), chopped

Advieh 2 (page 31) 2 tsp

Lemon juice to taste

Sugar to taste

Basmati rice 600 g (1 lb 5$^1/_3$ oz / 3 cups), soaked 1 hour

Chicken stock (page 80) 1 litre (32 fl oz / 4 cups)

Corn flour (optional) 1–2 Tbsp

GARNISHING

Lemon wedges

Parsley/mint

1. Rub turmeric, 1 tsp salt and black pepper on chicken. Cover and leave to stand for 1 hour.

2. Cherries need to be stoned and boiled whether they are fresh or dried. Rinse cherries clean and boil in 1 litre (32 fl oz / 4 cups) water till soft. Cool, then stone cherries. If cherries are large, chop and mash fruit to a coarse pulp and set aside. Reserve cherry water for cooking chicken but discard the bottom layer if there is any grit.

3. To prepare cherry and chicken layer, melt ghee in a saucepan and brown onion. Add garlic and tomato and fry till fragrant. Stir in *advieh* first, then add chicken, 500 ml (16 fl oz / 2 cups) cherry water and remaining 1 litre (32 fl oz / 4 cups) water and bring to the boil. Turn down heat and simmer till chicken is cooked. There should be a rich-coloured gravy. Adjust sweetness and sourness with lemon juice and sugar to taste. It should be more sour than sweet and with a hint of saffron in this particular *advieh*.

4. Combine rice with remaining 2 tsp salt, chicken stock and 500 ml (16 fl oz / 2 cups) cherry water and cook rice using your preferred method until rice is tender. When rice is done, fluff it up.

5. Layer rice with chicken and half the cherries ending with a layer of rice. Infuse pilaf using your preferred method (page 62).

6. Make a sauce with the gravy by either thickening with corn flour mixed in some water or blending the remaining half of cherries into the gravy with a stick blender to get a smooth sauce.

7. Serve cherry rice garnished with lemon wedges, a sprinkling of chopped parsley/mint and cherry sauce.

Shirini Polo (persian chicken pilaf)

This particular pilaf is a good way to use up any leftover grilled or roasted chicken or turkey while the rice is perked up with whatever dried fruit and nuts you may have in the larder. Jazz up the flavour with orange flower water or rose water, a common Mughlai and West Asian way of flavouring rice dishes. The fragrant dried roses sold in bottles for flower tea can also be steeped in hot water to get rose water. Artificial rose essence is commonly found in many parts of Asia and if used very sparingly, it can be quite good.

Ghee 4 Tbsp

Cinnamon stick 4-cm (1¹/₂-in)

Sultanas 30 g (1 oz / ¹/₄ cup)

Pistachios 30 g (1 oz / ¹/₄ cup), shelled and slivered

Almond slivers 30 g (1 oz / ¹/₄ cup)

Cooked chicken/turkey 500 g (1 lb 1¹/₂ oz / 2¹/₂ cups)

Lemon juice 2 Tbsp

Sugar 2 tsp

Basmati rice 600 g (1 lb 5¹/₃ oz / 3 cups), soaked 1 hour

Advieh 1, 2 or 3 (page 31) ¹/₂ tsp

Water 1.5 litres (48 fl oz / 6 cups)

Salt 2 tsp

Orange flower water/rose water (optional) ¹/₂ Tbsp

Mint leaves

1. Melt ghee in a frying pan and fry cinnamon stick, sultanas, nuts and cooked chicken. Add lemon juice and sugar and fry till sugar has dissolved. Adjust sourness and sweetness to taste. Remove cinnamon stick for cooking with rice.

2. Combine rice with cinnamon stick, *advieh*, water and salt and cook rice using your preferred method until rice is tender. When rice is done, fluff it up and stir in orange flower water/rose water if using.

3. Layer rice, chicken and nuts ending with a layer of rice. Infuse pilaf using your preferred method (page 62).

4. Garnish with chopped mint. Serve with a salad or pickles (pages 57–58).

West Asian Rice with Broad Beans

Although common in West Asia, fresh broad beans are less easily available elsewhere. Try looking for frozen baby fava beans as these are more tender than some dried broad beans which can be rather tough and take hours to soften. What's more, the skins can be so chewy that even after long boiling, you have to skin the broad beans. This is a rather tedious process. The broad beans can also be cooked in a slow cooker overnight till they are tender.

Broad beans 200 g (7 oz)

Lamb 500 g (1 lb 1¹/₂ oz), cubed

Salt 2¹/₂ tsp

Any *baharat* (pages 32–33) 2 tsp

Olive oil 60 ml (2 fl oz / ¹/₄ cup)

Water 2 litres (64 fl oz / 8 cups)

Onion 50 g (1²/₃ oz), peeled and cubed

Garlic 3 cloves, peeled and chopped

Fresh dill ¹/₂ cup, chopped

Basmati rice 600 g (1 lb 5¹/₃ oz / 3 cups), soaked 1 hour

1. Boil beans in a large pot of water till just tender. Alternatively, cook overnight in a slow cooker.

2. Rub lamb with ¹/₂ tsp salt and 1 tsp *baharat* and set aside.

3. Heat 2 Tbsp olive oil and fry onion till soft. Add seasoned lamb and brown it. Add 500 ml (16 fl oz / 2 cups) water and simmer till meat is tender. Remove and set meat aside. Reserve 125 ml (4 fl oz / ¹/₂ cup) gravy and combine remaining gravy with enough water to get 1.5 litres (48 fl oz / 6 cups) for cooking rice.

4. Put remaining olive oil into frying pan and fry garlic till fragrant but not brown. Add cooked beans, dill and remaining 1 tsp *baharat* and stir-fry for 2 minutes. Set aside half the broad beans and stir lamb cubes into beans remaining in pan. Fry for 5 minutes, adding the reserved gravy. Bring the lamb-beans mixture to the boil and simmer for another 5 minutes to meld flavours. Turn off heat, cover pan and keep stew warm.

5. Combine reserved beans with rice, 1.5 litres (48 fl oz / 6 cups) watered down gravy and remaining 2 tsp salt and cook rice using your preferred method until rice is tender.

6. Dish out rice and crown it with lamb and broad bean stew. Serve with pickles (pages 57–58), a salad or yoghurt sauce (page 47).

WEST ASIAN RICE WITH SPINACH

Spinach originated from Iran but is now found everywhere. If you can get pre-washed ready-to-eat baby spinach, fixing this West Asian rice is a snap. If not, cleaning fresh spinach is tedious because not only do you have to get rid of the coarse stems and tough leaves, you also have to strip off the tough thin membrane that covers the stems. Once you are done, the final amount of spinach can sometimes be reduced by at least 30 per cent. Spinach must also be rinsed in several changes of cold water. The cooking time depends on the kind of spinach, with baby spinach being fairly quick.

Long-grain rice *600 g (1 lb 5^1/$_3$ oz / 3 cups)*

Water *1.5 litres (48 fl oz / 6 cups)*

Ghee *60 ml (2 fl oz / ^{1}/$_4$ cup)*

Advieh *3 (page 31) 1^1/$_2$ tsp*

Salt *2^1/$_2$ tsp*

Onion *150 g (5^1/$_3$ oz), peeled and finely sliced*

Garlic *2 cloves, peeled and julienned*

Spinach *2 kg (4 lb 6 oz), cleaned and coarsely chopped*

GARNISHING

Lemon wedges/sumac

1. Cook rice first before preparing spinach. Combine rice with water, 2 Tbsp ghee, 1 tsp *advieh* and 2 tsp salt and cook using your preferred method until rice is tender.

2. Melt remaining ghee in a saucepan big enough to contain cooked rice. Fry sliced onion till fragrant and beginning to brown. Add garlic and continue frying till garlic is a pale golden colour. Stir in remaining salt, *advieh* and spinach. Fry till spinach changes colour. If using baby spinach, turn off heat now. If not, simmer till spinach is at preferred texture. The spinach should be moist but not swimming in liquid.

3. When rice is done, fluff it up and transfer rice to the saucepan. Press rice down gently so rice takes the shape of the pan.

4. Cover pan with a clean dishcloth wrapped round the lid or with several layers of paper towels and the lid clamped on tightly. Have the heat on low to infuse the flavours for 10 minutes. The spinach and rice can also be baked in an ovenproof dish in a 160°C (325°F) oven for 20 minutes. Do this in two batches if you don't have a large enough ovenproof dish.

5. To serve, turn rice out onto a large deep serving bowl so spinach is on top of rice. Serve with lemon wedges or a dish of sumac powder and yoghurt sauce (page 47).

WEST ASIAN MUSHROOM PILAF

This mushroom pilaf gets its light sour touch from sumac. However, if sumac is not available, serve the pilaf with a small bowl of lime or lemon juice to be added to taste and stirred into the rice. Another way is to serve the pilaf with yoghurt sauce (page 47) or any of the tangy Persian-style stews such as khoresht fesenjaan (page 150).

Olive oil *60 ml (2 fl oz / ^{1}/$_4$ cup)*

Onion *150 g (5^1/$_3$ oz), peeled and finely chopped*

Garlic *3 cloves, peeled, chopped*

Tomatoes *250 g (9 oz), skinned and chopped*

Capsicum (bell pepper) *1, seeded and sliced into strips*

Salt *2^1/$_2$ tsp*

Baharat *2 (pages 32–33) 2 tsp*

Fresh mushrooms *500 g (1 lb 1^1/$_2$ oz), cleaned and thickly sliced*

Long-grain rice *600 g (1 lb 5^1/$_3$ oz / 3 cups)*

Water *1.5 litres (48 fl oz / 6 cups)*

GARNISHING

Sumac/lime/lemon juice *to taste*

Mint/coriander leaves

1. Heat olive oil in a frying pan and fry onion and garlic till fragrant. Add tomatoes, capsicum, ^{1}/$_2$ tsp salt and baharat and fry for 2 minutes till tomatoes begin to dry out. Stir in mushrooms and mix well to coat mushrooms with tomatoes and spices. Heat mushrooms through but do not boil.

2. Combine rice with water and remaining 2 tsp salt and cook rice using your preferred method. When rice is done, fluff it up and stir in mushroom mixture. Cover and rest rice for 10 minutes before serving.

3. Before serving rice, mix in sumac and garnish with chopped mint/ coriander leaves.

4. Serve with a yoghurt sauce, pickles (pages 56–58), kebabs (pages 44–46) or any Persian-style stew (pages 149–150).

Note:

To clean mushrooms, wipe each mushroom gently with paper towels. Trim off and discard the stems.

Dajaj Wa Timman Ahmer (iraqi chicken with red rice)

The *timman ahmer* or "red rice" is a result of the tomato paste colouring the rice red. Any culture that eats rice as a staple, typically combines rice and chicken. This is the Iraqi version and what a treat it is because the chicken is fried! The chicken can also be cut into large pieces and grilled or into smaller pieces and deep-fried. Grilling is easier with large pieces, deep-frying with small ones. Alternatively, cook the red rice and serve it with *shish ta'uk* (page 45) or any basic roasted or grilled chicken (page 53).

Chicken 1 kg (2 lb 3 oz), chopped into pieces

Long-grain rice 600 g (1 lb 5$^1/_3$ oz / 3 cups)

Ghee/olive oil 3 Tbsp

Tomato paste 2 Tbsp

Tomatoes 100 g (3$^1/_2$ oz), skinned and chopped

Salt 2 tsp

Chicken stock (page 80) 1.5 litres (48 fl oz / 6 cups)

Za'atar 1 (page 34) 1 tsp

Cooking oil for deep-frying

MARINADE

Any *baharat* (pages 32–33) 2 tsp

Salt 1 tsp

Onion juice (page 36) 2 Tbsp

1. Combine ingredients for marinade and season chicken. Cover and leave for a few hours or overnight in the refrigerator.

2. Combine rice, ghee/olive oil, tomato paste, tomatoes, salt and chicken stock and cook rice using your preferred method until rice is tender. When rice is done, fluff it up and sprinkle *za'atar* into rice. Cover and rest rice for10 minutes before serving.

3. If frying chicken, heat enough oil in a small pot and deep-fry chicken to a golden brown. Alternatively, grill chicken for 30 minutes or more depending on the size of the pieces.

4. Serve rice topped with chicken, yoghurt sauce (page 47), and pickles (pages 57–58) or a salad.

Kedgeree (indian dhal rice)

Use any quick-cooking dhal for this dish. Mung dhal which is skinned, split mung beans cooks quickly as does masoor dhal, the common but distinctive reddish-pink dhal. Both are cheap as well. They soften quickly at almost the same rate as rice if soaked in advance. While the fresh dhal cooks quite quickly, they can take quite a while to soften if they have been stored for more than a year (as I found out one day). Pre-soaking and pre-boiling will equalise the different cooking times between rice and dhal.

Ghee 75 ml (2$^1/_2$ fl oz / $^1/_3$ cup)

Mustard seeds 1 tsp

Onion 50 g (1$^2/_3$ oz), peeled and thinly sliced

Ginger 2-cm (1-in) knob, peeled and chopped

Tomatoes 100 g (3$^1/_2$ oz), diced

Dhal 200 g (7 oz / 1 cup), soaked 30 minutes

Indian bay leaves 2

Water 2 litres (64 fl oz / 8 cups)

Long-grain rice 600 g (1 lb 5$^1/_3$ oz / 3 cups)

Salt 2 tsp

Any garam masala (page 30) $^1/_2$ tsp

Coriander leaves 1 bunch, chopped

1. In a saucepan, heat 2 Tbsp ghee and fry mustard seeds till they pop. Pour into a small bowl and set aside.

2. Using the same pan, heat remaining 3 Tbsp ghee and fry onion and ginger till pale brown and fragrant. Add tomatoes, dhal, bay leaves and 1 litre (32 fl oz / 4 cups) water and bring to the boil. Lower heat and simmer dhal till nearly tender and still whole. The length of time needed will depend on the dhal.

3. Measure out dhal liquid and add enough water to get 1.5 litres (48 fl oz / 6 cups) liquid. Add this liquid to rice and dhal. Season with salt and cook rice using your preferred method.

4. When rice is done, fluff it up and stir in garam masala, mustard seeds and chopped coriander leaves if using. Rest rice for 10 minutes before serving.

5. Serve kedgeree hot with some raita (page 59) or pickles (pages 56–58) and an Indian-style curry (page 43).

KUWAITI CHICKEN RICE

Arabs in the Persian or Arabian Gulf states such as Kuwait, Oman, Qatar, United Arab Emirates and Bahrain like their food spicier than elsewhere in West Asia. Gulf spice mixes are more likely to have chilli powder than sweet paprika which has the colour without the heat. Another almost standard ingredient is dried limes or lime powder which is sometimes called *noomi* or *loomi basra* presumably because it was once imported from this port on the Persian Gulf. Once in ancient Sumer and now Iraq's main port, Basra has been touted by some as the site of the Biblical Garden of Eden and the home of the mythical Sinbad of *Arabian Nights* fame. Substitute *noomi Basra* with fresh or freeze-dried lime juice.

Gulf *baharat* (page 33) $^1/_2$ tsp

Salt 2 tsp

Basmati rice *600 g (1 lb 5$^1/_3$ oz / 3 cups), soaked 1 hour*

Ground turmeric $^1/_2$ tsp

Olive oil *60 ml (2 fl oz / $^1/_4$ cup)*

Onion *150 g (5$^1/_3$ oz), peeled and chopped*

Raisins $^1/_4$ cup

Pine nuts $^1/_4$ cup

Lime wedges

CHICKEN STOCK

Chicken *1 kg (2 lb 3 oz), cut into large pieces*

Cinnamon stick *4-cm (1$^1/_2$-in)*

Cardamom *4 pods*

Cracked black pepper $^1/_4$ tsp

Cloves *2*

Noomi Basra 2

Salt *1 tsp*

Water *2 litres (64 fl oz / 8 cups)*

TOMATO-GARLIC SAUCE

Olive oil *1 Tbsp*

Onion *25 g (1 oz), peeled and finely chopped*

Garlic paste (page 36) *1 Tbsp*

Tomatoes *300 g (11 oz), skinned and chopped*

Tomato paste *1 Tbsp*

Red chilli powder $^1/_2$ tsp

Gulf *baharat* (page 33) $^1/_2$ tsp

Sugar *1 Tbsp*

Lime juice *1 Tbsp*

Salt *1 tsp*

Water *125 ml (4 fl oz / $^1/_2$ cup)*

1. Combine ingredients for chicken stock in a large pot and bring to the boil. Remove the scum that rises to the top. Turn down heat and simmer for 30 minutes till chicken is just cooked.

2. Remove and drain chicken, then sprinkle $^1/_2$ tsp *baharat* and $^1/_2$ tsp salt all over it. Set aside.

3. Strain stock, discarding solids. Measure out 1.5 litres (48 fl oz / 6 cups) stock for cooking rice.

4. Combine stock with rice, ground turmeric and remaining 1$^1/_2$ tsp salt and cook rice using your preferred method until rice is tender. When rice is done, fluff it up. Cover and rest rice for 10 minutes before serving.

5. Heat olive oil in a pan and sear chicken. Remove chicken, then fry onions till nearly brown, then add raisins, pine nuts and chicken and fry for a few minutes to brown pine nuts and meld flavours with chicken. Set aside and keep warm.

6. To make tomato-garlic sauce, heat olive oil in a pot and fry onion till translucent. Add garlic paste and fry till fragrant. Stir in rest of ingredients and bring to the boil. Simmer for 10 minutes or till tomatoes are soft and mushy and sauce is thick. The sauce can be kept chunky or blended to a smooth sauce. Adjust seasoning to taste as well as the consistency of the sauce with more water if too thick or boiling down if too watery.

7. To serve rice, spread it on a large serving platter. Top with chicken, raisin and pine nut mixture, then garnish with lime wedges.

8. Serve tomato-garlic sauce as a condiment on the side or poured over chicken and rice.

Kabseh (bedouin chicken rice)

This rice dish is said to have been a Bedouin dish cooked on the move, and spiced differently by different cooks depending on what spices are available. However, there seems to be some agreement among bloggers on the Internet that dried limes called *noomi*, *loomi* or *limu Basra* should be in the spice mix. The chicken has to be a modern meat as lamb is more likely in the light of the traditional nomadic lifestyle of the Bedouins. This may explain why some *kabseh* recipes consist of stewed lamb on flavoured rice and wrapped in pita bread. This one is chicken *kabseh* cooked in chicken stock, but if you prefer lamb, the grilled or roasted chicken can be substituted with grilled or roasted lamb. Look for ready-mixed *kabseh* spices in West Asian stores or use the spice mix here.

Olive oil/cooking oil *3 Tbsp*

Onion *100 g (3¹/₂ oz), peeled and thinly sliced*

Tomatoes *100 g (3¹/₂ oz), skinned and chopped*

Green and red capsicums (bell peppers) *50 g (1²/₃ oz) each, seeded and thinly sliced*

Noomi Basra *1, crushed*

Basmati rice *600 g (1 lb 5¹/₃ oz / 3 cups), soaked 1 hour*

Salt *2 tsp*

Chicken stock (page 80)/water *1.5 litres (48 fl oz / 6 cups)*

SPICE MIX

Noomi Basra *1 Tbsp*

Ground turmeric *¹/₂ tsp*

Ground allspice *¹/₂ tsp*

Ground cardamom *¹/₄ tsp*

Ground cinnamon *¹/₄ tsp*

Ground white pepper *¹/₄ tsp*

Ground black pepper *¹/₄ tsp*

1. Mix together ground spices for spice mix.

2. Heat oil in a saucepan and fry onion till soft. Stir in tomatoes, capsicums and dried lime and stir-fry till tomatoes are soft. Add spice mix and fry for 2 minutes.

3. Combine mixture with rice, salt and chicken stock/water and cook rice using your preferred method until rice is tender.

4. Serve rice with grilled, fried or roasted chicken (page 53) or lamb (pages 47–48, 50) or kebabs (pages 44–46).

Sayadieh (syrian-lebanese rice and fish)

This rice dish is found in the Mediterranean coastal regions of Lebanon and Syria where fish, while expensive, is eaten more frequently than in the regions away from the coast. There appears to be quite a number of ways of preparing fish and rice going by what my research on the Internet found. The fish can be whole fish, seasoned and baked or grilled and served with a specially prepared rice or the fish can be fried fish fillet or seasoned fish cooked together with the rice. On a trip to Syria and Lebanon in 2009, I came across a rather plain Syrian version with crispy fried battered fish sitting atop rice that had been flavoured with a very light fish-chicken stock and garnished with fried onions and pine nuts. It was tasty enough, but the tastier version was the one in a Beirut hotel restaurant where the rice had been cooked with the fried onion and spices although the fish stock was so faint that I could not taste it. Whichever method is used, select a firm-fleshed fish so that it does not fall apart while cooking.

Olive oil *125 ml (4 fl oz / $^1/_2$ cup)*

Pine nuts *50 g (1$^2/_3$ oz / $^1/_2$ cup)*

Onions *200 g (7 oz), peeled and thinly sliced*

Boneless fish fillets *800 g (1$^3/_4$ lb), cut into large cubes*

Lemon juice *1 Tbsp*

Salt *2$^1/_2$ tsp*

Long-grain rice *600 g (1 lb 5$^1/_3$ oz / 3 cups)*

Flat-leaf parsley *$^1/_4$ cup, chopped*

Lemon wedges

FISH STOCK

Fish trimmings *500 g (1 lb 1$^1/_2$ oz)*

Flat-leaf parsley *1 bunch*

Garlic *1 clove, peeled and smashed*

Water *2 litres (64 fl oz / 8 cups)*

SPICE MIX (OR ANY SPICE MIX ON PAGES 31–33)

Ground cumin *$^1/_2$ tsp*

Ground black pepper *$^1/_2$ tsp*

Ground paprika/cayenne pepper *$^1/_2$ tsp*

Allspice *$^1/_2$ tsp*

SAUCE

Lemon juice *1 Tbsp*

Salt *$^1/_2$ tsp*

Corn flour (optional) *1–1$^1/_2$ Tbsp*

Flat-leaf parsley *$^1/_4$ cup, chopped*

1. Heat olive oil in a frying pan and brown pine nuts. Scoop out and set aside. Stir in sliced onions and brown to a golden-dark brown colour, but do not let it burn. Scoop out and reserve a quarter of fried onions for garnishing. Do not wash pan.

2. Combine the rest of fried onions with fish stock ingredients in a pot and boil for 30 minutes till stock turns brown and onions are mushy and pale. Strain away solids. Measure out 1.5 litres (48 fl oz / 6 cups) stock for cooking rice. Keep remainder for making sauce.

3. Mix together ground spices for spice mix and rub it into fish fillet together with lemon juice and 1 tsp salt. Marinate fish for 30 minutes.

4. Combine fish stock with rice, remaining 2 tsp salt and cook rice using your preferred method until rice is tender.

5. In the same oil and pan in which onions were fried, fry marinated fish on both sides till cooked through.

6. Strain oil to get rid of any solids and use it to make sauce. If it is less than 1 Tbsp, add more to make up 1 Tbsp. To make sauce, combine oil, fish stock, lemon juice and salt and bring to the boil. If desired, stir in corn flour mixed with a little water to thicken sauce. Bring to the boil, stirring in chopped parsley when sauce thickens.

7. To serve, top individual plates of rice with pieces of fish and a garnish of fried onion and pine nuts. The sauce may be poured directly on the rice or kept on the side in a sauce boat.

8. Serve rice with lemon wedges, yoghurt sauce (page 47) and garlic-flavoured olive oil (page 36).

Mensaf (bedouin roast lamb and tomato pilaf)

Imagine a whole lamb being roasted over the fire under a starry desert sky and the sounds of a flute or *rebabab* being played by a Bedouin. Waiting for this lamb topping is a large platter of flavoured rice. This dish of rice and roast lamb is now Jordan's national dish and the best place to enjoy it is to camp overnight at Wadi Rum, one of the country's best tourist attractions. Barring an open fire under desert skies, a good electric or gas oven is the way most of us roast lamb. Although leg of lamb sounds great, compacting the meat into a ball by removing the shin bone and tying the meat into a ball gives a more even juicy roast without the meat round the shin drying out before the thicker parts are done. Supermarkets now sell lamb as a boned and rolled chunk rather than as an actual leg. Roast the lamb on a flat roasting rack to prevent uneven cooking.

Ghee 3 Tbsp

Onion 50 g (1²/₃ oz), peeled and thinly sliced

Ripe tomatoes 500 g (1 lb 1¹/₂ oz), skinned and coarsely chopped

Salt 2 tsp

Cumin ¹/₂ tsp

Yakhni (page 114) 1.5 litres (48 fl oz / 6 cups)

Basmati rice 600 g (1 lb 5¹/₃ oz / 3 cups)

ROAST LAMB

Garlic 6 cloves, peeled and finely chopped

Olive oil 60 ml (2 fl oz / ¹/₄ cup)

Mint, coriander leaves or flat-leaf parsley ¹/₂ cup, chopped

Salt 2 tsp

Any *baharat* or *advieh* (pages 31–33) 3 tsp

Semi-boneless leg of lamb 3 kg (6 lb 11 oz)

1. Start by preparing roast lamb. Mix together garlic, olive oil, herb of choice, salt and *baharat/advieh*.

2. Place lamb on a large sheet of aluminium foil big enough to wrap meat up well. Make slits in lamb right to the deepest part and rub seasoning mix into meat. Press some of the seasoning into the slits. Wrap up lamb and leave to season overnight in the refrigerator.

3. Bring lamb back to room temperature some 4 hours before it is to be roasted. Prepare a large piece of foil big enough to cover lamb to finish up roasting later on.

4. Arrange roasting rack on the lowest rung in oven and preheat oven to 200°C (400°F). Arrange lamb without foil on a rack in a roasting pan and pour 125 ml (4 fl oz / ¹/₂ cup) water into roasting pan.

5. Put lamb into preheated oven and roast each side for 10 minutes, turning lamb each time to brown it. After 40 minutes, reduce temperature to 160°C (325°F) and roast for another hour, turning every 20 minutes or till internal temperature of lamb reaches 70°C (155°F). If you have a meat thermometer, press the tip into the deepest part of lamb to check the internal temperature. As lamb can be eaten rare, it does not matter if the centre is a little pink.

6. Remove roasting pan from oven and cover lamb with foil to let lamb finish cooking for another 45 minutes. Place something heavy around edges of foil to hold it down securely over lamb.

7. While lamb is resting, cook rice. Heat ghee in a frying pan and brown onion. Stir in chopped tomatoes, salt and cumin and mix together. Simmer with 250 ml (8 fl oz / 1 cup) stock till tomato sauce looks rich and thick.

8. Add enough stock to tomato sauce to get 1.5 litres (48 fl oz / 6 cups). Combine tomato sauce and rice and cook using your preferred method until rice is tender. When rice is done, fluff it up. Cover and rest rice for 10 minutes.

9. Slice lamb thinly against the grain. Serve with rice and cooked yoghurt sauce (page 47).

Note:

This roast lamb also goes well with West Asian rice with ghee (page 70) and mashkoul *(page 95).*

MASHKOUL (WEST ASIAN ONION RICE)

This is an everyday dish in many West Asian homes, being flavourful and quick to prepare. It goes well with kebabs and grilled meat as well as with fried or grilled fish and prawns. The onion rice can be flavoured with either ghee or olive oil, with olive oil being the more common and the cheaper alternative to ghee.

Ghee/olive oil 60 ml (2 fl oz / ¹/₄ cup)

Onions 200 g (7 oz), peeled and finely chopped

Long-grain rice 600 g (1 lb 5¹/₃ oz / 3 cups)

Water 1.5 litres (48 fl oz / 6 cups)

Salt 2 tsp

GARNISHING

Fried onions (page 35)

1. Heat ghee/olive oil in a wok and fry chopped onions till a pale golden brown. If you have no fried onions for the garnishing, fry them before frying chopped onions.

2. Combine fried chopped onions and oil with rice, water and salt and cook rice using your preferred method until rice is tender. When rice is done, fluff it up. Cover and rest rice for 10 minutes before serving.

3. Garnish rice with fried onions and serve with any of the West Asian stews (pages 48–50), kebabs or grilled meats (pages 44–45) or fried or grilled seafood, a salad and pickles (pages 57–58).

TURKISH AUBERGINE AND TOMATO PILAF

Aubergines (eggplants) and tomatoes! What could be more Turkish? This pilaf is the rare vegetarian pilaf. Serve it with a dhal curry or bean stew for a more balanced meal if you want to keep it vegetarian.

Aubergines (eggplants) 1 kg (2 lb 3 oz)

Olive oil 60 ml (2 fl oz / ¹/₄ cup)

Onions 200 g (7 oz), peeled and thinly sliced or cubed

Long-grain rice 600 g (1 lb 5¹/₃ oz / 3 cups)

Tomatoes 300 g (11 oz), thickly sliced

Salt 2 tsp

Water 1.5 litres (48 fl oz / 6 cups)

1. Cut aubergines into large cubes or thick slices with the skin on. Heat a cast-iron frying pan, brush lightly with oil and brown aubergine cubes or slices on all sides till aubergines are just soft.

2. Heat olive oil in a wok and brown onions. Stir in browned aubergines and mix well.

3. Combine rice, tomatoes, salt and water and cook rice using your preferred method until rice is tender. When rice is done, fluff it up and remove half the rice to a large bowl. Put aubergines and onions into the rice pot, then return rice from bowl to rice pot. Let rice rest for 10 minutes before serving.

4. Serve pilaf with a raita (page 59), yoghurt sauce (page 47), and kebabs (page 44–46) or a meat stew (pages 48 and 50).

DOMATESLI PILAVI (TURKISH TOMATO PILAF)

The mint-flavoured pilaf makes this a good pilaf with a lamb stew, lamb kebabs or a mutton curry. The glutamic acid in tomatoes and the rich red colour make this a tasty and attractive dish.

Ghee 60 ml (2 fl oz / ¹/₄ cup)

Onion 150 g (5¹/₃ oz), peeled and finely chopped

Garlic 2 cloves, peeled and finely chopped

Ripe tomatoes 500 g (1 lb 1¹/₂ oz), skinned and chopped

Salt 2 tsp

Ground black pepper 1 tsp

Water 1.5 litres (48 fl oz / 6 cups)

Basmati rice 600 g (1 lb 5¹/₃ oz / 3 cups)

Mint ¹/₂ cup, chopped

1. Heat ghee in a wok and fry onion and garlic till soft and transparent. Add tomatoes, salt, pepper and 1 litre (32 fl oz / 4 cups) water and simmer for 10 minutes.

2. Add enough water to sauce in wok to make up 1.5 litres (48 fl oz / 6 cups) liquid. Combine sauce with rice and cook rice using your preferred method until rice is tender.

3. When rice is done, fluff it up and stir in chopped mint. Cover and rest rice for 10 minutes before serving.

4. Serve rice with any West Asian stew (page 49) or kebabs (pages 44–46) and a salad or pickles (pages 57–58).

Roz Bil Tamar (date and almond pilaf)

What could be more typically West Asian than the combination of almonds and dates? West Asian dates appear in profusion in countries with any community of Muslims during the month of Ramadan when it is believed that the day's fasting should be broken at sunset with a few dates and a drink before consuming a bigger meal.

Ghee 60 ml (2 fl oz / ¹/₄ cup)

Almond halves ¹/₂ cup

Onion 100 g (3¹/₂ oz), peeled and thinly sliced

Basmati rice 600 g (1 lb 5¹/₃ oz / 3 cups)

Water 1.5 litres (48 fl oz / 6 cups)

Salt 2 tsp

Dates 8, seeded and chopped

Rose water/orange flower water/ lime juice/grated lime peel 1 Tbsp

Za'atar 2 (page 34)/sumac 2 Tbsp

1. Heat ghee and brown almonds. Scoop out and set aside. Stir in onion and fry till brown.

2. Combine browned onion and ghee with rice, water, salt, dates and half the almonds. Cook rice using your preferred method. When rice is done, fluff it up and stir in rose water/orange flower water/lime juice/grated lime peel and za'atar/sumac.

3. Garnish with the remainder of browned almond halves.

4. Serve rice with any West Asian stew (pages 149–150), pickles (pages 57–58) or yoghurt sauce (page 47).

Masala Bhaat (indian spiced rice)

Any mix of vegetables can be used in this dish but the kind chosen will affect the final flavour as well as texture. I rather like green beans and carrots. They add colour to the yellow rice.

Ghee/cooking oil 60 ml (2 fl oz / ¹/₄ cup)

Mustard seeds 1 tsp

Salt 2 tsp

Yoghurt 2 Tbsp

Water 1.5 litres (48 fl oz / 6 cups)

Mix of vegetables cut into bite-size pieces (cauliflower, green beans, peas, carrots, broccoli, etc.) 1 kg (2 lb 3 oz)

Long-grain rice 600 g (1 lb 5¹/₃ oz / 3 cups)

Fresh grated coconut ¹/₄ cup

Coriander leaves 1 large bunch, chopped

SPICE PASTE

Ground coriander 1 tsp

Ground cumin ¹/₂ tsp

Red chilli powder 1 tsp

Ground turmeric ¹/₂ tsp

Asafoetida 1 large pinch

Water 1 Tbsp

1. Combine ingredients for spice paste to get a thick paste.

2. Heat ghee/oil in a wok and fry mustard seeds till they start to pop. Turn down heat and add spice paste and stir-fry for 2–3 minutes till fragrant.

3. Add salt, yoghurt and 125 ml (4 fl oz / ¹/₂ cup) water and stir in vegetables. Stir-fry for 2 minutes.

4. Combine rice, vegetable mixture and the remainder of the water and cook rice using your preferred method.

5. When rice is done, fluff it up. Cover and rest rice for 10 minutes before stirring in grated coconut and coriander leaves.

6. Serve rice with dhal curry (page 43), dhal char (page 44) or a chicken curry (page 43).

TAMATAR PULAO 1 (INDIAN TOMATO RICE 1)

There are many combinations of tomatoes with rice from West to Southeast Asia. I have come across "Mexican rice" at a Mexican supermarket in St Paul, MN, which is nothing but tomato rice! All tomato and rice combinations would yield a reddish-coloured rice but would taste different because of the different spices and side dishes. The quality and colour of the tomatoes will also affect the rice. Some types of tomatoes, even when ripe, do not have a rich colour or flavour when cooked. Substitute with canned plum tomatoes and tomato paste which, being a concentrate, has excellent colour and intense flavour. If using canned tomatoes, include the juice as part of the liquid for cooking the rice.

Ghee 60 ml (2 fl oz / ¼ cup)

Onion 100 g (3½ oz), peeled and thinly sliced

Black cardamom (see Glossary) 4 pods

Garlic 1 clove, peeled, chopped

Ripe tomatoes 400 g (14⅓ oz), skinned and chopped

Ginger 1 small thumb-size knob, peeled and smashed

Ground turmeric ½ tsp

Any garam masala (page 30) 1½ tsp

Salt 2 tsp

Basmati rice 600 g (1 lb 5⅓ oz / 3 cups)

Water 1.5 litres (48 fl oz / 6 cups) or as needed

Toasted cashew nut halves/ slivered almonds

1. Heat ghee in a wok and brown onion. Scoop out onion and set aside.

2. Add cardamom and garlic to pan and fry till fragrant but not brown. Add tomatoes, ginger, ground turmeric, garam masala and salt and mix well. Bring sauce to the boil.

3. Add enough water to tomato mixture to get 1.5 litres (48 fl oz / 6 cups) liquid. Combine this with rice and cook rice using your preferred method until rice is tender.

4. When rice is done, fluff it up, then stir in fried onion. Cover and rest rice for 10 minutes before serving.

5. Before serving, garnish rice with toasted cashew nut halves or slivered almonds.

6. Serve with a raita (page 59) or pickle (page 56–57) and a meat or seafood curry (page 43) and poppadoms.

TAMATAR PULAO 2 (INDIAN TOMATO RICE 2)

Ghee 60 ml (2 fl oz / ¼ cup)

Garlic 2 cloves, peeled and finely ground

Ginger 1 thumb-size knob, peeled and finely ground

Tomatoes 400 g (14⅓ oz), skinned and chopped

Green chillies 2, seeded and coarsely chopped

Salt 1½ tsp

Ground cumin ½ tsp

Indian bay leaves 2

Water 1.5 litres (48 fl oz / 6 cups) or as needed

Basmati rice 600 g (1 lb 5⅓ oz / 3 cups)

GARNISHING

Coriander leaves

Spring onions

Toasted cashew nuts

1. Heat ghee in a pot and fry garlic and ginger till fragrant. Add tomatoes, chillies, salt, cumin and bay leaves and fry for 2 minutes.

2. Add enough water to mixture to get 1.5 litres (48 fl oz / 6 cups) liquid. Combine this mixture with rice and cook rice using your preferred method until rice is tender. When rice is done, fluff it up and stir down ingredients. Cover and rest rice for another 10 minutes.

3. Before serving rice, mix in chopped coriander and spring onions and garnish with toasted cashew nuts.

4. Serve pilaf with a chutney (page 59), dhal curry (page 43), dhal char (page 44) or a chicken curry (page 43).

ANANAS PULAO (SHAH JEHAN-STYLE PINEAPPLE PILAF)

This recipe was inspired by the recipe for *ananas pulao* in *Nuskha-e-Shahjahani* but Shah Jehan's cooks won't recognise my way of preparing it. Not that the emperor would have cared so long as it had sweet-sour flavours. The availability of canned pineapples and juice makes this pilaf do-able anywhere and yet exotic. If you can't find nigella or black cumin, substitute with cumin seeds. This is an especially good recipe to try out the Mughlai technique of flavouring rice and meat with smoke. See Mughlai-style smoked lamb biryani (page 116).

Ghee 3 *Tbsp*

Onion 50 g (1²/₃ oz), *peeled and finely chopped*

Canned pineapple rings 6 *slices, cut into wedges*

Lemon juice 2 *Tbsp*

Sugar 1 *Tbsp*

Salt 2¹/₂ tsp

Basmati rice 600 g (1 lb 5¹/₃ oz / 3 cups), *soaked 1 hour*

Nigella/black cumin/cumin seeds ¹/₂ *Tbsp*

Coriander leaves ¹/₂ *cup, chopped*

WHOLE SPICES

Cinnamon stick 6-cm (2¹/₂-in)

Cloves 6

Cardamom 6 *pods*

GROUND SPICES

Saffron ¹/₂ tsp, *soaked in 1 Tbsp water*

Ground turmeric ¹/₂ tsp

Ground paprika/chilli powder 1 tsp

SPICED CHICKEN STOCK

Chicken 1 kg (2 lb 3 oz), *cut into 6 pieces*

Water 1 litre (32 fl oz / 4 cups)

Pineapple juice 500 ml (16 fl oz / 2 cups)

Canning syrup

Cloves 3

Cinnamon stick 4-cm (1¹/₂-in)

Ginger 1 *large thumb-size knob, peeled and bruised*

Onion 50 g (1²/₃ oz), *peeled and quartered*

Salt 1 tsp

1. Prepare spiced chicken stock. Put chicken and water into a pot and bring to the boil. Skim off the scum that rises to the top. When water is scum-free, add rest of stock ingredients and simmer till chicken is cooked. Drain chicken, cool and strip meat off bones. Return bones to stock and continue boiling for another 10 minutes or so. Strain stock and discard solids. Measure out 1.5 litres (48 fl oz / 6 cups) stock for cooking rice. Keep 125 ml (4 fl oz / ¹/₂ cup) for flavouring meat.

2. Heat ghee in a wok and fry onion and whole spices till onion begins to brown. Stir in pineapple wedges, chicken meat, lemon juice, sugar, ¹/₂ tsp salt and the 125 ml (4 fl oz / ¹/₂ cup) stock and bring to the boil. Adjust sweetness and sourness to taste. Simmer till liquid is almost gone but chicken is still moist.

3. Combine rice with 1.5 litres (48 fl oz / 6 cups) stock and remaining 2 tsp salt and cook rice using your preferred method until rice is tender. When rice is done, fluff it up and stir in nigella/cumin and chopped coriander leaves. Divide rice into 3 equal portions.

4. Stir saffron water into one portion of rice, turmeric into another portion and paprika/chilli powder into remaining portion. The rice should be unevenly coloured.

5. Layer rice and meat starting and ending with rice and infuse for 20 minutes using your preferred method (page 62).

6. Serve with a raita (page 59), salad or chutney (page 59) or yoghurt sauce (page 47).

KASHMIRI MUTTON PILAF

What makes this a Kashmiri pilaf is the generous amount of dried fruit and the saffron which is grown for export in Kashmir. This beautiful valley in the Himalaya was once the playground of the Mughal court and the Persian-rooted Mughlai taste for sweet-sour flavours in Kashmiri food has remained in predominantly Muslim Kashmir. The Indian elements are the garlic and ginger pastes and the fried onions, a combination found in many Indian dishes.

Ghee 60 ml (2 fl oz / ¼ cup)

Onions 250 g (9 oz), peeled and thinly sliced

Mutton without bone 750 g (1 lb 11 oz), cut into large cubes

Water 1 litre (32 fl oz / 4 cups) + more as needed

Yoghurt 250 ml (8 fl oz / 1 cup)

Salt 3 tsp

Sugar 2 tsp

Basmati rice 600 g (1 lb 5⅓ oz / 3 cups), soaked 1 hour

Dried fruit (raisins, apricots etc.) 120 g (4 oz / 1 cup)

Saffron 1 tsp, soaked in 1 Tbsp water

SPICE PASTE

Ginger paste (page 36) 2 Tbsp

Garlic paste (page 36) 1 Tbsp

Chopped green chillies 1 Tbsp

WHOLE SPICES

Black cardamom 3 pods

Cardamom 3 pods

Cloves 3

Indian bay leaves 3

Cracked black peppercorns 1 tsp

Cinnamon stick 4-cm (1½-in)

GARNISHING

Toasted split almonds ½ cup

Lemon wedges

1. Heat ghee in a saucepan and fry onions till translucent. Add mutton and ingredients for spice paste. Stir-fry till meat changes colour and ginger and garlic smell fragrant. Add whole spices and stir-fry for another 2 minutes, then add 1 litre (32 fl oz / 4 cups) water and bring to the boil. Turn down heat and simmer till mutton is tender. There should be about 125 ml (4 fl oz / ½ cup) gravy left. Stir in yoghurt, 1 tsp salt and sugar and return to the boil. Turn off heat.

2. Spoon out 125 ml (4 fl oz / ½ cup) mutton gravy and add enough water to get 1.5 litres (48 fl oz / 6 cups) liquid. Combine this with rice, remaining 2 tsp salt and dried fruit and cook rice using your preferred method until rice is tender. When rice is done, fluff it up, sprinkling in saffron water at the same time. Save a few drops for sprinkling over the top of rice.

3. Layer rice and meat starting and ending with rice and infuse for 20 minutes using your preferred method (page 62).

4. Depending on how the pilaf was infused, sprinkle remaining drops of saffron water on top of rice and garnish with toasted almonds and lemon wedges.

5. Serve with a raita (page 59), salad or chutney (page 59).

INDIAN-STYLE PEA PULAO

Fresh peas are common in Indian markets and these peas are delicious cooked with rice because Indian fresh peas are picked when mature and keep their texture even when boiled vigorously. Although fresh green peas are not found in Singapore wet markets, there are the fresh streaky beans which make an excellent substitute for fresh green peas as they take about the same amount of time to soften as rice and have a cooked texture similar to Indian peas.

Ghee 3 Tbsp

Ginger 6 slices, peeled and finely shredded

Garlic 1 clove, peeled and finely chopped

Tomatoes 200 g (7 oz), skinned and coarsely chopped

Fresh green peas 500 g (1 lb 1½ oz)

Salt 2 tsp

Long-grain rice 600 g (1 lb 5⅓ oz / 3 cups)

Water 1.5 litres (48 fl oz / 6 cups)

GARNISHING

Coriander leaves/mint

1. Heat ghee in a frying pan and fry ginger and garlic till fragrant. Do not brown garlic. Add tomatoes and peas and stir-fry for 5 minutes to soften tomatoes. Stir in salt.

2. Combine tomato and pea mixture with rice and water and cook rice using your preferred method until rice is tender.

3. Before serving, stir chopped herb of choice into hot rice.

4. Serve with a dhal or meat curry (page 43), meatballs in yoghurt sauce (page 42), chutney (page 59) or pickles (page 57).

YOGHURT RICE

This can be either South or West Asian because the ingredients are the same. Change the spice mix from baharat to garam masala and the accompanying side dishes and you change the region.

Yoghurt 250 ml (8 fl oz / 1 cup)

Water 1.25 litres (40 fl oz / 5 cups)

Sugar 1 tsp

Salt 2 tsp

Long-grain rice 600 g (1 lb 5⅓ oz / 3 cups)

Ghee 1 Tbsp

Any baharat (pages 32–33) or garam masala (page 30) ½ tsp

WHOLE SPICES

Cinnamon stick 4-cm (1½-in)

Cardamom 2 pods

Cloves 2

GARNISHING

Mint 1 cup, chopped

1. Beat together yoghurt, water, sugar and salt. Combine with rice, ghee and whole spices and cook rice using your preferred method until rice is tender. When rice is done, fluff it up and sprinkle in either baharat or garam masala. Rest rice for 10 minutes before serving.

2. Just before serving, stir chopped mint into rice.

3. Serve rice with lamb kebabs (page 44) and with either West Asian aubergine stew (page 49), yoghurt sauce (page 47) or dhal curry (page 43).

KHEEMA-MATTAR PULAO (MINCED MEAT AND PEAS PILAF)

This Indian-style pilaf can be made with any kind of minced meat although lamb or mutton would be more usual. Either fresh or frozen peas should be used, never canned peas as they are too mushy and overcooked and some are unnecessarily dyed a weird green. If using mutton, even minced mutton must be cooked for some time to get the meat tender before the peas are added and the *kheema-mattar* put into the rice to cook together.

Ghee *3 Tbsp*

Cloves *4*

Cumin seeds *1 tsp*

Minced meat *300 g (11 oz)*

Salt *2 1/2 tsp*

Yoghurt *125 ml (4 fl oz / 1/2 cup)*

Water *2 litres (64 fl oz / 8 cups)*

Fresh/frozen peas *300 g (11 oz)*

Basmati rice *600 g (1 lb 5 1/3 oz / 3 cups), soaked 1 hour*

Any garam masala (page 30) *1/2 tsp*

Red chilli powder *1 tsp*

Coriander leaves *1/2 cup, chopped*

SPICE PASTE

Onion *50 g (1 2/3 oz), peeled*

Garlic *2 cloves, peeled*

Ginger *1 large thumb-size knob, peeled*

Water *2 Tbsp*

Red chilli powder *1 tsp*

Garam masala 1 (page 30) *2 tsp*

1. Prepare spice paste. Blend together onion, garlic and ginger with water to a fine paste. Mix in chilli powder and garam masala.

2. Heat ghee in a saucepan and fry cloves and cumin seeds till fragrant. Add spice paste and fry for 2 minutes. Stir in minced meat, 1/2 tsp salt, yoghurt and 500 ml (16 fl oz / 2 cups) water and bring to the boil. Turn down heat and simmer till meat is tender and there is a thick sauce. If using minced chicken, reduce water to 250 ml (4 fl oz / 1 cup).

3. Combine minced meat with peas, remaining 2 tsp salt, rice and remaining1.5 litres (48 fl oz / 6 cups) water and cook rice using your preferred method until rice is tender. When rice is done, fluff it up and stir in garam masala, chilli powder and chopped coriander leaves. Cover and rest rice for 10 minutes before serving.

4. Serve rice with pickles (page 57), chutney (page 59) or raita (page 59) and yoghurt sauce (page 47).

INDIAN VEGETARIAN PILAF

The vegetables used in this pilaf can be any of your choice, but it should include a generous serving of peas, beans or boiled dhal to include some protein in the meal if it is going to be a one-dish meal. This pilaf is easily cooked on a stove-top or in a rice cooker, the latter being the easier. If cooking the pilaf on the stove top, do the first step in a saucepan large enough to cook the rice in. Increase or decrease the water for the rice depending on whether you are using juicy vegetables or drier ones like carrots and peas.

Ghee 75 ml (2¹/₂ fl oz / ¹/₃ cup)

Onion 150 g (5¹/₃ oz), peeled and chopped

Tomatoes 200 g (7 oz), thickly sliced

Potatoes 100 g (3¹/₂ oz), peeled and cubed

Mixed vegetables 1 kg (2 lb 3 oz), cut into small pieces

Long-grain rice 600 g (1 lb 5¹/₃ oz / 3 cups)

Salt 2 tsp

Sugar ¹/₂ tsp

Asafoetida 1 large pinch

Water 1.5 litres (48 fl oz / 6 cups)

SPICE PASTE

Ginger paste (page 36) ¹/₂ Tbsp

Ground turmeric ¹/₂ tsp

Red chilli powder 1 tsp

WHOLE SPICES

Cumin seeds 1 tsp

Cloves 4

Indian bay leaves 2

Cardamom 4 pods

Cinnamon stick 4-cm (1¹/₂-in)

1. Mix together spice paste ingredients.

2. Heat ghee and fry onion with cumin seeds till onion is transparent. Add other whole spices and spice paste and fry till fragrant. Stir in tomatoes, potatoes and mixed vegetables and fry for 2 minutes. Add a little water if vegetables are drier ones.

3. Combine rice, salt, sugar, asafoetida and water and mix well before adding vegetable mixture. Cook rice using your preferred method until rice is tender.

4. When rice is done, fluff it up and mix well. Rest rice for 10 minutes.

5. Serve pilaf with a chutney (page 59) or yoghurt sauce (page 47).

Green Coriander Rice with Eggs

This is an economical yet festive dish that does not call for expensive meat. Instead it features inexpensive boiled eggs. Costs can be kept low by substituting ghee with oil and the more expensive basmati rice with a cheaper long-grain rice. Use waxy potatoes so that they hold their shape better. Tomatoes can be skinned by peeling with a sharp paring knife rather than the more tedious method of boiling to loosen the skins.

Ghee 3 Tbsp

Potatoes 200 g (7 oz), cubed

Onion 50 g (1²/₃ oz), peeled and thinly sliced

Tomato 50 g (1²/₃ oz), skinned and thickly sliced

Yoghurt 125 ml (4 fl oz / ¹/₂ cup)

Basmati/long-grain rice 600 g (1 lb 5¹/₃ oz / 3 cups), soaked 1 hour

Water 1.5 litres (48 fl oz / 6 cups)

Salt 2 tsp

Any garam masala (page 30) ¹/₂ tsp

Hard-boiled eggs 12, shelled and halved

SPICE PASTE

Coriander leaves 1 cup

Onion 25 g (1 oz), peeled and chopped

Green chillies 50 g (1²/₃ oz), seeded

Ginger 1 thumb-size knob, peeled and sliced

Garlic 3 cloves, peeled

Water 2 Tbsp

WHOLE SPICES

Cinnamon stick 4-cm (1¹/₂-in)

Cardamom 4 pods

Indian bay leaves 2

GARNISHING

Coriander leaves ¹/₂ cup, chopped

1. In a food processor, make spice paste by blending together all the ingredients to a fine paste.

2. Heat ghee in a frying pan and brown potato cubes. The potato does not need to be cooked through. Set aside.

3. In the same pan, fry sliced onion till golden brown. Set aside.

4. Reheat pan and stir whole spices in hot ghee for 1 minute, then add spice paste. Fry till oil surfaces, then stir in tomato slices and fry till oil surfaces again. Add yoghurt, mix well and cook for 2 minutes.

5. Combine yoghurt mixture with rice, water, potatoes and salt and cook rice using your preferred method until rice is tender.

6. When rice is done, fluff it up and stir in fried onion and garam masala. Rest rice for 10 minutes.

7. To serve, stir chopped coriander leaves for garnishing into hot rice, dish out and top rice with hard-boiled egg halves.

8. Serve with a raita (page 59), yoghurt sauce (page 47), chutney or dhal curry (page 43).

Prawn Biryani

Biryani and pilaf are two words for the same delicious dish. Prawn biryani and Indian-style prawn pilaf (page 112) are two different ways of making this tasty dish, prawn biryani being the easier of the two. Note that frozen prawns, the kind most of us get nowadays, tend to weep excessively and if you want to infuse the rice, the resulting curry may be too liquid. If this happens, take the prawns out once they are cooked and dry out the gravy with a few minutes of hard boiling. Return the prawns to the pan and cook for another minute or so. With prawn biryani there is no infusing and any extra liquid is converted into a sauce.

Red chilli powder 2 tsp

Salt 2 1/2 tsp

Shelled prawns with tails on 1 kg (2 lb 3 oz)

Ghee 60 ml (2 fl oz / 1/4 cup)

Onions 200 g (7 oz), peeled and thinly sliced

Basmati rice 600 g (1 lb 5 1/3 oz / 3 cups), soaked 1 hour

Cooking oil 2 Tbsp

Coriander leaves 1 cup, chopped

Yoghurt 250 ml (8 fl oz / 1 cup) + extra as needed

PRAWN STOCK

Prawn shells and heads

Water 2 litres (64 fl oz / 8 cups)

WHOLE SPICES

Cinnamon stick 6-cm (2 1/2-in)

Cardamom 6 pods

Cloves 6

1. Mix chilli powder and 1/2 tsp salt into shelled prawns. Cover and stand for 30 minutes in the fridge.

2. In a frying pan, heat ghee and fry whole spices for 2 minutes. Scoop out and set aside. Put sliced onions into hot ghee and fry till golden brown. Scoop out and set aside.

3. Combine prawn shells and heads with water and bring to the boil. Turn down heat and simmer for 20 minutes. Strain solids and discard.

4. Combine fried spices, half the fried onions, rice, 1.5 litres (48 fl oz / 6 cups) prawn stock and remaining 2 tsp salt and cook rice using your preferred method until rice is tender.

5. Add oil to ghee in pan and fry marinated prawns till they change colour. Stir in rest of fried onions, coriander leaves and yoghurt and stir-fry till coriander leaves are limp. Scoop out prawns and reserve some of the gravy.

6. To make a sauce, add remaining prawn stock to the leftover gravy. Adjust salt and yoghurt to taste, adding more yoghurt if needed. Bring sauce to the boil and turn off heat when bubbles appear.

7. When rice is done, fluff it up and stir in prawns and reserved gravy. Rest rice for 10 minutes.

8. Serve rice with a raita (page 59) or pickles (pages 57) and the prawn sauce.

herbs such as coriander leaves was a medieval practice in Islamic West Asia, ...ed by a delicious green curry recipe that my daughter, Shakuntala, brought ...end a college friend's wedding. Her friend's grandmother's curry had been ...s delicious and when I came across the reference to herb-flavoured rice in ...result.

. Prepare chicken curry first. Make spice paste by grinding together coriander leaves, onion, green chillies, mint leaves, tomatoes and garlic with water till fine. Stir in ground powdered spices.

. Heat ghee in a saucepan and fry sliced onion to a golden colour. Scoop out and set aside.

. Fry cinnamon stick and cardamom in hot ghee for a minute, then add spice paste and fry till fragrant and oil surfaces. Stir in chicken, yoghurt, 1 tsp salt, Indian bay leaves and 1 litre (32 fl oz / 4 cups) water and bring to the boil. Turn down heat and simmer till chicken is cooked. Stir occasionally to prevent chicken from sticking to the bottom of the saucepan. There should be at least 750 ml (24 fl oz / 3 cups) gravy left: 250 ml (4 fl oz / 1 cup) for flavouring the special yoghurt sauce, and 500 ml (16 fl oz / 2 cups) for preparing rice.

4. This step is optional. The chicken can be boned and the meat returned to the gravy. Or the pieces of chicken can be left with the bone on.

5. Blend 1 cup coriander leaves with 250 ml (8 fl oz / 1 cup) water. Combine this with 500 ml (16 fl oz / 2 cups) curry gravy and enough water to get 1.5 (48 fl oz / 6 cups) liquid.

6. Combine coriander leaf liquid with rice and remaining 2 tsp salt and cook rice using your preferred method until rice is tender. When rice is done, fluff it up and sprinkle garam masala into rice and stir in fried onions and coriander leaves from the garnishing.

7. Layer rice and chicken ending with a layer of rice and infuse biryani for 20 minutes using your preferred method (page 62).

8. To make special yoghurt sauce, beat together yoghurt, 250 ml (8 fl oz / 1 cup) curry gravy, salt and milk in a saucepan. Bring to the boil and turn off heat.

9. To serve, garnish top of rice with toasted almonds or cashew nuts.

10. Serve biryani with special yoghurt sauce and a chutney (page 59).

Pakistani Green Biryani

PRAWN BIRYANI

Biryani and pilaf are two words for the same delicious dish. Prawn biryani and Indian-style prawn pilaf (page 112) are two different ways of making this tasty dish, prawn biryani being the easier of the two. Note that frozen prawns, the kind most of us get nowadays, tend to weep excessively and if you want to infuse the rice, the resulting curry may be too liquid. If this happens, take the prawns out once they are cooked and dry out the gravy with a few minutes of hard boiling. Return the prawns to the pan and cook for another minute or so. With prawn biryani there is no infusing and any extra liquid is converted into a sauce.

Red chilli powder 2 tsp

Salt 2^1/$_2$ tsp

Shelled prawns with tails on 1 kg
   (2 lb 3 oz)

Ghee 60 ml (2 fl oz / ^{1}/$_4$ cup)

Onions 200 g (7 oz), peeled and
   thinly sliced

Basmati rice 600 g (1 lb 5^1/$_3$ oz /
   3 cups), soaked 1 hour

Cooking oil 2 Tbsp

Coriander leaves 1 cup, chopped

Yoghurt 250 ml (8 fl oz / 1 cup) +
   extra as needed

PRAWN STOCK

Prawn shells and heads

Water 2 litres (64 fl oz / 8 cups)

WHOLE SPICES

Cinnamon stick 6-cm (2^1/$_2$-in)

Cardamom 6 pods

Cloves 6

1. Mix chilli powder and ^{1}/$_2$ tsp salt into shelled prawns. Cover and stand for 30 minutes in the fridge.

2. In a frying pan, heat ghee and fry whole spices for 2 minutes. Scoop out and set aside. Put sliced onions into hot ghee and fry till golden brown. Scoop out and set aside.

3. Combine prawn shells and heads with water and bring to the boil. Turn down heat and simmer for 20 minutes. Strain solids and discard.

4. Combine fried spices, half the fried onions, rice, 1.5 litres (48 fl oz / 6 cups) prawn stock and remaining 2 tsp salt and cook rice using your preferred method until rice is tender.

5. Add oil to ghee in pan and fry marinated prawns till they change colour. Stir in rest of fried onions, coriander leaves and yoghurt and stir-fry till coriander leaves are limp. Scoop out prawns and reserve some of the gravy.

6. To make a sauce, add remaining prawn stock to the leftover gravy. Adjust salt and yoghurt to taste, adding more yoghurt if needed. Bring sauce to the boil and turn off heat when bubbles appear.

7. When rice is done, fluff it up and stir in prawns and reserved gravy. Rest rice for 10 minutes.

8. Serve rice with a raita (page 59) or pickles (pages 57) and the prawn sauce.

INDIAN-STYLE PRAWN PILAF

The prawn stock makes this a very flavourful rice although some may find it a little strong. If so, cook the rice with a mix of prawn stock and water instead of just prawn stock. This particular pilaf can also be made with pieces of firm boneless fish. Instead of prawn stock, substitute with chicken or a light fish stock.

Basmati rice 600 g (1 lb 5^1/$_3$ oz / 3 cups), soaked 1 hour

Ginger 1 thumb-size knob, peeled and bruised

Salt 2^1/$_2$ tsp

Ghee 60 ml (2 fl oz / ^{1}/$_4$ cup)

Onion 100 g (3^1/$_2$ oz), peeled and thinly sliced

Ripe tomatoes 200 g (7 oz), skinned and chopped

Shelled prawns with tails on (keep shells and heads for stock) 1 kg (2 lb 3 oz)

Garam masala 2 (page 30) 1 tsp

Coriander leaves 1 cup, chopped

SPICE PASTE

Red chilli powder 2 tsp

Ginger paste (page 36) 2 Tbsp

Garlic paste (page 36) 1 Tbsp

SPICED PRAWN STOCK

Prawn shells and heads

Ginger 1 large thumb-size knob, peeled and bruised

Cinnamon stick 6-cm (2^1/$_2$-in)

Cracked black pepper 1 Tbsp

Cardamom 6 pods

Dried red chillies 6

Water 2 litres (64 fl oz / 8 cups)

GARNISHING

Coriander leaves

1. To make prawn stock, put prawn heads and shells with other stock ingredients in a pot and boil for 20 minutes. Strain and discard solids. Measure out 1.5 litres (48 fl oz / 6 cups) prawn stock for cooking rice. Freeze any excess for use in other recipes.

2. Combine rice with bruised ginger, prawn stock and 2 tsp salt and cook rice using your preferred method until rice is tender. When rice is done, fluff it up and rest rice for 10 minutes.

3. Heat ghee in a frying pan and brown onion. Stir in tomatoes, remaining ^{1}/$_2$ tsp salt and spice paste, and cook till tomatoes are soft.

4. Add prawns and fry till prawns begin to change colour. Stir in garam masala and chopped coriander leaves. Turn off heat. If prawns are very weepy, dry out gravy first before adding coriander leaves.

5. Layer rice and prawns starting and ending with a layer of rice. Infuse rice using your preferred method (page 62).

6. Serve pilaf hot with some pickles (page 57).

Mahi Pulao (shah jehan-style fish pilaf)

The recipe for Mahi Pulao in *Nuskha-e-Shahjahani* seems unnecessarily complicated: the fish has to be first rubbed with mustard oil and gram flour before washing. It is then marinated in yoghurt for 2 hours and again washed with cool water that was first boiled with some spices! These steps seem to indicate that the fish was a kind of salted fish. All the washing and soaking would have helped to get rid of excess salt. My recipe for *mahi pulao* uses fresh fish. The two Shah Jehan elements here are in the *yakhni* (spiced chicken stock) to cook the rice and the sweet-sour sauce garnish poured on the rice before serving. The flavours would have taken the Mughal emperor back to his Persian roots!

Cooking oil for frying fish

Firm boneless fish *800 g (1¹/₂ lb), cut into large cubes*

Ghee *60 ml (2 fl oz / ¹/₄ cup)*

Onion *50 g (1²/₃ oz) peeled and sliced thinly*

Yoghurt *60 ml (2 fl oz / ¹/₄ cup)*

Basmati rice *600 g (1 lb 5¹/₃ oz / 3 cups), soaked 1 hour*

Salt *2 tsp*

FISH MARINADE

Ground cumin *1¹/₂ tsp*

Ground coriander *1¹/₂ tsp*

Ground turmeric *¹/₂ tsp*

Salt *¹/₂ tsp*

Sugar *¹/₂ tsp*

Yoghurt *2 Tbsp*

SPICE PASTE

Ginger paste (page 36) *1 Tbsp*

Garlic paste (page 36) *1 Tbsp*

Green chillies *2, seeded and chopped*

SPICED CHICKEN STOCK

Chicken stock (page 80) *2 litres (64 fl oz / 8 cups)*

Cloves *6*

Cardamom *6 pods*

Fennel seeds *1 tsp, crushed*

Cracked black pepper *¹/₂ Tbsp*

APRICOT SAUCE

Dried apricots *¹/₂ cup, thinly sliced*

Lemon juice *2 Tbsp*

Sugar *2 Tbsp*

Water *250 ml (8 fl oz / 1 cup)*

Cinnamon stick *4-cm (1¹/₂-in)*

1. Combine ingredients for fish marinade and marinate fish. Cover and refrigerate for at least an hour or overnight.

2. Prepare spiced chicken stock by putting all the ingredients together in a pot and bringing to the boil. Turn down heat and simmer for 10 minutes. Strain stock and discard solids. Measure out 1.5 litres (48 fl oz / 6 cups) for cooking rice and 250 ml (8 fl oz / 1 cup) for preparing fish.

3. Heat 3 Tbsp oil in a frying pan and brown fish. It does not have to cook through. Set aside.

4. Heat ghee in a pot and brown sliced onion. Scoop out and set aside. Mix ingredients for spice paste and add to pot. Fry till fragrant. Add browned fish, yoghurt, remainder of fish marinade and 125 ml (4 fl oz / ¹/₂ cup) spiced stock and simmer till fish is just cooked through. Keep gravy for apricot sauce.

5. Combine rice with 1.5 litres (48 fl oz / 6 cups) stock and salt and cook rice using your preferred method until rice is tender.

6. Prepare apricot sauce by boiling together apricots, lemon juice, sugar, water and cinnamon stick till fruit is soft and there is a thick syrup. Mash fruit to a coarse pulp. Adjust tartness and sweetness to taste. Add fish gravy to apricot sauce and mix well.

7. Layer rice with fish, fried onions and some of the apricot sauce, ending with a layer of rice. Infuse pilaf using your preferred method (page 62).

8. Serve pilaf topped with some apricot sauce to taste, and a raita (page 59), pickles (page 58) or chutney (page 59).

MUTTON BIRYANI WITH CHERRIES AND GARLIC

The garlic inspiration for this pilaf came from *Nuskha-e-Shahjahani* and the cherries from all that I had been reading about cherries being the "king of fruit" in ancient Persia. The bag of dried tart cherries prompted the combination. The result was a dry pilaf that a friend who once worked with Afghan refugees said tasted like Afghani pilaf. Shah Jehan's cooks would not recognise my way of preparing this pilaf. Substitute the cherries with any dried sweet-sour fruit such as cranberries or thinly sliced unsweetened apricots. If unsweetened tart dried fruit is not available, add some lemon juice to the available fruit to increase the tartness.

YAKHNI

Bone-in lamb/mutton 1 kg (2 lb 3 oz)

Water 2 litres (64 fl oz / 8 cups)

Ghee/cooking oil 3 Tbsp

Onion 100 g (3 1/2 oz), peeled and coarsely chopped

Garlic 4 cloves, peeled, smashed

Ginger 1 large thumb-size knob, peeled and smashed

Salt 2 tsp

WHOLE SPICES FOR YAKHNI

Cracked black pepper 1 Tbsp

Cinnamon stick 6-cm (2 1/2-in) stick

Cardamom 6 pods

Cloves 6

Coriander seeds 1 Tbsp, crushed

BIRYANI

Dried cherries 200 g (7 oz), stoned and chopped

Ghee 60 ml (2 fl oz / 1/4 cup)

Pine nuts 1/4 cup

Garlic 100 g (3 1/2 oz), peeled and finely chopped

Sugar to taste

Lemon juice to taste

Basmati rice 600 g (1 lb 5 1/3 oz / 3 cups), soaked 1 hour

Salt 2 tsp

Nigella (optional) 2 tsp

SPICE MIX FOR BIRYANI

Ground cinnamon 1/4 tsp

Ground cardamom 1/4 tsp

Ground cloves 1/4 tsp

1. Start by preparing *yakhni*. Place meat and bones and water in a stock pot and bring to the boil. Skim off the scum that rises.

2. In a frying pan, heat ghee/oil and fry chopped onion till lightly browned. Add garlic and ginger and fry for 2 minutes or till fragrant. Pour contents into stock pot. Add whole spices and simmer for an hour or till meat is tender and there is about 1.625 litres (52 fl oz / 6 1/2 cups) stock. Add more water if necessary.

3. Remove meat and keep in large pieces or shred as preferred. Set meat aside. Strain stock and discard other solids. Extra stock not used can be frozen for another day.

4. While *yakhni* is boiling, start preparations for biryani. Rinse cherries quickly under the tap and soak them in 125 ml (4 fl oz / 1/2 cup) water till cherries are soft. Stone cherries.

5. Heat ghee in a wok and brown pine nuts. Remove and set aside for garnishing. Reheat wok and fry garlic briefly. Do not let it brown. Add cherries, cooked mutton from *yakhni*, spice mix, sugar and 125 ml (4 fl oz / 1/2 cup) *yakhni*. If cherries are not tart enough, add some lemon juice to taste. Simmer to blend flavours and cook till liquid is mostly absorbed but mixture still very moist.

6. Combine rice with 1.5 litres (48 fl oz / 6 cups) *yakhni* and salt and cook rice using your preferred method until rice is tender. When rice is done, fluff it up and stir in nigella if using.

7. Layer rice and meat ending with a layer of rice. Infuse biryani using your preferred method (page 62).

8. Garnish rice with pine nuts and serve with yoghurt sauce (page 47) or a raita (page 59).

Note:

Rice cooked in stock is much more flavourful than rice cooked with water and when the stock is spiced, the flavour is even better. Cooking rice in spiced stock was the Mughal tradition according to Nuskha-e-Shahjahani: Pulaos from the Royal Kitchen of Shah Jahan, a Mughal era cookbook, although fewer spices were used back in the 17th century compared to today. As mutton has to be boiled for quite a while to become tender enough to be tasty, it makes sense that the resulting stock should be used to cook the rice. If mutton/lamb stock is too strong, make yakhni with chicken.

MUGHLAI-STYLE SMOKED LAMB BIRYANI

This particular biryani is a good opportunity to try the old Mughlai technique of smoking the meat, a technique called *dhunghar*. The smoking is done after the lamb is tender. To impart a smoked flavour to the biryani, you will need a live coal which in a modern kitchen poses something of a problem! One modern way to solve it is to use liquid smoke which comes bottled. Look for it in shops selling barbecue paraphernalia. Stir $1/2$ tsp liquid smoke into the cooked lamb before the biryani is assembled for infusing. In the days when food was cooked in clay pots, the pot would be smoked first before it was used for infusing the pilaf.

Lamb *1 kg (2 lb 3 oz), cubed*

Ghee *3 Tbsp*

Onion *150 g (5$1/3$ oz), peeled and thinly sliced*

Water *1 litre (32 fl oz / 4 cups)*

Tomatoes *100 g (3$1/2$ oz), skinned and quartered*

Basmati rice *600 g (1 lb 5$1/3$ oz / 3 cups), soaked 1 hour*

Yakhni *(page 114) 1.5 litres (48 fl oz / 6 cups)*

Salt *2 tsp*

Mint/coriander leaves *$1/2$ cup*

MEAT MARINADE

Yoghurt *60 ml (2 fl oz / $1/4$ cup)*

Red chilli powder *1 tsp*

Ground coriander *1 tsp*

Salt *$1/2$ tsp*

Sugar *1 tsp*

Ginger paste *(page 36) 1 Tbsp*

Garlic paste *(page 36) 1 tsp*

Asafoetida *1 large pinch*

WHOLE SPICES

Cardamom *6 pods*

Black cardamom *(see Glossary) 3 pods*

Cinnamon stick *4-cm (1$1/2$-in)*

SPICE PASTE

Onion *100 g (3$1/2$ oz), peeled and finely chopped*

Ginger paste *(page 36) 2 Tbsp*

Green chillies *4, seeded and finely chopped*

1. Combine ingredients for meat marinade and marinate lamb cubes. Cover and refrigerate for at least an hour or overnight.

2. To cook lamb, first heat ghee in a pot and fry sliced onion till golden brown. Scoop out and set aside. Add whole spices to hot pot and fry for 1 minute. Add spice paste and fry till fragrant before adding marinated lamb and water. Bring to the boil, add tomatoes and simmer till meat is tender. Add more water if necessary. There should be about 250 ml (8 fl oz / 1 cup) gravy left.

3. If you want to try smoking the meat, do it before you infuse the rice. See note below.

4. Combine rice with *yakhni* and salt and cook rice using your preferred method until rice is tender. When rice is done, fluff it up and stir fried onions and mint/coriander leaves into rice.

5. Layer rice and meat ending with a layer of rice and infuse using your preferred method (page 62).

6. Serve biryani with a chutney (page 59), raita (page 59) or pickles (pages 57–58).

Note:

To smoke the meat (dhunghar), have ready a small metal pot or bowl. Indian kitchen shops sell these stainless steel pots that are stacked the smaller inside the larger and they come in some very tiny sizes. These handle-less pots are sold by weight. A small one will be a good receptacle for the live coals.

You will need 2 large pieces of live coals, 1 tsp melted ghee and $1/2$ tsp ground cloves.

Make a space in centre of the pot of curried lamb for the small pot with live coals. The meat should surround the pot to maximise the smoking. Knock off the ashes, then place the live coals and ground cloves into the small metal pot. Pour melted ghee on the coals and immediately cover the large pot to let the smoke permeate meat. Let meat rest undisturbed for 20 minutes before infusing rice with lamb.

Maqloobeh (west asian upside down rice)

This dish is common all over West Asia with Iraqis, Lebanese, Syrians, Palestinians and Israelis claiming *maqloobeh* as special to them. Be that as it may, I had my first taste of *maqloobeh* while visiting the site of the ancient Phoenician seaport of Ugarit in Syria. Struck by a brainwave, I asked the woman running a small restaurant nearby if she could cook *maqloobeh* for me while I was in the site where the earliest Phoenician alphabet dating back to 1400 BCE and ancestor of the Western alphabet was found impressed on a tiny clay tablet. Yes, the *maqloobeh* was as tasty as Ugarit was illuminating. My Palestinian driver now resident in Syria said the *maqloobeh* was just like home cooking!

Aubergines (eggplants) *100 g (3¹/₂ oz), 1-cm (¹/₂-in) thick slices*

Salt *2 tsp*

Red and green capsicums (bell peppers) *1 each, seeded and cut into thick rings*

Long-grain rice *600 g (1 lb 5¹/₃ oz / 3 cups)*

CHICKEN STOCK

Chicken with bone *1 kg (2 lb 3 oz), cut into 6 pieces*

Salt *1 tsp*

Baharat 1, 2 or 3 (page 32) *1 tsp*

Olive oil *60 ml (2 fl oz / ¹/₄ cup)*

Onion *100 g (3¹/₂ oz), peeled and finely chopped*

Water *2 litres (64 fl oz / 8 cups)*

GARNISHING

Parsley

Toasted almond halves/pine nuts

1. Rub chicken for chicken stock with salt and *baharat*. Set aside.

2. Heat a heavy frying pan. Brush a little olive oil on it and brown aubergine slices. Set aside.

3. Heat remainder of olive oil in a large saucepan and brown chicken. Stir in chopped onion and fry till fragrant and onion is brown. Add water and bring to the boil. Turn down heat and simmer till chicken is just cooked. It should take about 30 minutes. Remove chicken and when cool enough to handle, bone it and set meat aside.

4. Return chicken bones to pan and bring stock to the boil for another 20 minutes. Measure out 1.5 litres (48 fl oz / 6 cups) stock and stir salt into measured stock.

5. Arrange chicken meat, capsicum slices and aubergine slices at the bottom of a rice pot and some aubergine slices up the sides of the pot. Cover chicken and vegetables with rice and measured stock.

6. Put a small plate or a round wire rack over rice to stop vegetables from floating up. Cook rice using your preferred method until rice is tender.

7. Rest rice for 10 minutes before turning *maqloobeh* over. To do this, cover the rice pot with a serving plate. With oven gloves on or protecting your hands with a thick dishcloth in each hand, turn the rice pot over, pressing pot and plate tightly together as you turn.

8. Garnish *maqloobeh* with chopped parsley and toasted almond halves/pine nuts.

Note:

An alternative way to serve maqloobeh is to cook the rice with the vegetables and stock. The chicken meat is arranged at the bottom of a large bowl and the cooked rice and vegetables pressed into the bowl. The bowl is then turned over.

A faster way is to arrange the raw bone-in chicken at the bottom of the rice pot together with the vegetables and cook the chicken and rice together with water.

TABYEET (JEWISH SLOW-COOKED CHICKEN WITH RICE)

Tabyeet means "cooked overnight" in Arabic and this is a Jewish Sabbath dish cooked all over West Asia but often attributed to Iraqi Jews. Jewish dietary laws prohibit cooking on the Sabbath which starts when the sun goes down on Friday and ends when the sun sets the next evening. So the meal for the Sabbath must be prepared ahead of time and yet be still warm when eaten. If available, use a hard rice such as Uncle Ben's parboiled rice. The slow baking can turn regular long-grain a little mushy. *Tabyeet* is traditionally baked in a slow oven. (The *tabyeet* in the picture on the right was cooled in a slow cooker.)

Salt 2½ *tsp*

Chicken thighs or drumsticks
  6 *pieces, about 1 kg (2 lb 3 oz)*

Onion 100 g (3½ oz), *peeled and
  thickly sliced*

Tomatoes 250 g (9 oz), *cut into
  thick wedges*

Basmati rice 600 g (1 lb 5⅓ oz /
  3 cups)

Ghee/olive oil 3 *Tbsp*

Cardamom 6 *pods*

Eggs 6

Water 1.5 litres (48 fl oz / 6 cups)

SPICE MIX

Any *baharat* (pages 32–33) 3 *tsp*

Parsley 1 *cup, chopped*

Ground cumin 1 *tsp*

1. Mix together *baharat*, 1 tsp salt, chopped parsley and ground cumin. Divide into 3 equal parts. Rub one part into chicken, mix another part with onion and tomatoes, and the last part with rice.

2. Coat the bottom of a slow cooker with melted ghee/olive oil and sprinkle with cardamoms. Top with chicken, then layer with half the onion and tomato mixture. Rinse eggs clean and tuck eggs in with onion and tomato mixture. Add rice and top with remaining onion and tomato mixture.

3. Dissolve remaining 2 tsp salt with water and pour it into slow cooker. Cover and leave to cook overnight.

4. The dish can also be baked in a 120°C (250°F) oven overnight. The baking dish should have a lid and the lid can be sealed with dough made of flour and water.

5. If the rice is baked, it will have a rice crust. To loosen the rice crust, soak the bottom of the pot in cold water or place on a very damp towel for 10 minutes.

6. Loosen rice crust with a flat spatula before turning the rice and chicken over onto a serving platter. Serve with pickles (pages 57–58).

Sar Poh Fan (cantonese clay pot rice)

The traditional way to prepare this dish was to steam the rice with everything mixed together in a clay pot. With the widespread use of the electric rice cooker, however, the name "clay pot rice" has become a misnomer. The best reason for not bothering with the clay pot version which takes twice as long to do is that there is little difference in the flavour. However, the clay pot steps have been included here for those who prefer to do it the traditional way.

Dried shiitake mushrooms 4, *large, softened in water*

Chicken 500 g (1 lb 1 1/2 oz), *boned*

Chinese sausages 2, *thinly sliced*

Salted fish (optional) 3 *thin slices, chopped or shredded*

Cooking oil 2 *Tbsp*

Garlic 2 *cloves, peeled, chopped*

Long-grain rice 600 g (1 lb 5 1/3 oz / 3 cups)

Salt 1 1/2 tsp

Water/chicken stock (page 80) 1.5 *litres (48 fl oz / 6 cups) or as needed*

Chopped spring onion

Chopped coriander leaves

CHICKEN MARINADE

Oyster sauce 3 *Tbsp*

Dark soy sauce 1 *tsp*

Sesame oil 2 *tsp*

Ginger juice (page 36) 1 *Tbsp*

1. Quarter or slice mushrooms thickly according to preference. Keep water used for soaking mushrooms for cooking rice.

2. Combine ingredients for marinade and marinate chicken for 10 minutes.

3. In a clay pot or frying pan if cooking the rice in a rice cooker, first fry sliced Chinese sausage till oil comes out from it, then add cooking oil and stir in chopped or shredded salted fish if using, then stir in chopped garlic. Fry till fragrant, then add mushrooms and marinated chicken and fry for 5 minutes or so.

4. If using rice cooker, pour contents of frying pan into rice pot, add rice, salt and 1.5 litres (48 fl oz / 6 cups) water/stock and cook as usual.

5. If cooking rice in a clay pot, add rice, salt and 1.25 litres (40 fl oz / 5 cups) water/stock to meat and mushrooms in clay pot and steam covered clay pot for 1 hour or till rice is done.

6. When rice is done, stir in chopped spring onion and coriander leaves before serving.

7. Serve with a soup (page 51) and stir-fried vegetables (page 55).

Hokkien Yam Rice

This is a traditional Hokkien rice that I recall eating as a child although I have had Teochew friends tell me it is Teochew. What we call yam (*Colocasia esculenta*) is also known as taro, cocoyam or dasheen elsewhere (see Glossary). The taro or yam pads out the rice and the dried prawns add flavour. For this rice to be tasty, the yam has to be fluffy, rather like Russet potatoes and never like waxy potatoes. One old-fashioned test used by a wet market stallholder to check if the yam is going to be fluffy is to cut a thin slice from the bottom of the yam. If a powdery white residue forms on the blade, the yam will be fluffy. However, you won't need this test when you buy the very tubby Thai yams.

Cooking oil 3 *Tbsp*

Garlic 1 *clove, peeled, chopped*

Dried prawns 2 *Tbsp, finely chopped*

Yam (taro) 500 g (1 lb 1 1/2 oz), *peeled and cubed*

Salt 2 *tsp*

Water 1.625 *litres (52 fl oz / 6 1/2 cups)*

Long-grain rice 600 g (1 lb 5 1/3 oz / 3 cups)

Chopped spring onion

Chopped coriander leaves

1. Heat oil in a wok and sauté garlic and dried prawns till fragrant.

2. Add cubed yam, 1 tsp salt and 125 ml (4 fl oz / 1/2 cup) water. Mix well and cover wok. Turn down heat and simmer gently till yam is half-cooked or about 10 minutes. The time will depend on the yam and the size of the cubes. Stir occasionally to prevent yam from sticking. When done, there should be no liquid left.

3. Combine rice, yam and remaining 1 tsp salt with remaining 1.5 litres (48 fl oz / 6 cups) water and cook rice using your preferred method until rice is tender. When rice is done, fluff it up gently without mashing up yam cubes. Rest rice for 10 minutes before serving.

4. Serve rice hot with a garnish of chopped spring onion and coriander leaves and a dish of stir-fried vegetables (page 55) or a vegetable soup (page 51).

Loh Mai Kai (cantonese glutinous rice with chicken)

Loh mai kai is a popular dim sum dish and is often eaten along with dumplings and spring rolls as part of many a dim sum meal. At a fancier meal, the *loh mai kai* is steamed wrapped in dried lotus leaf to give the rice a special fragrance. *Loh mai kai* makes a good meal by itself especially if you serve it together with a dish of stir-fried vegetables.

Chicken meat *200 g (7 oz),
skinned and cubed*

Dark soy sauce *2 tsp*

Oyster sauce *2 Tbsp*

Dried shiitake mushrooms *4,
softened in water*

Dried prawns *1 Tbsp, softened in
water and chopped, or 2 dried
scallops, softened in water and
shredded*

Cooking oil *3 Tbsp*

Shallots *25 g (1 oz), peeled and
thinly sliced*

White glutinous rice *600 g
(1 lb 5^1/$_3$ oz / 3 cups), soaked
overnight*

Salt *^{1}/$_2$ tsp*

Leeks *150 g (5^1/$_3$ oz), thickly sliced*

Chinese sausage *1, thinly sliced*

Water *375 ml (12 fl oz / 1^1/$_2$ cups)
or as needed*

1. Marinade chicken cubes with dark soy sauce and oyster sauce. Cover and stand for 1 hour refrigerated.

2. Slice, quarter or halve softened mushrooms according to preference. Save water used for soaking mushrooms for cooking rice.

3. If using scallops, set aside water used for softening scallops. If using dried prawns, they can be chopped or left whole. Any bits of shell should be discarded.

4. Heat oil in a wok and fry sliced shallots. When it begins to brown, add dried prawns or scallops and fry till shallots are golden brown. Add chicken and mushrooms and fry till chicken is almost cooked. Stir in drained rice with salt. Put all ingredients into a clay pot.

5. Measure mushroom and scallop or dried prawn soaking water and top up to get 375 ml (12 fl oz / 1^1/$_2$ cups) water and add to clay pot. Cover clay pot and steam for 30 minutes.

6. Lift lid and stir rice and ingredients. Continue to steam for another 30–40 minutes until rice is tender.

7. Dish out and serve hot.

Loh Mai Kai in Lotus Leaf

Lotus leaves *4*

Twine for tying

1. The lotus leaves must be softened by blanching in boiling water or soaking for several hours in cold water till pliable. Rinse leaves clean carefully to avoid tearing leaves.

2. Prepare rice as above until step 5. Remove clay pot from steamer after 30 minutes of steaming.

3. Cut leaves in half, overlap 2 halves of a leaf and spoon a quarter of steamed rice on leaf. Fold into a parcel and tie with some twine.

4. Repeat to get 4 parcels. Or if preferred, wrap into 2 large parcels.

5. Place parcels in a steamer and steam for 30 minutes. If a softer texture is preferred, steam for longer.

6. Just before serving, use a pair of scissors and cut into the top of leaves to expose rice.

7. Serve hot.

KONGNAMULPAP (KOREAN RICE WITH BEAN SPROUTS AND BEEF)

Soy bean sprouts are easily found in East and Southeast Asian markets and even the larger Asian stores in the US. They are distinguished from mung bean sprouts by the much larger yellow head. Substitute with mung bean sprouts or any kind of sprouts if bean sprouts are not available. If using more delicate sprouts, just stir them into the rice after the rice is cooked. Remove the tails from the soy sprouts for a more attractive presentation.

Shredded beef 200 g (7 oz)

Ginger 4 slices, peeled and finely shredded

Sesame oil 1 Tbsp

Light soy sauce 1 Tbsp

Sugar 1 tsp

Salt 1 tsp

Short-grain rice 400 g (14^1/$_3$ oz / 2 cups)

Water 625 ml (20 fl oz / 2^1/$_2$ cups)

Cooking oil 2 Tbsp

Soy bean sprouts 300 g (11 oz), tailed

GARNISHING

Chopped spring onion

Korean sesame salt (page 34)

1. Season beef with ginger, sesame oil, light soy sauce, sugar and salt. Cover and stand for 30 minutes or overnight in the refrigerator.

2. Cook rice with water using your preferred method until rice is tender.

3. Heat oil and fry beef for 1 minute on high heat. Add bean sprouts and fry for another minute. Fluff up rice and stir beef and sprouts into it.

4. Garnish rice with chopped spring onion and a sprinkling of sesame salt. Serve rice hot with kimchi or kimchi soup (page 51).

OGOKPAP (KOREAN FIVE-GRAIN RICE)

Five-grain, six-grain and even seven-grain rice is common in East Asia and packages of rice mixed with grains are found in East Asian supermarkets and its popularity appears to be spreading. In 2009, not only did I find them in some supermarkets in the US, I was also seeing them in some small neighbourhood supermarkets in Singapore. Mixed rice may have originated as a way of padding out scarce rice but it has come to be enjoyed for its own sake. One of the typical grains added to rice is millet which was first cultivated in East Asia thousands of years ago and long before rice. Others are sorghum, wheat, barley or corn, with dried beans as the protein element. As milled rice cooks fairly quickly, pre-cook the dried beans first before cooking them with rice. If brown rice is used in place of white rice, the dish will have a more chewy texture.

Short-grain rice 100 g (3^1/$_2$ oz / ^{1}/$_2$ cup)

Glutinous rice 50 g (1^2/$_3$ oz / ^{1}/$_4$ cup)

Barley 100 g (3^1/$_2$ oz / ^{1}/$_2$ cup)

Pre-cooked black beans 100 g (3^1/$_2$ oz / ^{1}/$_2$ cup)

Pre-cooked red beans 100 g (3^1/$_2$ oz / ^{1}/$_2$ cup)

Ginger 1 small thumb-size knob, peeled and smashed

Sesame oil 1 Tbsp

Salt ^{1}/$_2$ tsp

Water 625 ml (20 fl oz / 2^1/$_2$ cups)

GARNISHING

Chopped spring onion

1. Combine rice with other ingredients and cook rice using your preferred method until rice is tender.

2. Before serving, stir in chopped spring onion. The rice can be served at room temperature or warm with kimchi and kimchi soup (page 51).

Adzuki Gohan

This flavoured rice is prepared with short-grain rice and water for a quick nutritious rice meal. It can also be made into rice balls for packed lunches or picnic boxes because it can be eaten cold. The difference between adzuki gohan and sekihan (below) is that the latter is made with white glutinous rice.

White short-grain rice *400 g (14 oz / 2 cups)*

Pre-cooked adzuki beans *100 g (3¹/₂ oz / ¹/₂ cup)*

Ginger *4 slices, shredded finely*

Water *625 ml (20 fl oz / 2¹/₂ cups)*

Japanese vinegar *1 Tbsp*

Spring onion *1, just the green tips*

Japanese sesame salt (page 34) *to taste*

1. Combine rice with adzuki beans, ginger strips and water and cook rice using your preferred method until rice is tender. When rice is done, stir in vinegar and spring onion tips.

2. Serve in bowls or make into rice balls.

3. To make rice balls, divide rice into 12–14 portions. Put a portion of rice on a muslin cloth soaked first with Japanese vinegar and roll rice into a ball or shape rice into a triangle or a roll.

4. Sprinkle with Japanese sesame salt.

Sekihan (Japanese celebration rice)

Sekihan, the name for this dish of red beans and rice, also means "celebration" so common is its appearance at celebratory meals perhaps in part because of its attractive colour and ease of preparation? This is particularly so if you have a rice cooker with a sticky rice setting and if you have pre-cooked adzuki beans in the freezer. If not, pre-boil the beans the day before preparing the glutinous rice and keep the bean stock for cooking the rice.

Pre-cooked adzuki beans *100 g (3¹/₂ oz / ¹/₂ cup)*

White glutinous rice *400 g (14 oz / 2 cups)*

Adzuki stock from cooking adzuki beans/water *625 ml (20 fl oz / 2¹/₂ cups)*

1. Combine adzuki beans, rice and stock/water and cook rice using your preferred method until rice is tender.

2. Serve hot with sprinkling of sesame salt.

GARNISHING

Japanese sesame salt (page 34)

Kuri Gohan (Japanese Chestnut Rice)

Chestnuts appear in East Asian markets in profusion in autumn and the smell of roasting chestnuts fills the air in street corners. Cooks come up with ways to serve up this sweet nut in stews, soups and rice dumplings. In Japan, chestnuts are combined with rice to give *kuri gohan* with the delicate flavours of autumn.

Fresh chestnuts *300 g (11 oz)*

Short-grain rice *600 g (1 lb 5¹/₃ oz / 3 cups)*

Mirin *2 Tbsp*

Ginger *6 thin slices, peeled and finely shredded*

Water *1.25 litres (40 fl oz / 5 cups)*

1. If using fresh chestnuts that have not been shelled, cut into the soft stiff shell with a small paring knife and peel it off. To remove the thin papery skin, first boil the nuts in water for 10 minutes, then peel off loosened skins. Quarter chestnuts if they are large.

2. Combine rice, mirin, ginger and chestnuts with water and cook rice using your preferred method until rice is tender. When rice is done, fluff it up and rest rice for 10 minutes before serving.

3. Dish rice out into rice bowls. Sprinkle with some sesame salt and spring onion tips. Serve with a miso soup and pickles (page 56).

CONDIMENT

Japanese sesame salt (page 34)

Spring onion *1, green tips only, finely chopped*

One of the most common ways to use up leftover boiled rice is to fry it, a dish long attributed to the Chinese. Whether Chinese cooks were the first to come up with fried rice, the fact is that today most rice-eating families will have fried rice at least once a week if not more frequently. Frying rice is not the only way to dress plain rice. It can be dressed with oils and vinegars to make rice salads, or a freshly prepared sauce or a large serving of stew can be ladled on top of it. The Iranians have numerous classic stews known as *khoreshts* that are served on rice. The Cantonese have such classics as *char siew fan* or duck rice while the Japanese have sushi, now so accepted worldwide that many supermarkets outside Japan offer sushi as a standard daily fast food item. The recipes in this section on Fried and Dressed Rice differs from Flavoured Rice in that the starting point here is always a plain boiled rice whether long-grain or short-grain. Unlike a flavoured rice like biryani, a fried rice is more quickly put together. Ingredients can be substituted, left out or added on, depending on what your refrigerator or larder has hidden away. Even making a Persian-style stew or *khoresht* just means assembling all the ingredients and throwing them into a pot—well almost.

FRIED AND DRESSED RICE

While the rice to be served with a stew would be any cooked rice boiled using a rice to water ratio of between 1:1.5 and 1:2 (depending on the rice), keeping in mind certain pointers helps get you that plate of perfect fried rice. Naturally, the definition of perfection varies with the culture. If you use cooked short-grain rice for fried rice, the resulting dish won't be in neat, tender separated grains as it would be if you made the dish with long-grain rice. This is because short-grain is more sticky. Nevertheless, short-grain fried rice can be firm yet tender, dry and full of flavour rather than mushy and damp, if you keep certain rules in mind. The first rule to remember is that fried rice must never be made with freshly cooked rice but always with cold and even overnight rice whether you are using long-grain or short-grain rice. Rice that has been left too long in the fridge can even be revived by sprinkling some water into the rice as you fry so that the dried rice plumps up again. Another rule to remember is that if your meat or seafood gives out too much juices, you have to dry it out before you add rice—unless it is rice that is really dried out and somewhat hard. The heat also has to be high so that unnecessary liquids evaporate quickly. The third rule is to avoid over-frying. All the ingredients must be cut and measured out and on hand before you turn on the heat. Once you start frying, the ingredients have to be added very quickly in a particular sequence for one reason and that is to avoid over-cooking any of the ingredients including the rice. You want the rice to be hot but still firm and yet tender but not soft. And, of course, perfect fried rice starts with rice that is cooked perfectly. As an aside, many of the recipes in this section would be very tasty if prepared with brown rice.

SALTED FISH FRIED RICE/BURMESE FRIED RICE

To give this dish oomph, the bean sprouts must be kept very crunchy and the salted fish must be used very sparingly so less is better. The salted fish can be fried and pounded or shredded ahead of time and kept refrigerated till needed. However, the flavour of the fried rice is enhanced if the oil used for frying the salted fish is used to fry the rice as well. As an aside, salted fish are not all alike. Some are soft and melt in your mouth, others are crisp and shred easily. This is salted threadfin, also known as Mergui salted fish as the best was said to come from this Burmese archipelago fronting the Andaman Sea. This dish is similar to Burmese fried rice but the Burmese typically eat their fried rice with an onion chutney. The recipe is provided below. This chutney is good with pilafs too! Salted fish fried rice is generic to other parts of Southeast Asia as well as China.

Cooking oil *60 ml (2 fl oz / ¹/₄ cup)*

Salted threadfin *100 g (3¹/₂ oz), thinly sliced*

Garlic *2 cloves, peeled and chopped*

Bean sprouts *500 g (1 lb 1¹/₂ oz)*

Salt *¹/₂ tsp*

Cold cooked long-grain rice *1 kg (2 lb 3 oz / 6 cups)*

Dark soy sauce *2 drops*

Chopped spring onion

BURMESE ONION CHUTNEY (OPTIONAL)

Onion *100 g (3¹/₂ oz), peeled and finely chopped*

Green chillies *3, seeded and finely chopped*

Large lime juice *1¹/₂ Tbsp*

Salt *¹/₄ tsp*

Coriander leaves *1 bunch, chopped*

1. Prepare Burmese onion chutney first, if desired. Combine ingredients for chutney together and adjust seasoning to taste. Set aside.

2. Heat oil in a wok and fry thinly sliced salted fish till crisp and brown. Cool, then pound crisp fish to a coarse powder.

3. Reheat oil used for frying salted fish and sauté chopped garlic till fragrant but not brown, then add bean sprouts and fry for 1 minute before adding salt, rice and dark soy sauce to colour rice.

4. Stir-fry for a few minutes till rice is heated through. Stir in chopped spring onion last.

5. Dish out and serve hot with Burmese onion chutney for a Burmese flavour.

MALAY NASI GORENG (MALAY/STRAITS CHINESE FRIED RICE)

I like adding a vegetable to Malay *nasi goreng* because that makes it a complete meal. At the same time, the vegetables add colour and crunch. Carrots or green beans are particularly good.

Cooking oil 3 Tbsp

Onion 100 g (3¹/₂ oz), peeled and cubed small

Green beans/carrots 200 g (7 oz)

Prawns/chicken/beef 200 g (7 oz)

Sambal *belacan* (page 59) 1 Tbsp

Salt 1 tsp

Cold cooked long-grain rice 1 kg (2 lb 3 oz / 6 cups)

GARNISHING

Chopped spring onion

1. Heat oil in a wok and fry onion till it begins to colour. Stir in beans/carrots, then prawns/meat and fry till prawns begin to change colour or meat is nearly cooked. If using beef, take care not to overcook beef.

2. Before prawns or meat is cooked, add sambal *belacan* and fry for another minute or so, then stir in salt and rice and heat through.

3. Stir in chopped spring onion last. Dish out and serve hot.

KHAO PHAD (THAI FRIED RICE)

Basic Thai fried rice is an invaluable standby when you want something very tasty and yet don't want to spend an hour in the kitchen. It never fails to satisfy although if you do Thai food frequently and your ventilators are not powerful enough, your kitchen can develop an "Indochinese" kitchen odour because of all that frying fish sauce. But I think it is worth it!

Cooking oil 60 ml (2 fl oz / ¹/₄ cup)

Garlic 6 cloves, peeled and chopped

Boneless chicken 100 g (3¹/₂ oz), sliced into strips

Shelled prawns 200 g (7 oz)

Fish sauce 3 Tbsp

Cold cooked long-grain rice 1 kg (2 lb 3 oz / 6 cups)

Lime juice to taste

Bird's eye chillies 3, finely chopped

Bean sprouts 100 g (3¹/₂ oz)

Spring onion 1 large bunch, coarsely chopped

Basil leaves 2 cups

CONDIMENT

Fish sauce with chopped bird's eye chillies

1. Heat oil in a large wok and sauté garlic till fragrant.

2. Add chicken and prawns and fry till prawns turn pink and meat changes colour.

3. Stir in 1 Tbsp fish sauce, add rice, then remaining 2 Tbsp fish sauce. Fry for 2 minutes over high heat, then turn off heat.

4. Stir in lime juice, chopped chillies, bean sprouts, spring onion and basil leaves.

5. Dish out and serve hot with a saucer of fish sauce and chopped chillies on the side.

KHAO PHAD PRIK KHING (THAI FRIED CURRIED RICE)

This fried rice is a little tricky because the curry paste can be too damp. If so, you need to dry out the curry paste before you add the meat or seafood: stir-fry it well over high heat before adding the rice. A quick alternative to making the spice paste here is to use 2–3 Tbsp of the ubiquitous packaged Thai red or green curry paste. If using one of these packaged pastes, taste the fried rice before adding any fish sauce. Some pastes are very well-salted. One advantage is that kaffir lime is also included. Although a poor substitute for kaffir lime leaves, some fresh lemon zest is better than none. Either blend the zest with the spice mix or add it in large pieces and discard after frying the rice.

Cooking oil 5 Tbsp

Chicken/pork/beef/prawns 300 g
(11 oz), thinly sliced/shelled

Long beans/French beans/
carrots/peas 300 g (11 oz),
cut into short finger lengths/
julienned

Salt 1/2 tsp

Cold cooked long-grain rice 1 kg
(2 lb 3 oz / 6 cups)

Kaffir lime leaves 3 leaves,
crushed

Fish sauce 2 Tbsp

SPICE PASTE

Galangal 4 thin slices

Lemon grass 1 small stalk, thinly
sliced

Ground white pepper 1/4 tsp

Ground coriander 1/2 tsp

Dried red chillies 4, seeded and
soaked

Shallots 25 g (1 oz)

Water 2 Tbsp

GARNISHING

Coriander leaves 1 sprig,
chopped

Lime wedges

1. Blend all ingredients for spice paste together in a food processor till fine.

2. Heat oil in a wok and fry spice paste till fragrant and dry before adding meat or prawns. Fry till meat is cooked or prawns change colour before adding chosen vegetable together with salt. Mix well and fry for 1–2 minutes. The vegetables should still be crisp.

3. Add rice, crushed lime leaves and fish sauce and mix well, coating the grains with the curry. Heat rice through.

4. Dish out and garnish with coriander leaves and lime wedges. Serve hot.

KIMCHI FRIED RICE

This very Korean dish should be done with short-grain rice but frying long-grain rice this way is also very tasty. The kimchi should first be squeezed very dry before it is cut up. Save the juices for making kimchi soup (page 51) to serve with the rice. The fried rice can also be served with a plate of perilla leaves for wrapping the rice if these leaves are cheaply available.

Kimchi 400 g (14¹/₃ oz / 2 cups)

Cooking oil 3 Tbsp

Garlic 6 cloves, peeled and chopped

Shelled prawns/chicken/pork slivers 200 g (7 oz)

Salt 1 tsp

Red chilli 1, sliced

Cold cooked short-/long-grain rice 1 kg (2 lb 3 oz / 6 cups)

Sesame oil 1 Tbsp

GARNISHING

Chopped spring onion

Chopped coriander leaves

1. Dry kimchi by squeezing juices into a bowl, then cut into thin slices.

2. Heat cooking oil in a wok and sauté half the chopped garlic till fragrant but not brown. Stir in prawns/meat into hot oil and fry till prawns change colour or meat is cooked.

3. Add kimchi, salt and chilli and mix well. Fry for 1 minute, then add rice, sesame oil and remaining raw garlic and fry till rice is heated through.

4. Stir in chopped spring onion and coriander leaves. Serve with a light soup.

EURASIAN CORNED BEEF FRIED RICE

As a schoolgirl, I once talked about corned beef with a Eurasian school friend. I had never eaten corned beef before and she said that it was very good with rice and that the canned corned beef could be fried with chilli and onion. Years later when I had left home and was cooking for myself, I finally prepared this delicious corned beef fried rice which to me will always be "Eurasian fried rice" because of that long-ago chat about corned beef with a Eurasian girl whose name I no longer remember. Note that the flavour of the fried rice will depend greatly on the quality of the corned beef.

Cooking oil 3 Tbsp

Onion 100 g (3¹/₂ oz), peeled and cubed small

Red chillies 2, seeded and sliced

Canned corned beef 1 can, 326 g (11¹/₂ oz)

Lime juice 1 Tbsp

Cabbage 300 g (11 oz), finely shredded

Cold cooked long-grain rice 1 kg (2 lb 3 oz / 6 cups)

1. Heat oil in a wok and fry onions and chillies for 2 minutes, then add corned beef and lime juice and fry till corned beef is well-heated through. Stir in cabbage and fry to preferred texture. (I like mine crunchy.)

2. Stir in rice, mix well and fry till rice is heated through.

3. Dish out and serve hot.

MILLIONAIRES' FRIED RICE

This fried rice with crabmeat was the speciality of two sisters who ran a food stall in a coffeeshop located opposite the Chinese Millionaires' Club in Bukit Pasoh in Singapore in the 1980s. It was said to be the most expensive fried rice in Singapore then. The stall has since disappeared and the crabmeat fried rice is now franchised. Fry your own and you can be generous with the fresh crabmeat. For that original taste, you have to add MSG. Years ago when I tasted the sisters' fried rice for the first time at the coffeeshop, there were several huge bags of the flavour enhancer stacked against the wall and I could taste the MSG in the rice!

Cooking oil 3 Tbsp

Shallots ¹/₂ cup, peeled and thinly sliced

Cold cooked long-grain rice 1 kg (2 lb 3 oz / 6 cups)

Salt 1¹/₂ tsp

MSG (optional) ¹/₄ tsp

Ground white pepper 1 tsp

Fresh crabmeat 500 g (1 lb 1¹/₂ oz / 3 cups)

GARNISHING

Chopped coriander leaves

Chopped spring onion

1. Heat oil in a wok and fry sliced shallots till golden brown, taking care not to burn it.
2. Stir in rice, salt, MSG, if using, and pepper and mix well. Fry till rice is heated through.
3. Stir in crabmeat and mix well. Fry till heated through.
4. Stir in chopped coriander leaves and spring onion last.
5. Dish out and serve hot.

BEEF FRIED RICE

Strange as it may sound, given the ubiquity of hamburgers and steaks today, I grew up without having ever eaten beef until I was old enough to go out on dates and thus gained exposure to café food. In the 1960s, the only places that served beef were the restaurants and cafés patronised by the British troops who were based in Singapore up till 1968. It was in a pub-restaurant in Serangoon Gardens, where many British families were housed, that I came across this unusual fried rice. It became my favourite way of enjoying beef, a meat that I still rarely eat, although now more for environmental reasons than anything else.

Rump steak 500 g (1 lb 1¹/₂ oz)

Bicarbonate of soda ¹/₂ tsp

Light soy sauce 1 Tbsp

Dark soy sauce 1¹/₂ tsp

Ground white pepper ¹/₂ tsp

Cooking oil 3 Tbsp

Shallots 100 g (3¹/₂ oz), peeled and thinly sliced

Cold cooked long-grain rice 1 kg (2 lb 3 oz / 6 cups)

Salt 1 tsp

Coriander leaves 1 large bunch, chopped

CONDIMENT

Light soy sauce with chopped red chillies

1. Trim off any fat and gristle from meat, slice thinly across the grain and marinate with bicarbonate of soda, ¹/₂ Tbsp light soy sauce, 1 tsp dark soy sauce and ¹/₄ tsp pepper for 30 minutes in the fridge.
2. Heat oil in a wok and fry shallots till it begins to colour. Stir in beef and after 1 minute, add rice, salt and remaining ¹/₂ tsp dark soy sauce to colour rice. Fry for another 5 minutes to cook beef and heat rice through. Do not overcook beef. Fry on high heat so rice will be dry.
3. Stir in coriander leaves last.
4. Serve hot with a condiment of light soy sauce and chopped red chillies.

YONG CHEW FRIED RICE/YANGZHOU FRIED RICE

I was once told that this particular fried rice should be delicately coated with beaten egg during the frying to give this dish a pale golden colour. However, I have also noticed that the Yong Chew fried rice served up in many Chinese restaurants often comes without the delicate yellow colour and just has bits of fried egg clinging to the rice. What is de rigueur is red roast pork and small shelled prawns. The trick is in very fast frying in a very hot wok and having all the ingredients ready at hand before you start heating up your wok. And frying this amount of rice in two or three lots will give a better result than doing it in one go.

Cold cooked long-grain rice 1 kg
   (2 lb 3 oz / 6 cups)
Sesame oil 2 Tbsp
Ground white pepper $^1/_2$ tsp
Salt 1 tsp
Cooking oil 60 ml (2 fl oz / $^1/_4$ cup)
Small shelled prawns $^1/_2$ cup
Eggs 4, beaten
Carrot 100 g (3$^1/_2$ oz), peeled and
   cubed small
Green peas $^1/_2$ cup
Red roast pork (page 140) $^1/_2$ cup,
   cubed small
Spring onion 1, large, chopped

1. In a mixing bowl, prepare rice by coating it well with sesame oil, pepper and salt.
2. Heat oil in a wok and fry prawns till they change colour. Scoop out and set aside.
3. Reheat oil till very hot, then pour in beaten eggs and let it set a little, then add prepared rice on top of the still liquid eggs and stir-fry rice quickly to coat grains with egg.
4. Add carrot, green peas, red roast pork and prawns in that order.
5. Stir-fry for a couple of minutes, then add spring onion.
6. Dish out and serve hot.

OYSTER SAUCE FRIED RICE

This dish actually started out being prepared with rice noodles but one of my daughters, Savitri, tried it out with rice and we thought it was delicious. So oyster sauce fried rice became part of the family menu. It is especially delicious with a squeeze of lime or lemon juice over it. You can make it vegetarian by substituting firm tofu for prawns and using vegetarian oyster sauce instead.

Cooking oil 60 ml (2 fl oz / $^1/_4$ cup)
Garlic 6, peeled and chopped
Red chillies 3, seeded and thinly
   sliced
Shelled prawns 500 g (1 lb 1$^1/_2$ oz)
Cabbage 500 g (1 lb 1$^1/_2$ oz),
   shredded
Oyster sauce 3 Tbsp
Salt 1 tsp
Ground white pepper 1 tsp
Cold cooked long-grain rice 1 kg
   (2 lb 3 oz / 6 cups)

GARNISHING
Chopped spring onion
Lime halves/lemon wedges
   (optional)

1. Heat oil in a wok and sauté garlic and sliced chillies till fragrant, then add prawns and cabbage. Fry till prawns begin to change colour.
2. Stir in oyster sauce, salt and pepper and mix well, then stir in rice and fry till heated through.
3. Lastly, stir in chopped spring onion.
4. Dish out and garnish each serving with lime halves/lemon wedges.

Char Siew Fan (rice with red roasted pork, Cantonese-style)

In Singapore and Malaysia, this is a popular quick-serve meal available wherever there is a coffeeshop stall selling Cantonese roast meats. The red roast pork is sliced, placed atop an individual serving of hot rice and a large spoonful of fragrant sauce poured over the meat and rice. The sauce is made with the juices of the roasted meats, hence its delicious smoked flavour. Traditional red roast pork is made with a well-marbled piece of pork to keep the lean meat juicy.

RED ROAST PORK (CHAR SIEW)

Pork, preferably with some fat
  800 g (1³/₄ lb)
Red food colouring *a few drops*
Sugar/honey *1 Tbsp*
Dark soy sauce *1 Tbsp*
Light soy sauce *1 Tbsp*
Hot cooked long-grain rice *1 kg
  (2 lb 3 oz / 6 cups)*
Cucumber *1, sliced*

SAUCE

Water *375 ml (12 fl oz / 1¹/₂ cups)*
Thick dark soy sauce *1 Tbsp*
Sweet dark soy sauce *1 Tbsp*
Light soy sauce *1 Tbsp*
Five-spice powder *1 large pinch*
Corn flour *1 Tbsp*

CONDIMENT

Any bottled garlic chilli sauce
  or chicken rice chilli sauce
  (page 52)

1. Prepare red roast pork. Cut pork into thick strips about 5 cm (2 in) across and about 3 cm (1 in) thick.

2. Mix food colouring, sugar/honey, soy sauces and marinate pork. Cover and stand for a few hours or overnight in the fridge.

3. When ready to cook, drain marinade from meat and set aside for making sauce.

4. Heat a grill to 220°C (428°F) and grill both sides of meat till done. The cooking time will depend on the thickness of the meat.

5. Prepare sauce. Mix together reserved meat marinade with soy sauces and five-spice powder. In a separate bowl, mix corn flour with some water and set aside for the last step.

6. Halfway through grilling, pour half the soy sauce mixture into the roasting pan to prevent the pan dripping from drying out. Continue grilling till meat is done. Remove grilled meat and pour pan dripping into a small saucepan.

7. Combine pan dripping with remainder of sauce mixture and bring to the boil. Stir corn flour and water well and add to the boiling sauce. Adjust seasoning to taste with more light soy sauce or sweet dark soy sauce. Turn off heat when sauce thickens.

8. To serve, slice roast pork to preferred thickness and arrange on top of a plate of rice garnished with sliced cucumbers. Dress with some of the sauce.

9. Serve rice hot with a condiment of chilli sauce.

DUCK RICE

In Singapore and Hong Kong, the stalls in coffeeshops and restaurants selling Cantonese-style roast meats are usually the ones that also offer duck rice. The duck can be braised or roasted, the former being easier to do at home. A whole duck is rather large and will certainly leave you with more than enough for one meal. In Singapore, some supermarkets offer half a duck. This duck rice is prepared with braised duck and the condiment is the classic Teochew garlic-vinegar chilli sauce.

Hot cooked long-grain rice *1 kg (2 lb 3 oz / 6 cups)*

SAUCE FOR RICE
Corn flour *1 Tbsp*
Water *60 ml (2 fl oz / 1/4 cup)*
Dark soy sauce *2 tsp*

BRAISED DUCK
Duck *1/2*
Five-spice powder *1 tsp*
Dark soy sauce *2 tsp*
Light soy sauce *2 Tbsp*
Salt *1 tsp*
Ground white pepper *1/2 tsp*
Ginger *1 large thumb-size knob, peeled and smashed*
Water *2 litres (64 fl oz / 8 cups)*

GARNISHING
Spring onion *1, cut to finger lengths*
Coriander leaves *1 bunch, chopped*

CHILLI AND GARLIC VINEGAR SAUCE
Red chillies *30 g (1 oz), seeded*
Garlic *4 cloves, peeled*
Chinese rice vinegar *3 Tbsp*
Salt *1/4 tsp*
Sugar *1/2 tsp*
Water *2 Tbsp*

1. To braise duck, put all ingredients together into a large pot and bring to the boil. Turn down heat and simmer for 2 hours or till duck is tender. There should be at least 500 ml (16 fl oz / 2 cups) gravy for making sauce for rice. Adjust seasoning to taste. Drain duck from gravy.

2. Prepare chilli and garlic vinegar sauce. Put all ingredients for sauce together in a food processor and blend till fine. Rest for at least an hour before serving.

3. To make sauce for rice, stir together corn flour, water and dark soy sauce. Bring duck gravy to the boil, then stir in corn flour mixture. Return to the boil and turn off heat when sauce thickens. Adjust thickness of the gravy with more corn flour if necessary.

4. To serve, chop duck into pieces. Place some pieces of duck atop an individual serving of hot rice, then ladle a generous helping of sauce over. Garnish with spring onion and coriander leaves.

5. Serve duck rice with chilli and garlic vinegar condiment.

MUI FAN (CANTONESE RICE IN SEAFOOD SAUCE)

What makes *mui fan* so tasty is the *wok hei* (literally "wok's breath") which basically refers to the fragrance from the light singeing of the ingredients with the high flames. This is hard to duplicate at home but if you want to try it, you need to be dexterous with the wok and be sure to have all the ingredients at hand before you start cooking. With a home preparation, getting the *wok hei* is easier if you cook with gas and divide the cooking into smaller portions. Use a wok with a long handle. This allows you to tip the wok towards the flames to sear its contents. This is easier, too, if the food is oily!

Cooking oil 60 ml (2 fl oz / 1/4 cup)

Garlic 3 cloves, peeled and chopped

Pork/chicken 100 g (3 1/2 oz), thinly sliced

Mustard greens 300 g (11 oz), cut into finger lengths

Shelled prawns with tails on 200 g (7 oz)

Squid 100 g (3 1/2 oz), cleaned and cut into rings

Cooked long-grain rice 1 kg (2 lb 3 oz / 6 cups)

SAUCE

Water 500 ml (16 fl oz / 2 cups)

Corn flour 1 Tbsp

Dark soy sauce 1 tsp

Light soy sauce 2 Tbsp

Salt 1/2 tsp

Ground white pepper 1/2 tsp

CONDIMENT

Light soy sauce with pickled green chillies

1. Mix together ingredients for sauce in a bowl. Stir well just before adding to wok.

2. Heat oil in a wok over high heat and sauté garlic till fragrant. Stir in pork/chicken and fry till meat is cooked. Add mustard greens, then prawns and when prawns begin to change colour, add squid.

3. This step is optional. When squid begins to turn opaque, hold wok such that the oil in the wok will catch the flames. Stir vigorously as you do so.

4. Quickly add rice, mix well and add sauce. Bring to the boil.

5. Serve *mui fan* straight away with a condiment of light soy sauce with pickled green chillies.

SALMON KEDGEREE

Unlike the kedgerees in the Biryanis, Pilafs and Other Flavoured Rice section, this particular kedgeree is more a dressed rice than the cooked-together kind. It starts as plain hot rice to which you add any kind of boned fried or grilled fish. Even leftovers will do if there is enough of it. I prepare it with salmon because it is such a lovely colour and flavour.

Salmon 300 g (11 oz)

Salt 1 1/2 tsp

Cooking oil for frying salmon

Ghee/butter 60 ml (2 fl oz / 1/4 cup)

Garlic 3 cloves, peeled and chopped

Red chilli powder 2 tsp

Hot cooked long-grain rice 1 kg (2 lb 3 oz / 6 cups)

Parsley 1/2 cup, chopped

Hard-boiled eggs 2, shelled and chopped

Ground black pepper 1/4 tsp

1. Rub salmon with 1/2 tsp salt.

2. Heat some oil in a wok or frying pan and cook fish through, browning both sides. To test for doneness, insert a toothpick into the thickest part. If the toothpick slides in easily, the fish is cooked. Alternatively, the fish can be grilled. Cool, then flake fish and discard any bones. Set aside.

3. Drain oil from wok or pan, then heat ghee/butter and fry garlic and chilli powder for 1 minute, taking care not to burn chilli powder.

4. Stir in remaining 1 tsp salt followed by rice. Mix well, then add fish, parsley and lastly, chopped boiled eggs. Try not to mash all the yolk into rice.

5. Serve salmon kedgeree hot with a raita (page 59), pickles (page 57) or a salad.

Sesame Rice, Indian-style

This is basically a fried rice but flavoured with nuts and spices and with the added tang of lime juice. It is dressy enough to make its appearance on a festive occasion, served with fancy side dishes such as meat curries and kebabs. This is yet another tasty brown rice recipe.

White sesame seeds ¹/₂ cup

Cooking oil 3 Tbsp

Cashew nuts 200 g (7 oz / 1 cup)

Cold cooked long-grain/brown rice 1 kg (2 lb 3 oz / 6 cups)

Red chilli powder 1 tsp

Asafoetida 1 large pinch

Lime juice 1 Tbsp

Salt 1¹/₂ tsp

Garam masala 1 (page 30) ¹/₂ tsp

Chopped spring onion

Chopped coriander leaves

1. In a dry wok over low heat, stir-fry sesame seeds till pale golden in colour, taking care not to over-brown sesame seeds or it will taste bitter. Pound sesame seeds to release fragrant oils.

2. In the same wok, heat oil and fry cashew nuts till golden brown. If nuts are halved, they will brown faster. Scoop out nuts and set aside.

3. Put rice, chilli powder, asafoetida, lime juice and salt into wok and fry till rice is heated through. Mix in sesame seeds, cashew nuts and garam masala.

4. Dish out and garnish with chopped spring onion and coriander leaves.

5. Serve rice with pickles (page 57), poppadom and a dhal curry (page 43) or a chutney (page 59).

Indian Fried Rice

This fried rice uses the classic combination of ginger, garlic and onion often seen in Indian curries and rice dishes. The addition of the garam masala at the end of the frying keeps the fragrance of the spices fresh.

Cooking oil 3 Tbsp

Onion 100 g (3¹/₂ oz), peeled and finely sliced

Red chilli powder 1 tsp

Chicken slivers 100 g (3¹/₂ oz)

Salt 1¹/₂ tsp

Green peas 200 g (7 oz / 1 cup)

Tomatoes 200 g (7 oz), seeded and cubed

Cold cooked long-grain rice 1 kg (2 lb 3 oz / 6 cups)

Green chillies 2, seeded and sliced

Garam masala 1 (page 30) 1 tsp

GINGER-GARLIC PASTE

Ginger 1 small thumb-size knob, peeled and finely chopped

Garlic 30 g (1 oz), peeled and finely chopped

1. Make ginger-garlic paste first by pounding ginger and garlic to a fine paste.

2. Heat oil in a wok and sauté ginger-garlic paste and cubed onions till fragrant but not brown. Stir in chilli powder and chicken and fry till meat is cooked.

3. Stir in salt, peas and tomato cubes and fry till tomatoes begin to get soft. If the seasoning is too damp, dry it out a little.

4. Add rice and green chillies and fry till rice is heated through. Stir garam masala in last.

5. Dish out and serve hot.

RICE WITH LIME DRESSING, INDIAN-STYLE

It is best to do a taste test while you are making the dressing as you may want more or less tartness. Fresh coconut tastes best but if you can't get fresh grated coconut, use canned desiccated coconut. Be sure however that it is unflavoured. If you don't want your dressing so tart, plump up the coconut with some water instead. Unlike fried rice, this dressed rice starts with hot cooked rice. This is another recipe that would be tasty if made with brown rice.

Hot cooked long-grain rice 1 kg
(2 lb 3 oz / 6 cups)

Ground turmeric ¼ tsp

Ghee/cooking oil 2 Tbsp

Ginger 10 thin slices, peeled and finely shredded

Red chilli powder 1 tsp

Boiled chana dhal (chickpeas) 3 cups

Salt 1½ tsp

Grated coconut without skin ½ cup

Finely grated lime zest 1 tsp

Green chillies 2, seeded and thinly sliced

Lime juice 60 ml (2 fl oz / ¼ cup)

Coriander leaves 1 bunch, chopped

Toasted cashew nuts

1. Sprinkle hot rice with ground turmeric and mix together. The rice does not have to be evenly coated all over. Spoon onto a serving dish and keep rice warm. Alternatively, leave it in the rice pot till you are ready to dress the rice.

2. Heat ghee/oil in a wok and fry ginger, chilli powder, boiled chana dhal and salt. Smash up some of the chickpeas.

3. Stir in grated coconut and lime zest, turning constantly till coconut is on the dry side. If using desiccated coconut, you have to add some water or lime juice instead to plump it up.

4. Stir in green chillies and lime juice. Mix well. Adjust seasoning to taste. Divide chana dhal among servings of warm rice.

5. Garnish with chopped coriander leaves and cashew nuts.

6. Serve with a meat dish (page 42) and a salad, chutney (page 59) or pickles (page 57).

INDIAN COCONUT FRIED RICE

You can use desiccated coconut to prepare this particular fried rice if you cannot get fresh grated coconut easily. In India, little boys with trays of shelled coconut crowd bus and railway stations selling pieces of shelled coconut as a snack. Whole coconuts complete with husk and shell are sometimes seen in Mexican supermarkets in the US. As the process of husking and shelling a coconut is rather complicated, just use canned desiccated coconut, if fresh is unavailable. This recipe works well with cooked brown rice too.

Ghee/cooking oil 3 Tbsp

Mustard seeds 1 tsp

Ginger 3 slices, finely shredded

Fresh peas/beans 1 cup, blanched or boiled till tender

Grated coconut without skin ½ cup

Red/green chillies 2, seeded and chopped

Asafoetida 1 large pinch

Salt 1½ tsp

Cold cooked rice/brown rice 1 kg
(2 lb 3 oz / 6 cups)

Toasted cashew nuts/almonds ½ cup

Coriander leaves 1 bunch, chopped

1. Heat ghee/oil in a wok. Add mustard seeds and ginger strips and fry till mustard seeds pop. Add peas/beans, grated coconut, chillies, asafoetida and salt.

2. Fry till coconut begins to brown, taking care not to blacken coconut or rice will taste bitter.

3. Stir in rice, mix well and fry till heated through. Add toasted cashews/almonds and chopped coriander leaves last.

4. Serve hot with a dhal curry (page 43).

Puliyodarai (south indian tamarind rice)

This South Indian dressing for rice is going to taste a little like *resam*, a South Indian tamarind soup eaten with rice. Unlike *resam*, however, there is dhal and chickpeas in it and plenty of spice paste. When making chana dhal or any dhal curry, you can always boil extra and set it aside for preparing this dressed rice. Look for ground fenugreek in Middle Eastern stores. If unavailable, substitute ground fenugreek with 1 tsp whole fenugreek seeds and fry that with the mustard seeds.

Ghee/oil 60 ml (2 fl oz / ^{1}/$_4$ cup)

Hot cooked long-grain rice 1 kg (2 lb 3 oz / 6 cups)

Garam masala 1 (page 30) ^{1}/$_2$ tsp

White sesame seeds 1 Tbsp, toasted

Tamarind pulp 75 g (2^1/$_2$ oz)

Water 1 litre (32 fl oz / 4 cups)

Curry leaves 1 sprig

Mustard seeds 2 tsp

Onion 50 g (1^2/$_3$ oz), peeled and thinly sliced

Mung beans/mung/masoor dhal 100 g (3^1/$_2$ oz / ^{1}/$_2$ cup), soaked 1 hour

Boiled chana dhal (chickpeas) 3 cups

Salt 1^1/$_2$ tsp

Sugar to taste

SPICE PASTE

Ground turmeric ^{1}/$_2$ tsp

Red chilli powder 2 tsp

Ground coriander 2 tsp

Ground fenugreek ^{1}/$_2$ tsp

Asafoetida 1 large pinch

Water 3 Tbsp

GARNISHING

Toasted cashew nuts

Mint leaves

1. Stir 2 Tbsp ghee/oil into hot cooked rice together with garam masala and keep rice warm.

2. Dry-fry sesame seeds to brown them but take care not to burn them. Pound to release oils. Set aside.

3. Mix all spice paste ingredients together.

4. Mix tamarind pulp with 1 litre (32 fl oz / 4 cups) water and strain away solids. Set aside tamarind juice until needed.

5. Heat remaining 2 Tbsp ghee/oil in a wok and fry curry leaves and mustard seeds till mustard seeds pop. Add sliced onion and spice paste and stir-fry till fragrant.

6. Add tamarind juice, soaked dhal, boiled chana dhal and salt and simmer gently till dhal is tender. There should be at least 750 ml (24 fl oz / 3 cups) thick gravy in the stew. Stir in sugar and sesame seeds when dhal is cooked.

7. To serve, dish out rice onto a serving dish and top with dhal dressing. (Note that if dressing is left to cool down, it will thicken. If so, stir in some water or tamarind juice to thin it out again.)

8. Garnish with cashew nuts and mint leaves.

DAHI JAU (ORISSA CURD RICE)

Variations of yoghurt and rice are eaten all over India, the simplest being yoghurt seasoned with salt poured over rice. This one from Orissa is rather like a cucumber raita on rice. Called *dahi* in Hindi and *tyroo* in Tamil, yoghurt is regarded in India as an easily digested food and the traditional way is to have the rice on the soft side so that the curds and rice will be suitable for everyone from young to old, as well as anyone under the weather. If no one is under the weather, you might want to keep the rice firm instead.

Cucumber *500 g (1 lb 1¹/₂ oz)*

Salt *2 tsp*

Sugar *1 tsp*

Yoghurt *1 litre (32 fl oz / 4 cups)*

Green chillies *2, seeded and chopped*

Hot cooked long-grain rice *1 kg (2 lb 3 oz / 6 cups)*

YOGHURT TOPPING

Ghee *3 Tbsp*

Mustard seeds *1 tsp*

Dried red chillies *2, seeded and coarsely cut*

Curry leaves *1 sprig, crushed*

GARNISHING

Coriander leaves/mint leaves *1 large bunch, chopped*

1. Quarter cucumber and slice away soft core of seeds. Slice thinly. Salt cucumber slices with ¹/₂ tsp salt and stand for 15 minutes, then squeeze out juices.

2. Mix sugar and remaining 1¹/₂ tsp salt into yoghurt, then add green chillies and cucumber.

3. To make yoghurt topping, heat ghee in a small frying pan and fry mustard seeds, dried red chillies and curry leaves till mustard seeds pop.

4. Divide rice into individual serving plates, spoon cucumber and green chilli raita on rice and top with hot ghee mixture. Garnish with chopped coriander/mint leaves.

5. Serve with a dry curry such as seeni sambol (page 56), fried fish (page 40) and poppadoms also called *appalam* in South India.

DOI BHAAT (BENGALI CURDS AND RICE)

This dish of curds and rice is unusual in being a cooked yoghurt sauce poured over the rice. Although the yoghurt can be cooked with the rice, I don't like the way that the yoghurt separates. This sauce has sugar added to it, the Bengalis being famous for their sweet tooth. Kolkata, the capital city of West Bengal, is known in India for its many sweet shops. Halve the sugar or omit if you prefer your rice more tangy.

Long-grain rice *600 g (1 lb 5¹/₃ oz / 3 cups)*

Water *1.5 litres (48 fl oz / 6 cups)*

Salt *1¹/₂ tsp*

Lime/lemon zest *1 Tbsp, finely chopped*

Garam masala 1 or 2 (page 30) *¹/₂ tsp*

YOGHURT SAUCE

Yoghurt *750 ml (24 fl oz / 3 cups)*

Milk *250 ml (8 fl oz / 1 cup)*

Salt *1¹/₂ tsp*

Sugar *¹/₂ Tbsp*

GARNISHING

Ghee *2 Tbsp*

Almond/cashew nut slivers *¹/₂ cup*

Cumin seeds *¹/₂ tsp*

1. Cook rice with water, salt and lime/lemon zest using your preferred method until rice is tender. When rice is done, fluff it up and sprinkle in garam masala.

2. Prepare yoghurt sauce. Beat together yoghurt, milk, salt and sugar together in a saucepan and heat sauce up. Stir continuously till bubbles appear. Turn off heat as soon as it starts to boil.

3. Prepare garnishing. Heat ghee in a frying pan and fry nuts. Scoop out and set aside. Fry cumin seeds for 1 minute.

4. To serve, spoon yoghurt sauce over individual plates of rice and garnish with some ghee and cumin seeds and fried nuts.

5. Serve with a salad or pickles (page 57).

KHORESHT GHAIMEH (PERSIAN LAMB STEW WITH LIME)

Make this with mutton if you cannot get lamb. The more gamey flavour of mutton will be moderated by the *noomi Basra*. Adjust the amount of water to get the right tenderness and time the addition of the split peas into the stew such that the peas are not boiled to mush before the meat is tender. Traditionally flavoured with *noomi Basra*, you can substitute with lime or lemon juice or even freeze-dried lime juice if you don't have dried limes. The kind of limes and lime juice you add to the stew will affect its flavour as limes are not all alike. The stew should taste sour but adjust this to personal taste.

Olive oil *90 ml (3 fl oz / 6 Tbsp) + more for brushing aubergines (eggplants)*

Onions *250 g (9 oz), peeled and thinly sliced*

Lamb *600 g (1 lb 5¹/₃ oz), cubed*

Advieh 3 (page 31) *2 tsp*

Water *1.5 litres (48 fl oz / 6 cups)*

Salt *2 tsp*

Tomatoes *250 g (9 oz), quartered*

Tomato paste *¹/₂ Tbsp*

Noomi Basra 3

Lime juice *to taste*

Yellow/green split peas *360 g (13 oz / 1¹/₂ cups), soaked 1 hour*

Aubergines (eggplants) *400 g (14¹/₃ oz), sliced 1-cm (¹/₂-in) thick*

Hot cooked long-grain rice *1 kg (2 lb 3 oz / 6 cups)*

1. Heat olive oil in a saucepan and fry onions till pale brown, then add meat and *advieh* and stir-fry till meat changes colour.

2. Add water, salt, tomatoes, tomato paste, *noomi Basra* and lime juice and bring to the boil. Turn down heat and simmer. When meat is beginning to get tender, add split peas. Add more water if necessary to continue simmering. There should be plenty of thick gravy. This stew benefits from being rested for several hours to meld the flavours before serving.

3. Brush olive oil lightly on both sides of aubergine slices. Grill or pan-fry till aubergines are soft and brown outside.

4. To serve, heap individual serving plates with some hot rice, add some aubergine slices and top with stew.

KHORESHT-E-HULU (PERSIAN CHICKEN PEACH STEW)

This is one of the savoury fruity stews for which Persian cuisine is famous. Saffron is said to be the world's most expensive spice and it adds an interesting and somewhat unidentifiable fragrance to this stew. Not everyone likes the flavour of saffron though and a little goes a long way. If fresh unripe peaches are not available, use any fresh sour fruit such as sour plums or nectarines. The Southeast Asian version would be with sour belimbing or unripe starfruit.

Saffron threads ¹/₂ tsp

Olive oil 60 ml (2 fl oz / ¹/₄ cup)

Onion 150 g (5¹/₃ oz), peeled and thinly sliced

Chicken 1 kg (2 lb 3 oz), cut into pieces

Advieh 2 (page 31) 2 tsp

Lime juice 60 ml (2 fl oz / ¹/₄ cup)

Sugar 1 Tbsp

Salt 1¹/₂ tsp

Water 1 litre (32 fl oz / 4 cups)

Fresh unripe peaches 500 g (1 lb 1¹/₂ oz), pitted, thinly sliced

Hot cooked long-grain rice 1 kg (2 lb 3 oz / 6 cups)

1. Steep saffron threads in 1 Tbsp water and set aside.

2. Heat olive oil in a saucepan and brown onion. Add chicken and fry till meat changes colour, stirring constantly to avoid burning onion.

3. Add advieh and stir-fry for 2 minutes, then add lime juice, sugar, salt, water and sliced peaches to pan. Bring to the boil, then simmer for an hour till a thick chunky sauce forms and chicken is tender.

4. Adjust seasoning to taste, then stir in saffron water with saffron threads and mix well. Simmer for another 5 minutes, then turn off heat.

5. Rest stew for a couple of hours at least before serving it on top of boiled rice.

KHORESHT FESENJAAN (PERSIAN MEAT STEW IN POMEGRANATE-WALNUT SAUCE)

In medieval times, the meat in this stew was duck. These days, it is lamb, beef or chicken rather than duck. Pomegranate juice is becoming trendy as a health food and 100 per cent pomegranate juice can be seen in health food sections of supermarkets or in supermarkets specialising in organic and whole foods. The stew can also be made with pomegranate molasses if you can find it. Both pomegranate juice and molasses are very tart, so you have to do a taste test when you add the sugar to the stew. If you can find ground pomegranate seeds, add this thickener to the ground walnuts. Adjust the amount of juice in the stew to the meat you are cooking as chicken gets tender more quickly than lamb or beef. The stew should have a thick sweet-sour gravy.

Chicken 1 kg ((2 lb 3 oz) or 750 g (1 lb 11 oz) lamb/beef

Olive oil 60 ml (2 fl oz / ¹/₄ cup)

Onions 200 g (7 oz), peeled and thinly sliced

Ground walnuts 200 g (7 oz / 2 cups)

Salt 1¹/₂ tsp

Advieh 2 (page 31) ¹/₂ Tbsp

Pomegranate juice 1 litre (32 fl oz / 4 cups)

Sugar to taste

Hot cooked long-grain rice 1 kg (2 lb 3 oz / 6 cups)

1. Chop chicken into pieces. If using lamb or beef, cube meat.

2. Heat olive oil in a pot and brown onions lightly, then add ground walnuts, salt and advieh and stir-fry till oil surfaces. Add meat, mix well and fry till meat begins to change colour.

3. Add pomegranate juice to meat and bring to the boil. Turn down heat and simmer till meat is tender. The sauce should be thick and oil should rise to the top. Add sugar to taste. Stand stew for a couple of hours to meld flavours before serving. The stew will taste even better left overnight.

4. To serve, ladle stew over individual plates of boiled rice.

CHELO KEBAB (PERSIAN GRILLED LAMB AND RICE)

Chelo is the Farsi word for Persian-style plain cooked rice with *tah-deeg* (rice crust). Yet this seemingly simple combination of cooked rice with grilled lamb topped with raw egg yolk is so popular that there are Iranian restaurants specialising in it. Much depends on the tenderness of the lamb and the way the rice is cooked. *Chelo kebab* is eaten with the egg yolk stirred into the hot rice to form a rich coating, this particular combination being very traditional. If eating raw egg bothers you, try poaching the egg. Without the egg yolk, the *chelo kebab* will be rather dry.

Lamb fillet *300 g (11 oz)*

Onion juice (page 36) *2 Tbsp*

Lemon juice *2 tsp*

Salt *1 tsp*

Ground black pepper *1/2 tsp*

Advieh 2 (page 31) *1 tsp*

Melted ghee/olive oil *2 Tbsp*

Small tomatoes *1–3 per person*

Very hot cooked Persian-style boiled rice (page 23) *1–1 1/2 cups per person*

Egg yolks *1 per person*

Sumac

Bamboo skewers *as needed*

1. If using a tougher cut of lamb other than fillet, prepare meat and marinate it overnight with the addition of a large pinch of bicarbonate of soda to tenderise meat. If using fillet, 1–2 hours will do. If there is gristle or fat on the meat, trim it off and slice meat thinly across the grain.

2. Mix together onion juice, lemon juice, salt, black pepper and *advieh* with slices of lamb. During marinating, stir meat occasionally.

3. Before threading meat into skewers, stir 1 Tbsp melted ghee/olive oil into meat. Divide meat into 6 portions and thread meat through skewers.

4. Thread tomatoes on separate skewers. Brush some melted ghee/olive oil on tomatoes and time the grilling of tomatoes and meat such that both are cooked at the same time. If tomatoes are large, start grilling them first and grill till they burst their skins. Do not overcook meat.

5. To serve, spoon hot rice and any *tah-deeg* on a plate. The rice should be very hot. Quickly remove grilled lamb from skewers and place on top of rice, add grilled tomatoes, raw egg yolk and a generous sprinkling of sumac.

6. Serve at once with yoghurt sauce (page 47), a raita (page 59) or pickles (pages 57–58).

INDONESIAN NASI GORENG (INDONESIAN FRIED RICE)

To Singaporeans, Indonesian *nasi goreng* is incomplete without the two sticks of succulent satay sitting next to the fried egg on top of the fried rice. Grill the satay in the oven or over the gas jets if you have a stove top grill pan or grid. It will take less trouble than starting up the barbecue. Alternatively, do a simple fried chicken seasoned with salt and pepper and the *nasi goreng* will taste as good. If you can't find bottled sambal *oelek*, make the chilli paste below. By the way, fried *krupuk* is a standard garnish in Indonesian *nasi goreng*, a fact I forgot when doing the picture!

Boneless chicken *300 g (11 oz), cubed*

Cooking oil *75 ml (2¹/₂ fl oz / 5 Tbsp)*

Onion *100 g (3¹/₂ oz), peeled and cubed*

Shelled small prawns *200 g (7 oz)*

Salt *1 tsp*

Cold cooked long-grain rice *1 kg (2 lb 3 oz / 6 cups)*

Eggs *1 per serving*

Fried *krupuk* (fish/prawn crackers) *a few pieces per serving*

Bamboo skewers *12*

MARINADE FOR CHICKEN

Indonesian thick dark soy sauce (*kicap manis*) *2 tsp*

Lemon grass *1 stalk, thinly sliced and finely ground*

Ground coriander *1 tsp*

Cooking oil *1 Tbsp*

Salt *1 tsp*

Sugar *2 Tbsp*

CHILLI PASTE (OPTIONAL)

Red chillies *3, seeded*

Shallots *3, peeled and chopped*

Dried prawn (shrimp) paste (*belacan*) *¹/₂ tsp*

Sugar *¹/₂ tsp*

1. Mix ingredients for marinade together and marinate chicken cubes. Cover and stand for a couple of hours or overnight refrigerated. Divide into 12 portions and thread chicken cubes through bamboo skewers. Start grilling satay before frying rice. The two tasks should be finished at about the same time so that the satay and fried rice can be enjoyed while hot. When grilling the satay, brush some oil on the meat to keep it moist.

2. If sambal *oelek* is not available, make chilli paste. Pound all ingredients together till fine. Alternatively, blend all the ingredients in a food processor with a bit of water. Set aside.

3. Heat 3 Tbsp oil in a wok and fry onion till it begins to soften. Add sambal *oelek* or chilli paste, prawns and salt and fry till prawns change colour. Stir in rice and mix well, heating rice through. Turn off heat and keep rice warm.

4. In a frying pan, heat ¹/₂ Tbsp oil and fry eggs one at a time sunny-side up. Fry each egg according to individual taste. Some like their eggs fried to death!

5. To serve, divide rice among individual serving plates and top each mound of rice with a fried egg, a few pieces of fried *krupuk* and a couple of sticks of satay.

Rice Salad

Black medium-grain rice has a nutty texture much like any brown rice and the best will have the fragrance of black glutinous rice. It should be soaked for at least an hour or overnight, then cooked with at least three times the amount of water for cooking white rice. It can also be cooked in a rice cooker but be sure that there is room for boiling up because of the increased amount of water. In other words, 1 cup of black rice should be cooked in a rice cooker with capacity for at least three or more cups. This rice is a modern take on the Indian-style dressed rice dishes (pages 144, 146 and 148) and those dressings will also be very tasty when made with black or brown rice. This salad can also be made with both long- and short-grain brown rice. This is one salad that benefits from being left to sit around and makes great picnic food.

Black/brown rice 150 g (5^1/$_3$ oz / ^{3}/$_4$ cup), soaked 1 hour or overnight

Water 500 ml (16 fl oz / 2 cups)

Onion 50 g (1^2/$_3$ oz), peeled and thinly sliced

Cucumber 1, small, seeded and cubed

Red capsicum (bell pepper) 1, small, seeded and cubed

Parsley/coriander leaves ^{1}/$_2$ cup, chopped

Carrot 100 g (3^1/$_2$ oz), peeled and cubed or sliced

DRESSING

Olive oil 3 Tbsp

Lemon juice 2 Tbsp

Salt 1 tsp

Red chilli powder 1 tsp

1. Cook rice with water using your preferred method until rice is tender. When rice is done, fluff it up and let it rest for 10 minutes.

2. Mix ingredients for dressing together in a mixing bowl. Stir onion and warm rice into dressing and mix well before adding cucumber, capsicum and chopped parsley/coriander. Adjust dressing to taste.

3. Rest salad for at least an hour in the refrigerator and serve cold.

Malay Nasi Ulam

Malay or Straits Chinese, the beauty of *nasi ulam* is that you can stretch the amounts with whatever vegetables and fish that you may have on hand. The rice can also be increased at will. It is an excellent way to use up any leftover fried fish. Even the fresh herbs can be changed according to what you have available.

Cabbage 100 g (3^1/$_2$ oz), thinly shredded

Cucumber 1 cup, cubed small

Hot cooked rice 1 kg (2 lb 3 oz / 6 cups)

Fried fish 200 g (7 oz), flaked

Salted fish 50 g (1^2/$_3$ oz), fried and finely pounded

Turmeric leaf 1 large, thinly shredded

Shredded torch ginger bud 1 Tbsp

DRESSING

Shallots ^{1}/$_2$ cup, peeled and thinly sliced

Sambal *belacan* (page 59) 2 Tbsp

Lime juice 2 Tbsp

Salt 1 tsp

1. Mix together dressing ingredients in a large bowl.

2. Stir in cabbage and cucumber. Mix well.

3. Stir in hot cooked rice, flaked fried fish and pounded salted fish and mix well.

4. Mix in shredded herbs.

5. Serve warm or cold.

LONTONG (RICE CAKES WITH VEGETABLE CURRY)

Lontong is a popular dish consisting of a vegetable curry with rice cakes. Traditionally, the rice cakes, known as *ketupat* in Malay, are cooked in small casings woven from coconut palm fronds. The casings are half-filled with broken rice and then boiled in water till the soft rice is compressed into a cake inside the casing. The rice cake hardens when it cools. Today, ready-to-boil *ketupat* packed into little plastic bags is sold in supermarkets in Singapore and Malaysia.

RICE CAKE (KETUPAT)
Long-grain rice 600 g (1 lb 5¹/₃ oz / 3 cups)
Water 1.75 litres (56 fl oz / 7 cups)

QUICK SERUNDING
Cooking oil 1 Tbsp
Lemon grass 1 stalk, bruised
Onion 30 g (1 oz), peeled and sliced
Dried chillies 3, seeded and sliced
Grated coconut 200 g (7 oz / 2 cups)
Kaffir lime leaves 3, bruised
Salt ¹/₂ tsp
Sugar 1 Tbsp

SPICE PASTE
Dried chillies 30 g (1 oz), seeded
Shallots 100 g (3¹/₂ oz), peeled
Garlic 2 cloves (3¹/₂ oz), peeled
Turmeric 1 thumb-size knob
Dried prawn (shrimp) paste (*belacan*) ¹/₂ Tbsp
Candlenuts 8, rinsed
Water 60 ml (2 fl oz / ¹/₄ cup)

SAYUR LODEH
Cooking oil 3 Tbsp
Firm bean curd 200 g (7 oz)
Galangal 1 thumb-size knob, peeled and smashed
Chicken (page 80)/prawn stock (page 110) 2 litres (64 fl oz / 8 cups)
Long beans/green beans 200 g (7 oz), cut into finger lengths
Cabbage 150 g (5¹/₃ oz), chopped
Carrot 100 g (3¹/₂ oz), peeled, sliced
Jicama (yam bean) 200 g (7 oz), peeled and sliced
Coconut cream 250 ml (8 fl oz / 1 cup)
Glass noodles 50 g (1²/₃ oz), softened in cold water
Prawns 400 g (14¹/₃ oz), shelled

CONDIMENT
Straits Chinese *nasi lemak* chilli sauce (page 41)

1. Prepare rice cake and serunding a day ahead of making *sayur lodeh*.

2. The rice can be broken up before boiling or mashed while boiling. The rice must be soft for it to form into a cake.

3. Cook rice using your preferred method until tender. Scoop hot, cooked rice into a glass or plastic container with a well-fitted lid. The size of the container should be such that the rice will be compressed tightly once the lid is on. If possible, put a heavy weight on top of the covered container.

4. An alternative way to make *ketupat* is to roll it like sushi but more tightly. Cut some pieces of cleaned banana leaves a little larger than the size of the sushi mat. Place a piece of leaf on the sushi mat, spoon the hot, cooked rice onto the leaf and roll up tightly (page 161). Push the soft rice at the ends towards the centre and close the ends with bamboo skewers. Cool rice for several hours before serving.

5. Another way is to have ready a dampened piece of muslin. Divide the hot rice into several portions and make the rice cakes by wrapping each portion of hot rice tightly in the muslin cloth. Squeeze and shape the rice into the traditional *ketupat* shape like square cushions. Work quickly so that the rice is still warm and soft when you are compressing it.

6. Prepare serunding. Heat oil and fry lemon grass, onion and chilli for 2 minutes. Add all other ingredients and stir-fry over low heat till coconut is fragrant and a golden colour. Bottle and keep refrigerated until needed.

7. To make spice paste, put all the ingredients into a food processor and blend to a smooth paste.

8. In a large saucepan, heat oil and brown both sides of bean curd. Cut into 1-cm (¹/₂-in) cubes or slices and set aside.

9. Reheat oil in pan and stir-fry spice paste till fragrant and oil surfaces. Add galangal and stock and bring to the boil. Add vegetables, half the coconut cream and return to the boil. Simmer gently till vegetables are of preferred tenderness.

10. Stir in fried bean curd, glass noodles and prawns and simmer till prawns change colour. Add the remaining coconut cream and return to the boil. Turn off heat as soon as bubbles start to appear on the surface of the curry.

11. To serve lontong, cut rice cakes into bite-size pieces with a knife moistened with cold water to avoid sticking. Place rice cubes in a large individual soup dish or bowl. Ladle a serving of vegetable curry onto rice cubes.

12. Serve hot with a topping of serunding and chilli sauce.

SUSHI

Sushi is one rice preparation that allows your artistic side to show itself as there are numerous possibilities when making these rice rolls. Sushi is not to be confused with sashimi which is raw seafood eaten with soy sauce and wasabi dips. Sushi is vinegared rice pressed or moulded with either raw seafood or various cooked ingredients. Naturally, sushi with raw seafood is the premium sushi because the seafood has to be super-fresh and of the best quality, and the conditions for preparation and consumption such that the raw seafood stays fresh. Those with cooked ingredients, on the other hand, is standard fare for the average Japanese housewife fixing a *bento* or lunch box for the spouse and schoolchildren.

Sushi can be eaten with your fingers. It is classic finger food and usually rolled with a covering, has some grilled nori stuck on it or with a leaf to make it easy to handle. But if preferred and the piece is small enough to be eaten in one bite, you can also pick it up with your chopsticks. Traditional sushi is usually eaten in two bites at most and so is made quite small. If you want a condiment with your bite, do not dip the rice part of the sushi into the soy sauce to avoid the rice falling apart. If adding wasabi, pick up a dollop and smear it on your sushi before popping it into your mouth.

The first stage in making any kind of sushi starts with preparing the vinegared rice or *sumeshi*. Given the ubiquity of Japanese rice cookers all over Asia, I will assume the availability of a rice cooker. Not so available is a *hangiri*, the Japanese word for a wooden tub usually made of cedar wood which is used to mix salt and rice vinegar into the hot rice. A *hangiri* has a flat base and a wide mouth to cool the rice without condensation forming on the rice and is made of wood so that the moisture is more easily absorbed while at the same time easily dampened to prevent the rice from sticking to the wood. This *hangiri* must not be used for anything else other than making sushi rice to avoid any odd odours clinging to the wood. For this reason, the *hangiri* should also be carefully stored to avoid the wood picking up any unpleasant odours.

The other piece of equipment is a rice paddle called *shamoji*. Again, wood is recommended because it is easily dampened to prevent the rice sticking to the paddle. The last piece of traditional equipment is a hand-held paper fan to cool the rice quickly while the vinegar is being stirred into the rice. This is a manoeuvre calling for some dexterity because it is not easy to get your hands to perform entirely different motions at the same time! If you have a table fan, the easiest way is to position the *hangiri* facing the fan turned on its lowest setting while you make your *sumeshi*. Another alternative is to make the *sumeshi* standing below a ceiling fan. The aim is to cool the rice quickly to prevent condensation forming on it.

Sumeshi is sticky and the way to counteract this stickiness is to dampen the *hangiri* and rice paddle by soaking it in cold water for 1–2 hours before the equipment is used to mix the hot rice. To prevent the rice from sticking to your hands when making sushi, dampen your hands in vinegared water. Keep a clean kitchen towel nearby, wet hands, then thump the back of your hands on the towel to get rid of excess moisture. If after several rolls, the rice begins to stick, either dampen your hands again in the vinegared water or wash your hands clean in cold water, then dampen them with vinegared water.

SUMESHI (SUSHI RICE) Makes about 670 g (11¹/₃ oz / 4 cups)

Sumeshi or sushi rice is cooked with a rice to water ratio of between 1:1.5 and 1:2 depending on your particular short-grain rice. The rice should be fairly firm and yet be tender without being mushy. There are several kinds of Japanese vinegar, so be sure to pick the kind for making sushi rice and not pickles. The stirring of vinegar into the hot rice should be done for no more than 3 minutes to avoid over-handling the rice.

Short-grain rice 400 g (14¹/₃ oz / 2 cups)

Water 750 ml–1 litre (24–32 fl oz / 3–4 cups)

Japanese rice vinegar for sushi 60 ml (2 fl oz / ¹/₄ cup)

1. Soak *hangiri* (wooden rice tub with a cover) and *shamoji* (rice paddle) in cold water for 1–2 hours. Just before using, discard water and wipe *hangiri* and *shamoji* dry. In place of *hangiri*, use your rice pot with a suitable lid.

2. Have the vinegar ready in a bowl near you in front of the table fan.

3. Cook rice with water using your preferred method until rice is tender.

4. Spread hot cooked rice in *hangiri*/rice pot, sprinkle vinegar over and quickly mix rice and vinegar together. Have the table fan on as you mix. Within a couple of minutes, the rice should start to look glossy. Stop after 3 minutes but keep the fan on to cool the rice.

5. Cover *sumeshi* with a clean kitchen towel, put the lid on and continue with other preparations.

Flavoured Sumeshi

Sumeshi can be flavoured in a variety of ways. Some flavours are cooked in together with the rice; others are stirred into the cooked rice at the same time as the vinegar. Note that the Japanese never add salt to rice. Rather, any salty flavours come from a soy sauce dip served with the sushi or from other flavourings.

1) Konbu

Konbu (kelp) 10-cm (4-in)

1. Wipe konbu with a damp kitchen towel, make a few slashes in the seaweed and put it in to cook with the rice. Remove konbu once water has started to boil.

2) Sake

Sake 60 ml (2 fl oz / ¼ cup)

1. Substitute 60 ml (2 fl oz / ¼ cup) water with sake and cook as usual.

3) Mirin

Mirin 1 Tbsp

1. Add mirin to the water for cooking the rice and cook as usual.

4) Toasted Sesame Seeds (with or without salt)

Toasted white or black sesame seeds with or without salt as desired

1. Sprinkle the sesame seeds into the sumeshi while mixing in the vinegar.

5) Pickled Ginger

Pickled ginger as desired, shredded finely

1. Stir the shredded pickled ginger into the sumeshi with the vinegar.

6) Umeboshi (pickled plum)

Umeboshi (pickled plums) 1–2, seeded and mashed

1. Stir mashed plums into the vinegar and mix into the rice.

7) Coriander Leaves

Coriander leaves to taste, finely chopped

1. Leave rice to cool before stirring coriander leaves into the rice. Note that this is not a Japanese flavour so use just a small amount to hint at the coriander flavour.

8) Perilla Leaves (shiso)

Perilla leaves (shiso) a few leaves, finely shredded or left whole

1. Stir finely shredded leaves into the sumeshi or place moulded sushi on whole leaves as a base.

ROLLED SUSHI

To make rolled sushi, you must have a bamboo mat called a *makisu*. The mat, which is made of thin pieces of bamboo tied together with string, should be the size of your sheets of seaweed or larger. If you already have a small *makisu*, buy seaweed sheets to fit the size of your mat. Small mats are easier to handle than a large one.

Japanese cucumber *1 or about 8 crabsticks*

Sumeshi/sushi rice *(page 159) 670 g (11¹/₃ oz / 4 cups)*

Toasted nori (seaweed) *4 sheets, each 17 x 20 cm (6¹/₂ x 8-in),*

Wasabi *¹/₂–1 Tbsp*

VINEGARED WATER

Water *750 ml (24 fl oz / 3 cups)*

Japanese rice vinegar for sushi *6 Tbsp*

GARNISHING

Black sesame seeds (optional)

CONDIMENTS

Pickled young ginger

Wasabi

Light soy sauce

1. Mix together water and vinegar and have the bowl of vinegared water near you as you make the sushi.

2. If using cucumber, quarter it into 4 long wedges. Cut the lengths to match the width of the seaweed sheet. If cucumber is short, it can be joined end to end in the roll. Alternatively, use crabsticks. Remove plastic wrapping from crabsticks.

3. Using vinegared water-dampened hands, divide rice into 6 portions.

4. Place a sheet of nori on bamboo mat and spread rice evenly on one-third of seaweed sheet.

5. Spread a thin line of wasabi along the rice. Top with cucumber or crabsticks in a straight line.

6. To roll up sushi, have one edge of the seaweed aligned with the edge of the sushi mat nearest to you. Holding the edge of the mat, turn the seaweed sheet inwards over the rice, rolling the rice with the seaweed and pressing gently as you roll to compress the rice. The rice roll should be tight enough to hold all the ingredients together, but not so tight that the seaweed tears. Getting it the right tightness is a matter of becoming sensitive to the amount of pressure needed. When roll of rice is all covered, trim off edge of seaweed that flaps open. Alternatively, moisten end to stick it to rice roll. Repeat till *sumeshi* and cucumber/crabsticks are used up.

7. To cut a seaweed-covered sushi roll, use a sharp chef's knife and avoid any sawing motions. Start by pricking the seaweed with the tip of the knife, then press the knife downwards into the roll and forwards. Cut the roll into even pieces.

8. Lie pieces on its side to show off the filling. If garnishing, sprinkle some black sesame seeds on top of each piece.

9. Serve rolled sushi with pickled young ginger, wasabi and light soy sauce.

FILLED AND PRESSED SUSHI

Filled and pressed sushi is what Japanese mothers turn out for their children and picnic *bento* boxes. The filling can be whatever leftovers that are dry enough to be used as a filling or specially prepared fillings. Once the ball of rice is filled, it is pressed into special Japanese sushi moulds or into vinegared cookie cutters to shape the rice ball. Besides moulding, filled sushi can also be shaped into triangles or rolled into balls. See also *adzuki gohan* (page 126).

Sumeshi/sushi rice (page 159)
  670 g (11¹/₃ oz / 4 cups)
Cooked seafood/dried bonito
  flakes/seeded *umeboshi*/
  flavoured seaweed/pickled
  vegetables *as needed*

VINEGARED WATER

Water *250 ml (8 fl oz / 1 cup)*
Japanese rice vinegar for sushi
  2 Tbsp

1. Mix together water and vinegar and have the bowl of vinegared water near you as you make the sushi.

2. Dampen a cookie cutter of the right depth and size in vinegared water. Dampen hands in vinegared water, then press enough *sumeshi* to cover the bottom of the cookie cutter and up the sides, leaving a depression the in centre for the filling. Spoon your choice of filling, then top with enough rice to cover the filling. Pop the shaped sushi out of the cutter.

3. Sushi can also be formed by shaping a small handful of *sumeshi* into an oval and pressing a piece of cooked or raw seafood on it. Each piece should only be big enough preferably for just one bite but not more than two bites.

TRIANGLES AND BALLS

Japanese rice vinegar for sushi
  as needed
Sumeshi/sushi rice (page 159)
  670 g (11¹/₃ oz / 4 cups)
Cooked seafood/dried bonito
  flakes/seeded *umeboshi*/
  flavoured seaweed/pickled
  vegetables *as needed*
Toasted nori (seaweed) *4 sheets,*
  each 17 x 20 cm (6¹/₂ x 8-in),
  cut into 2.5-cm (1-in) strips

1. Have ready a small piece of muslin soaked in Japanese vinegar. Spread the muslin on one palm and spoon 2–3 Tbsp sumeshi into it.

2. Press or roll the rice to compact it, then make a cavity and fill it up with chosen filling. Cover up the filling and roll the sushi into a ball or shape the rice into a triangle.

3. Wrap a strip of nori round the triangle or ball for easy handling of the sushi.

An assortment of sushi

CHIRASHI-ZUSHI

There is no rolling or pressing in this particular sushi and the flavourings can be stirred into the sushi rice like a salad or arranged artistically on top of the rice with some seasoned vegetables, a mushroom or two, and pieces of cooked or fresh raw seafood to give a very attractive meal. Fish roe always looks good. Pickled vegetables are easily available in Japanese supermarkets. *Chirashi-zushi* is casual family fare and so is made in the *hangiri* which is brought to the table.

Sumeshi/sushi rice (page 159)
 670 g (11 1/3 oz / 4 cups)

Cooking oil for frying

Egg *1, beaten*

Sashimi/cooked seafood *200 g (7 oz)*

Seasoned or pickled vegetables/ seaweed *1/4 cup per bowl of rice*

GARNISHING

Green tips of spring onions, finely cut

Toasted nori (seaweed) *1 sheet, cut into fine strips*

Japanese sesame salt (page 34) *to taste*

CONDIMENTS

Wasabi

Light soy sauce

1. Prepare *sumeshi* and leave it in the *hangiri*/rice pot.

2. Heat oil in a frying pan and fry egg into a thin omelette. Roll up and slice thinly.

3. Arrange egg strips, sashimi/cooked seafood and seasoned or pickled vegetables/seaweed on *sumeshi*. Garnish with a light sprinkling of spring onion tips and nori strips.

4. Serve with wasabi, light soy sauce and a miso soup.

Ochazuke (rice in green tea)

This rice preparation is sometimes also called *chazuke*. While the Chinese fry leftover rice, the Japanese will typically pour hot green tea over leftover rice and garnish it with whatever cooked leftovers may be in the fridge. However, do not use raw or smoked seafood. The freshly-made green tea will heat up the leftovers somewhat but it is best to warm the leftovers briefly in a microwave oven first.

Cooked chicken/fish

Cooked short-grain rice

Shredded pickled ginger

Toasted nori (seaweed) *1 sheet, cut into fine strips*

Chopped perilla/spring onions

Freshly-made green tea

CONDIMENTS

Japanese sesame salt (page 34)

Wasabi

Japanese-style pickles (page 56)

1. Shred or flake chicken/fish. Put chicken/fish with rice, shredded ginger, nori strips and chopped perilla/spring onions in a rice bowl. Heat briefly in the microwave oven.

2. Pour freshly-made hot green tea over mixture.

3. Serve with sesame salt and wasabi to taste and a dish of Japanese-style pickles. (Make Quickie Daikon Pickle (page 56) but without the garlic.)

Timman Queemah (iraqi minced meat stew with rice)

"Timman" means rice while "*queemah*" means minced in Arabic and is close to the Hindi word "*kheema*" which also means minced. So timman queemah is "Iraqi-style minced meat stew with rice". Both Indian *kheema* and Iraqi *queemah* are minced meat curries or stews that are eaten with rice or flatbread. Dried limes called *noomi Basra* give Iraqi dishes a citrus-y accent. If you can't get dried limes, substitute with lime or lemon juice and zest. The chickpeas must be boiled ahead of time as it takes much longer to cook than minced meat. A large pinch of bicarbonate of soda with the soaking water will speed up cooking of the chickpeas.

Chickpeas *100 g (3¹/₂ oz)*

Olive oil *60 ml (2 fl oz / ¹/₄ cup)*

Onion *100 g (3¹/₂ oz), peeled and chopped*

Garlic *2 cloves, peeled and chopped*

Minced lamb/mutton/chicken *500 g (1 lb 1¹/₂ oz)*

Tomatoes *200 g (7 oz), chopped*

Tomato paste *1 Tbsp*

Any *baharat* (pages 32–33) *1 Tbsp*

Noomi Basra 2, crushed

Salt *1¹/₂ tsp*

Water *about 750 ml (24 fl oz / 3 cups)*

Flat-leaf parsley/coriander leaves *¹/₂ cup, chopped*

1. Start preparations a day ahead. Soak chickpeas overnight. The following day, boil in a pot of water till tender. Alternatively, cook unsoaked chickpeas overnight in a slow cooker till tender. Drain and set aside.

2. Heat olive oil in a saucepan and fry onion till soft and translucent. Stir in garlic, chickpeas, meat, tomatoes, tomato paste, *baharat*, crushed dried limes and salt and mix well. Add water. The amount of water will vary according to the meat used. Chicken will need less water than mutton. Add more water as needed.

3. Bring to the boil, turn down heat and simmer till meat is tender and sauce is rich and thick.

4. Stir in parsley/coriander leaves and cook for another 10 minutes. Let stew rest for an hour or more for flavours to meld.

5. Serve stew ladled over boiled rice, and with a salad, chutney or pickles on the side.

Porridge can be cooked in several ways: in a rice cooker with a porridge setting, in a slow cooker and on a stove top. The first two are easiest and need almost no attention. All you have to do is put the rice and water into the pot, turn on the heat or press the right buttons and the porridge will be cooked with no fuss or mess. With a slow cooker, you can start making the rice porridge the night before for a breakfast of rice porridge the next morning. A fuzzy-logic rice cooker also allows you to do the same, although this will depend on how long the "keep warm" setting stays on. If porridge is cooked on a stove-top, it must be stirred to prevent the bottom from catching and scorching. If there is more control over the diffusion of heat such as by using a heat diffusion plate, there is less risk of scorching the porridge if you forget to give it the occasional stir. Whatever your method of cooking porridge, pre-soak the rice for an hour or so and your porridge will cook faster.

RICE PORRIDGES AND RICE SOUPS

You can stop boiling the porridge once it has reached your preferred consistency. Some like their porridge more like watery soft-cooked rice; others prefer their porridge almost like thick soup. The consistency of porridge can be adjusted by the addition of hot water or boiling down, but note that porridge thickens when it cools down. The amount of water for making porridge depends on the type of rice used, the cooking method as well as whether the porridge is to be thick and fairly smooth or more granular and like soft rice. A ratio of 1:3 is a good starting point. You can add hot—not cold—water to the porridge as it boils, if you think it is too granular or too thick. Cooled porridge that has thickened may be thinned with boiling water stirred into it and brought briefly to the boil.

Then there are rice soups which are basically soft-cooked rice added to a pot of soup. These are just as digestible although much less bland than rice porridge. Rice soups can be very rich when the stock is good and other ingredients are added to it. Rice porridge starts out plain but its very plainness increases its attraction for rich trimmings and richer flavours. Almost all of the recipes in this section start out with plain porridge or plain soft-cooked rice. When you are done adding the trimmings, the flavours are far from plain.

RICE PORRIDGE THREE WAYS

In Southeast and East Asia, rice porridge is considered breakfast food. All three kinds of porridge use long-grain rice but each is flavoured differently. Taiwan porridge, which is sometimes called Hokkien porridge because the Hokkiens are the dominant dialect group in Taiwan, has sweet potatoes, so it is sometimes called sweet potato porridge. The Thais, on the other hand, like their porridge spicy and sour. The Teochews, a dialect group from southern China like their porridge plain and more like very soft watery rice to be enjoyed with fresh fish simply steamed, the Teochews being noted as fishermen and fishmongers in days of old. In Singapore, traditional Teochew rice porridge stalls still serve plain steamed fish with rice porridge. Otherwise, the dishes that these different communities eat with rice porridge are fairly similar, many being canned preserved vegetables, soy sauce-flavoured meat and fish, fermented soy bean curd (*tau joo*) and salted eggs.

1) TEOCHEW MUAY (TEOCHEW PORRIDGE)

Long-grain rice *300 g (11 oz / 2 cups)*

1. Cook rice porridge using your preferred method to get a very soft rice. The porridge should still look fairly granular and it should be watery, not thick and gluey. If the porridge thickens after cooling, thin it with boiling hot water.
2. Serve hot with a choice of side dishes (page 172).

2) TAIWAN PORRIDGE

Long-grain rice/short-grain rice *250 g (9 oz / 1¼ cups)*
Sweet potatoes *200 g (7 oz), peeled and cut into large chunks*

1. Cook rice porridge using your preferred method. When porridge is about 15 minutes from reaching your preferred texture, add sweet potato chunks. Continue simmering till sweet potatoes are done, adding more water if necessary. The porridge should be fairly thick, the rice broken down and not as watery as Teochew porridge.
2. Serve hot with a choice of side dishes (page 172).

3) THAI RICE PORRIDGE

Long-grain rice *250 g (9 oz / 1¼ cups)*
Fish sauce *to taste*
White vinegar *to taste*
Bird's eye chillies *to taste, chopped*
Fried garlic and garlic oil *(page 37) to taste*

1. Cook rice porridge using your preferred method. The porridge should be softer and thicker than Teochew porridge but not as thick and starchy as Taiwan porridge.
2. The rest of the ingredients are stirred into the porridge according to taste or set out as condiments to be mixed and matched.

Clockwise from top left: Steamed Pork with Salted Mustard Greens, Onion and Chilli Omelette, Steamed Pork with Salted Egg, Thai Rice Porridge, Salted Eggs, Stewed Preserved Vegetables, Teochew Muay, Taiwan Porridge

4) Sides Dish Suggestions for Teochew Muay, Taiwan Porridge and Thai Rice Porridge

- Chinese canned mustard pickles and vegetables
- Canned or bottled stewed preserved vegetables
- Bottled fermented soy bean curd (*tau joo*)
- Steamed minced pork with salted egg (page 54)
- Steamed minced pork with salted mustard greens (page 54)
- Onion and chilli omelette (page 55)
- Salted radish omelette (page 55)
- Salted eggs. (Rinse eggs clean and boil for 15 minutes. To serve, cut boiled eggs in half.)
- Stewed belly pork with dark soy sauce (Stew 500 g (1 lb 1¹/₂ oz) belly pork slices or cubes with 750 ml (24 fl oz / 3 cups) water, 2 Tbsp dark soy sauce, 60 ml (2 fl oz / ¹/₄ cup) light soy sauce and ground white pepper to taste till pork is soft.)

Century Egg Porridge

This is a Cantonese dish found in dim sum restaurants but it is easy to make at home. While the pork is cooked with the porridge, the century eggs should only be added when the pork and porridge have boiled up. Boiling century egg with the porridge for too long turns the porridge watery. Some kind of chemical reaction must be taking place! The pork balances the sharpness of the century eggs.

White short-grain rice *250 g (9 oz / 1¹/₄ cups)*
Century eggs *2*
Cooking oil *1 Tbsp*
Ginger *4 slices, shredded*
Minced pork *100 g (3¹/₂ oz)*
Salt *1 tsp*
Water *125 ml (4 fl oz / ¹/₂ cup)*
Fried garlic (page 37) *1 tsp*

GARNISHING
Chinese fried crullers *2 pieces, cut into thin rings*
Chopped spring onion

CONDIMENT
Light soy sauce

1. Cook rice using your preferred method to get a thick porridge.

2. Prepare century eggs by scraping away rice husks and shelling eggs. Rinse clean under running water and pat dry with a paper towel. Cut eggs into small wedges and set aside in a bowl.

3. In a large saucepan, heat oil and sauté ginger, minced pork and salt till meat is cooked. Add water, fried garlic, porridge and bring to the boil. Lastly, stir in century egg and mix well. Turn off heat.

4. To serve, dish out porridge into bowls and garnish with crullers and spring onion. Serve hot with a condiment of light soy sauce.

KAI CHOK (CANTONESE CHICKEN PORRIDGE)

There are several ways to prepare chicken porridge. The simplest way is to make the porridge and add minced chicken to the boiling rice porridge. Another is to prepare a soup with the stock, meat and seasoning and add hot porridge to that. The more elaborate way, which is done by some chicken rice stalls, is to serve dressed hot porridge with steamed chicken. In the 1990s, I came across a particularly tasty version of this at a Petaling Street road-side stall in Kuala Lumpur, Malaysia. I thought it was the best-tasting *kai chok* ever. Sadly, when I went in search of it some 10 years ago, Petaling Street had changed beyond recognition and the street stall had disappeared.

White short-grain rice 200 g (7 oz / 1 cup)

White glutinous rice 50 g (1²/₃ oz / ¹/₄ cup)

Sesame oil 1 Tbsp

Ginger 3 thin slices, finely shredded

Chicken stock (page 80) 250 ml (8 fl oz / 1 cup)

Salt 1 tsp

Light soy sauce 1 Tbsp

Steamed chicken, Singapore-style (page 52)

GARNISHING

Sesame oil 1 Tbsp

Light soy sauce 1 Tbsp

Chopped spring onion

Chopped coriander leaves

1. Cook short-grain rice and glutinous rice using your preferred method to get a thick smooth porridge.

2. In a large pot, heat sesame oil and fry ginger for a few minutes. Add chicken stock, salt and light soy sauce and bring to the boil. Add porridge to stock and return to the boil.

3. Prepare garnishing by mixing sesame oil and light soy sauce in a bowl. Garnish each bowl of rice porridge with a teaspoon of the mixture and some spring onion and coriander leaves.

4. Serve porridge with a dish of chopped steamed chicken on the side. Garnish chicken with a generous drizzle of sesame oil and light soy sauce, chopped spring onion and coriander leaves.

Arroz Caldo (filipino rice soup)

This is Filipino chicken rice porridge by its Spanish name which means "rice soup". This Filipino rice porridge resembles Thai porridge in flavour but where the Thais add vinegar, *arroz caldo* has calamansi lime juice. (The resulting flavour is remarkably like a Mexican chickpea chicken soup that I once had in Mexico City!) Calamansi lime is a small, very juicy and very sour lime indigenous to the Philippines. While the Thais spice their rice porridge with chopped chillies, this porridge is spiced with plenty of ground black pepper.

White short-grain rice *200 g (7 oz / 1 cup)*

White glutinous rice *50 g (1²/₃ oz / ¹/₄ cup)*

CHICKEN SOUP

Chicken *500 g (1 lb 1¹/₂ oz)*

Chicken bones *500 g (1 lb 1¹/₂ oz)*

Onion *50 g (1²/₃ oz), peeled and quartered*

Tomatoes *100 g (3¹/₂ oz), quartered*

Garlic *4 cloves, peeled and smashed*

Fish sauce *2 Tbsp*

Cracked black peppercorns *¹/₂ Tbsp*

Water *2.5 litres (80 fl oz / 10 cups)*

Coriander leaves *1 small bunch*

Spring onions *3*

Chinese celery *1 small bunch*

GARNISHING

Chopped spring onion

Chopped coriander leaves

Fish sauce

Ground black pepper

Calamansi lime halves

1. Put all the ingredients for chicken soup into a stock pot and bring to the boil. Skim off the scum that rises to the top, turn down heat and simmer for 45 minutes.

2. Remove chicken when it is cooked. Cool and shred meat. Set meat aside in a covered bowl to prevent it from drying out or immerse meat in some stock. Return bones to the stock pot and simmer for another 30 minutes. Strain stock and discard solids.

3. Cook short-grain and glutinous rice using your preferred method into a soft porridge.

4. To serve the rice soup, dish porridge out into bowls and stir in a generous helping of hot soup.

5. Garnish with shredded chicken, chopped spring onion, coriander leaves, a drizzle of fish sauce, ground black pepper and lime halves to taste. Serve with more fish sauce on the side.

TEOCHEW FISH PORRIDGE

This Teochew porridge is more like a soft-cooked rice in fish soup than a thick porridge cooked with slices of fish, which is another way of making fish porridge. It is a good way to use up leftover boiled rice. Just add some water to the rice and boil till you get a soft granular porridge. Be generous with the ginger and Chinese celery when making the fish soup. Add vinegar to get a Thai rice soup and lime juice to get a Filipino rice soup.

White long-grain rice *250 g (9 oz / 1¼ cups)*

Ginger *8 thin slices, finely shredded*

Boneless fish *500 g (1 lb 1½ oz), thickly sliced*

FISH SOUP

Cooking oil *1 Tbsp*

Garlic *2 cloves, peeled and chopped*

Ginger *1 large thumb-size piece, peeled and smashed*

Water *1 litre (32 fl oz / 4 cups)*

Fresh fish bones and trimmings *500 g (1 lb 1½ oz)*

Chinese celery *1 large bunch*

Salt *1 tsp*

Light soy sauce *1 Tbsp*

GARNISHING

Chopped coriander leaves

Chopped spring onion)

Chopped Chinese celery

Fried garlic *(page 37) to taste*

CONDIMENTS

Light soy sauce

Chopped red chillies (optional)

Ground white/black pepper (optional)

Calamansi lime halves (optional)

White vinegar (optional)

1. Cook rice into a soft, granular porridge or very soft rice using your preferred method.

2. Prepare fish soup. Heat oil and fry garlic and ginger in a large pot till garlic is golden brown. Add water, fish bones and trimmings, and all other ingredients for fish soup and bring to the boil. Turn down heat and simmer for 30 minutes. Strain and discard solids.

3. To make fish porridge, return fish soup to the boil. Add shredded ginger, fish slices and soft rice and return to the boil.

4. Garnish and serve rice soup with chopped coriander leaves, spring onion, Chinese celery and fried garlic.

5. Serve individual saucers of light soy sauce with or without chillies with the rice soup. If Thai or Filipino fish porridge is preferred, also serve with white vinegar or lime halves.

Korean Shellfish Porridge

Any kind of shellfish may be used for this dish but the ones where the meat is easily extracted such as scallops or clams are best. If using live shellfish such as clams, the sand in them needs to be cleaned out. However, I have never had any success with the regularly recommended method of soaking shellfish in several changes of cold water for several hours to get rid of the grit. The method that works for me is to lightly boil the shellfish in water and let the grit settle to the bottom of the pot. It is astonishing the amount of grit there is.

White short-grain rice 250 g (9 oz / 1¼ cups)

Water 750 ml (24 fl oz / 3 cups)

Live shellfish 1 kg (2 lb 3 oz)

Sesame oil 1 Tbsp

Ginger 6 slices, finely shredded

Chopped garlic 1 tsp

Chopped spring onion 1 Tbsp

Salt to taste

Korean sesame salt (page 34)

GARNISHING

Chopped spring onion

Chopped coriander leaves

1. Cook rice into a thick rice porridge using your preferred method.

2. In a pot, bring the water to the boil. Add cleaned shellfish and return water to the boil. Stir and boil for 5 minutes. Turn off heat, cover pot and let shellfish cook in the residual heat. When shellfish is cool enough to handle, extract meat and swish it in some of the shellfish stock. Drain and set aside shellfish. Cover to avoid drying out. Reserve stock.

3. To get grit-free shellfish stock, leave stock for at least 30 minutes to let grit settle to the bottom of the pot. Carefully spoon out the stock without stirring up the grit. Discard the bottom one-third of the stock with the sand.

4. In a saucepan, heat sesame oil and add ginger, garlic and spring onion and fry for 1 minute without browning garlic. Add stock, salt and porridge and return to the boil before putting in shellfish.

5. Dish out and sprinkle sesame salt to taste. Garnish with some chopped spring onion and coriander leaves.

6. Serve porridge hot with some kimchi.

Korean Prawn Porridge

South Korean markets are full of all kinds of very fresh seafood which accounts for the delicate rather than robust flavour of this prawn (shrimp) porridge. Most seafood do not take kindly to the long boiling needed to make porridge, so cook the porridge first. The prawns can be kept whole or chopped coarsely.

White short-grain rice 250 g (9 oz / 1¹/₄ cups)

Sesame oil 1 Tbsp

Ginger 6 slices, finely shredded

Garlic 1 clove, peeled and finely chopped

Shelled prawns 300 g (11 oz)

Salt 1 tsp

Light soy sauce 1 Tbsp

GARNISHING

Chopped spring onion

Shredded perilla leaf

Korean sesame salt (page 34)

1. Cook rice using your preferred method to get a smooth thick porridge.
2. Heat sesame oil in a pot and fry ginger strips, garlic and prawns together till prawns begin to change colour.
3. Add porridge, salt and soy sauce and bring to the boil.
4. Garnish with chopped spring onion or shredded perilla leaf and sesame salt to taste. Serve hot.

Korean Kimchi Rice Soup

White short-grain rice 250 g (9 oz / 1¹/₄ cups)

KIMCHI SOUP

Kimchi with pickling liquid 500 ml (16 fl oz / 2 cups), cut into pieces

Pork/chicken/beef stock 750 ml (24 fl oz / 3 cups)

Toenjang or brown miso 1 tsp

Garlic 2 cloves, peeled and finely chopped

Soft tofu 200 g (7 oz), cubed

Salt ¹/₂ tsp

1. Cook rice using your preferred method until rice is soft.
2. Combine kimchi with pickling liquid, stock, toenjang or miso and garlic in a saucepan and bring to the boil. Add tofu and salt to taste.
3. Spoon rice into individual serving bowls and ladle soup over. Serve hot.

PENANG OYSTER PORRIDGE

In the days before globalised trade, dried oysters were considered a luxury and something of a treat. Oyster porridge was made when the cook was feeling extravagant, wanted something that went a long way and yet was easy to prepare. Anyone who finds fresh seafood strong-tasting will find dried seafood even more so. When it comes to dried seafood such as oysters and prawns, a little goes a long way. The porridge can be made more delicate by not boiling the oysters for too long in the porridge or by cutting down on the number of oysters. The addition of minced pork or chicken improves the flavour of the porridge. So does serving it Thai-style with cur bird's eye chillies and vinegar or Flilpino-style with calamansi lime juice and ground black pepper.

Long-grain rice 250 g (9 oz / 1¼ cups)

Dried oysters 4–6, rinsed

Old ginger 1 large thumb-size piece, peeled and smashed

Chinese celery 1 bunch, chopped

Minced pork/chicken 100 g (3½ oz)

Salt 1 tsp

Light soy sauce 1 Tbsp

Garlic oil (page 37) 2 tsp

GARNISHING

Garlic oil (page 37)

Salted Tientsin cabbage (tang chye)

Chopped spring onion

Ground black/white pepper

1. Cook rice porridge with dried oysters, ginger and celery using your preferred method to your preferred consistency. Alternatively, add the oysters only when the rice porridge is half-cooked.

2. Stir minced meat, salt, light soy sauce and garlic oil into the hot porridge and continue simmering till meat is cooked.

3. Serve porridge hot with a light garnish of garlic oil, salted Tientsin cabbage, chopped spring onion and a sprinkling of ground pepper.

VIETNAMESE RICE PORRIDGE WITH GARLIC PORK

While garlic and rice porridge is an unbeatable combination in many Southeast Asian rice porridges, this one has the added flavour of green onion oil, a Vietnamese specialty. Instead of pork, the rice porridge can be made with chicken, shelled prawns or fish slices prepared the same way as pork.

Long-grain rice 250 g (9 oz / 1¹/₄ cups)

Pork/chicken/fish/shelled prawns 200 g (7 oz), cut into strips or slices

Fish sauce 2 Tbsp

Sugar 2 tsp

Cooking oil 2 Tbsp

Chopped garlic 2 Tbsp

GREEN ONION OIL

Cooking oil 60 ml (2 fl oz / ¹/₄ cup)

Thinly sliced spring onions ¹/₄ cup

NUOC CHAM

Fish sauce 2 Tbsp

Pounded garlic ¹/₂ Tbsp

Pounded red bird's eye chillies 1 Tbsp

Lime juice 2 Tbsp

Sugar 1 tsp

GARNISHING

Chopped spring onions

Coriander leaves

1. Cook rice using your preferred method to get a porridge that is somewhat watery.

2. Marinate meat/seafood with fish sauce and sugar.

3. To make green onion oil, heat oil in a wok and fry spring onions till fragrant and whites of spring onions have turned golden brown. Turn off heat just before spring onions are golden brown or it will turn too dark in the residual heat. Scoop out into a bowl and set aside.

4. In the same wok, heat 2 Tbsp oil and add garlic. Just as the garlic begins to brown, add seasoned meat/seafood and stir-fry till meat/seafood is just cooked. Do not burn garlic or overcook seafood. Timing is important. One way to slow down the browning of garlic is to sprinkle some water into the pan.

5. To make nuoc cham, combine all ingredients together in a small jar and shake well to dissolve sugar. Adjust flavour to taste.

6. Just before serving porridge, return porridge to the boil. Add meat/seafood and heat it up again especially if meat/seafood has cooled down.

7. Garnish with a light sprinkling of chopped spring onions, coriander leaves and a dash of green onion oil, with individual dip saucers of nuoc cham.

EBI ZONI (RICE CAKE IN PRAWN SOUP)

This rice soup is often prepared as part of the Japanese New Year celebrations because the rice consists of a piece of mochi, a glutinous rice cake that is a traditional Japanese New Year treat. Although most think of mochi as a sweet, mochi is also eaten in a savoury soup. Traditionally, the mochi is grilled on a stick over hot coals to soften the hard dried mochi before it is added to the soup. However, as the mochi is frozen in this case, grilling is not necessary. Using a Japanese soup concentrate simplifies the preparation but the MSG flavour in these commercial soup concentrates may be too strong for some people. If so, make your own soup.

Dried shiitake mushrooms 6, *softened in water*

Prawns 6, *shelled leaving tails intact, shells reserved for making soup*

Chrysanthemum leaves *1 large bunch*

Mochi (page 206) 6, *each about 100 g (3¹/₂ oz)*

SOUP

Konbu (kelp) 20-cm (8-in) long *piece, about 10 g (¹/₃ oz), wiped with damp towel*

Water *1 litre (32 fl oz / 4 cups)*

Prawn (shrimp) shells and heads 6

Ginger *1 thumb-size piece, peeled and smashed*

Light soy sauce *2 Tbsp*

1. Prepare soup at least 5 hours in advance. With a pair of scissors, make cuts along both sides of the sheet of konbu but without cutting it right through. Put konbu and water in a saucepan and leave it to soak for 5 hours.

2. Bring konbu and water to the boil. Just as bubbles start to roll up, take out konbu and add prawn shells and heads and ginger.

3. Bring to the boil and simmer for 1 minute. Turn off heat and strain off solids. Stir in light soy sauce.

4. Trim stems off softened mushrooms and cut a pattern on the top of caps.

5. Return soup to the boil and add mushrooms. Simmer for 5 minutes, then add prawns. When prawns begin to change colour, stir in chrysanthemum leaves, and lastly mochi. When mochi softens, turn off heat.

6. Serve immediately in individual bowls.

BARLEY AND RICE, JAPANESE-STYLE

Barley and rice is a typical East Asian combination but the miso flavouring makes this one Japanese-style. Substitute the miso with spicy Korean *toenjang* and you get Korean-style barley and rice. Because rice with mixed grain is usually cooked till the harder grain is soft, any mixed grain rice will usually come out more like porridge because rice usually softens fairly quickly. Called *okayu* in Japanese, porridge is often eaten for breakfast with some pickles and perhaps soft tofu seasoned lightly with soy sauce. More elaborate side dishes would be grilled fish or meat. Garnish with chopped spring onions if perilla leaves are not available.

White short-grain rice *250 g (9 oz / 1¹/₄ cups)*

Pearl barley *100 g (3¹/₂ oz / ¹/₂ cup), soaked 1 hour*

Water *1 litre (32 fl oz / 4 cups)*

Pale miso *1 Tbsp*

Pickled young ginger *6 thin slices, finely shredded*

Spring onion *1, chopped*

Japanese sesame salt (page 34)

1. Cook rice and barley together in the water till barley is soft using the mixed grain setting if your rice cooker has one. Add more water if needed to soften barley. Alternatively, boil rice and barley on the stove top or overnight in a slow cooker.

2. When barley is soft, stir in miso, pickled ginger and chopped spring onion.

3. Garnish with a sprinkling of sesame salt and serve porridge hot with Japanese-style pickles.

THAI SEAFOOD RICE SOUP

In typical Thai fashion, this rice soup is flavoured with chillies, fish sauce and fresh herbs. However, these flavourings can be served up as condiments for guests to help themselves to whatever takes their fancy. The bare minimum, however, would be some chillies and lime juice. Use whatever seafood is available, but there should be some trimmings for making the stock. If using live shellfish, it should be lightly boiled and the meat extracted first (page 177). Prawns can be left in their shells but crabs should be partially shelled and halved. The shells can be used for stock.

Long-grain rice *250 g (9 oz / 1¹/₄ cups)*

Assorted seafood *1 kg (2 lb 3 oz)*

Chicken stock (page 80) *1 litre (32 fl oz / 4 cups)*

Garlic oil (page 37) *to taste*

Fried garlic (page 37) *to taste*

Fish sauce *to taste*

SEAFOOD STOCK

Seafood trimmings from cleaning seafood

Water *1 litre (32 fl oz / 4 cups)*

Garlic *1 head, peeled and smashed*

Chinese celery *1 large bunch*

Coriander leaves *1 large bunch*

Salt *1 tsp*

Fresh red bird's eye chillies *3*

White vinegar *1 Tbsp*

Fish sauce *2 Tbsp*

GARNISHING

Chopped coriander leaves

Chopped spring onion

Chopped Chinese celery

Whole or chopped basil leaves

Fried garlic (page 37)

Garlic oil (page 37)

CONDIMENTS

Fish sauce

Large lime wedges

Chopped bird's eye chillies

1. Cook rice using your preferred method to get a soft rice. The rice should not be watery.

2. Clean seafood before preparing stock. Squid should have ink sacks removed. Prawns may be shelled or not. If prawns are shelled, make a slit down the middle to remove the dirt track. Crabs should be scrubbed very clean. Remove top shell of crabs and use for stock. Halve or quarter crabs. Bone fish and keep trimmings for stock.

3. Put all ingredients for seafood stock with seafood trimmings into a large pot and bring to the boil. Turn down heat and simmer for 30 minutes. Strain stock and discard solids. If you have blanched mussels or clams in the boiling stock, let stock sit for 30 minutes or more to allow any grit to settle to the bottom. Discard last 2-cm (1-in) of stock in the pot. Ladle out stock carefully to avoid stirring up grit.

4. Mix chicken and seafood stock. Add some garlic oil and fried garlic and bring to the boil. Add fish sauce to taste. Add trimmed seafood to boiling stock and boil till seafood changes colour.

5. To serve rice soup, spoon a serving of rice into a soup bowl and ladle seafood soup over. Garnish with coriander leaves, spring onion, Chinese celery, basil leaves, fried garlic and a drizzle of garlic oil.

6. Serve immediately with individual dip saucers of fish sauce, lime wedges and chillies.

INDONESIAN BUBUR AYAM (INDONESIAN CHICKEN PORRIDGE)

This is another typical Southeast Asian breakfast available as street food in Indonesia. This dish can be a rice porridge or a rice soup depending on preference, so cook the rice accordingly. I like it as a rice soup. It is equally tasty made with either long- or short-grain rice. The soup is especially delicious because of the root herbs in it and because it is only mildly spicy.

White long- or short-grain rice
    250 g (9 oz / 1 1/4 cups)
Cooking oil 2 Tbsp
Salt 1/2 tsp

CHICKEN STOCK
Chicken 500 g (1 lb 1 1/2 oz),
    chopped into 4 pieces
Lemon grass 1 stalk, smashed
Water 1.5 litres (48 fl oz / 6 cups)
Salt 1 tsp

SPICE PASTE
Shallots 100 g (3 1/2 oz), peeled
Garlic 6 cloves, peeled
Galangal 4 slices, peeled
Turmeric 1 small knob, peeled
Dried chillies 6, seeded and
    soaked in water to soften
Candlenuts 3
Water 2 Tbsp

GARNISHING
Chopped coriander leaves
Chopped Chinese celery
Chopped spring onions
Fried shallots (page 37)

CONDIMENT
Kicap manis (Indonesian dark soy
    sauce)
Chopped red chillies

1. Cook rice using your preferred method to get a soft rice or thick porridge according to your preference.

2. To make chicken stock, put chicken, lemon grass, water and salt into a stock pot and bring to the boil. Skim off any scum that rises to the top. Turn down heat and simmer for 30 minutes. Remove pieces of chicken, cool and shred meat. Set aside in a covered bowl to prevent meat from drying out. Return bones to the stock and simmer for another 30 minutes. Strain and discard solids.

3. To make spice paste, put all ingredients into a food processor and blend to a fine paste. Heat 2 Tbsp oil in a wok and fry spice paste till fragrant and oil surfaces. Stir in shredded chicken and 1/2 tsp salt. Add 60 ml (2 fl oz / 1/4 cup) stock and bring to the boil. Adjust seasoning to taste.

4. To serve, put porridge into a individual soup bowl. Add a generous serving of chicken and sauce and top with some hot chicken stock.

5. Garnish to taste and serve with a condiment of kicap manis and chopped chillies in individual dip saucers.

LOBSTER RICE SOUP

In 2009, some friends introduced me to this high-end porridge that was the specialty of a seafood restaurant in Sembawang in north-western Singapore. The base of this rice soup with spiny lobsters is a chicken stock. If farmed spiny lobsters are not available, substitute with any other lobster or crab claws. Whether lobster or crab claws, the shellfish has to be cracked or chopped in a way that allows the flesh to be picked out. Small spiny lobsters can be chopped in half lengthwise but something large like a Maine lobster should be first boiled till it turns red and the meat extracted and cut into pieces. The shell can be further boiled for stock to add to the chicken stock.

Long-grain rice 250 g (9 oz / 1¼ cups)

Cooking oil 2 Tbsp

Ginger 8 slices, finely shredded

Garlic 2 cloves, peeled and finely chopped

Chicken stock (page 80) 2 litres (64 fl oz / 8 cups)

Salt 1½ tsp

Lobster 200–300 g (7–11 oz) per person, scrubbed clean

Chopped spring onion

1. Cook rice using your preferred method to get a very soft rice.

2. Heat oil in a large pot and fry ginger and garlic till brown, then pour in chicken stock. Add salt and bring to the boil before adding soft rice. Return stock to the boil.

3. When stock is boiling again, add prepared lobster and continue boiling till lobster turns red. Turn off heat and garnish with spring onion.

4. Serve immediately in a large soup tureen.

Nasi Rawon

This East Javanese speciality is an unusual-looking rice soup which lovers of *buah keluak* (Indonesian black nut) will recognise immediately. It has a distinctive black colour from the seeds of the *kepayang* (*Pangium edule*), a tropical tree native to Indonesia, Malaysia and Papua New Guinea. Called *keluak* in Malay and *kluwak* in Indonesian, the soft, fleshy oily meat that is extracted from the hard-shelled seeds is cooked into a number of iconic dishes of which *nasi rawon* is one. Preparing *buah keluak* is a long-winded process that starts when the seeds are plucked. They contain poisonous hydrocyanic acid which must be neutralised before the seeds are sold, a process that involves boiling and pickling in ashes. The cook preparing *buah keluak* then has to soak the seeds for several days, scrub them clean and crack the seeds open. Thankfully, shelled *keluak* can be bought from certain wet markets in Singapore such as Tekka and Geylang Serai. If abroad, look for *keluak* in stores patronised by Indonesian Chinese. For instance, it can be found in Amsterdam which has a large community of Indonesian Chinese. Oxtail or shin beef makes a tasty substitute for brisket. If preferred, the rice can be firm rather than a soft rice or porridge. If so, you might want to cook the beef into a thicker stew rather than a soup. In East Java, *nasi rawon* is served with raw, newly sprouted mung beans which have a nutty flavour rather than the more "green" taste of Singapore bean sprouts. The *keluak* soup is also lighter because the nut is used more sparingly. My *rawon* is darker because I love the flavour of *keluak*!

Long-grain rice 400 g (14¹/₃ oz / 2 cups)

Raw/blanched soy/mung bean sprouts 150 g (5¹/₃ oz)

Salted eggs 3, cleaned, boiled, shelled and cut into wedges

Lime halves

BEEF BRISKET IN BUAH KELUAK SOUP

Buah keluak (Indonesian black nut) meat 100 g (3¹/₂ oz)

Tamarind pulp 50 g (1²/₃ oz)

Water 1.5 litres (48 fl oz / 6 cups)

Cooking oil 3 Tbsp

Lemon grass 1 stalk, bruised

Beef brisket 750 g (1 lb 11 oz), cut into cubes

Salt 1¹/₂ tsp

Kaffir lime leaves 3

SPICE PASTE

Shallots 75 g (2¹/₂ oz)

Garlic 25 g (1 oz)

Dried chillies 30 g (1 oz), seeded and softened

Candlenuts 3

Ground coriander 2 tsp

Turmeric 1 thumb-size knob, peeled

Galangal 1 thumb-size knob, peeled

Dried prawn (shrimp) paste (belacan) 1 tsp

Water 2 Tbsp

CONDIMENT

Sambal belacan (page 59)

1. Blend together ingredients for spice paste in a food processor till fine.

2. Pick through shelled *buah keluak* meat to remove any shell splinters. Rinse quickly under a tap, then pound nut meat in a mortar and pestle to a smooth paste. Alternatively, blend with some water to get a smooth paste.

3. Mix tamarind pulp with 500 ml (16 fl oz / 2 cups) water and strain away solids.

4. Heat oil in a pot and fry bruised lemon grass and ground spice paste till fragrant. Add beef, salt, pounded nut meat, tamarind juice and remaining 1 litre (32 fl oz / 4 cups) water and bring to the boil. Turn down heat and simmer till beef is tender and liquid reduced to a rich, thick soup or stew if it is to be eaten with firm rice.

5. In the last 5 minutes of stewing, bruise kaffir lime leaves and add to stew. *Buah keluak* tastes better if allowed to age for several hours or overnight.

6. Cook rice using your preferred method to your preferred texture.

7. To serve, heap a helping of raw or blanched bean sprouts in a soup plate with rice. Ladle soup and beef on rice, garnish with a wedge of salted egg and serve hot with sambal *belacan* and lime halves.

Mujadara (west asian lentil porridge)

This is unusual in being either a porridge or a pilaf depending who you are cooking for. Your family may get it as a porridge while your guests are served pilaf. If making it as a pilaf, pre-soak or pre-cook the lentils so that it cooks at the same rate as rice. If made into porridge as in this instance, the rice and lentils are boiled together till, like Japanese *okayu*, the harder ingredients are soft. This porridge can also be made with leftover rice.

Brown lentils *100 g (3¹/₂ oz / ¹/₂ cup), soaked in cold water for 1 hour*

Water *2 litres (64 fl oz / 8 cups)*

Long-grain rice *400 g (14¹/₃ oz / 2 cups)*

Olive oil *2 Tbsp*

Onion *25 g (1 oz), peeled and chopped*

Garlic *2 cloves, peeled and chopped*

Tomatoes *100 g (3¹/₂ oz), chopped*

Ground turmeric *¹/₄ tsp*

Salt *1¹/₂ tsp*

Ground cumin *¹/₄ tsp*

GARNISHING

Chopped parsley/mint/coriander leaves

1. Boil lentils first in the water and skim off any scum that rises to the top. When water is scum-free, add rice and bring to the boil. Turn down heat and simmer till lentils are soft.

2. Heat olive oil in a frying pan and fry onion and garlic till fragrant. Add tomatoes, ground turmeric, salt and ground cumin and cook till tomatoes begin to get mushy. Pour contents of pan into porridge and continue boiling porridge for another 5 minutes.

3 Serve porridge with some pickles (page 57–58) and kebabs (page 44–46) or roast meat.

Rice—short-grain, long-grain and glutinous—is the basic ingredient in many Asian desserts, a large number of which are basically sweet porridges or puddings. These are usually made by boiling one or a combination of the three types of rice into a porridge which is then flavoured with various types of indigenous sugars such as coconut or date palm sugar and nuts and dried fruit added or used as garnishing. Short-grain and white glutinous rice gives porridge a thicker, smoother mouth-feel, and long-grain a lighter one. Which is preferable is a matter of cultural as well as personal preference. However, when it comes to making rice cakes, the right kind of rice must be used. This is almost invariably cooked white glutinous rice although there is also black glutinous rice, a much more chewy rice because it is a whole grain rice. Semi-cooked or cooked white glutinous rice is made into sweet treats as well as savoury snacks wrapped in banana or bamboo leaf or moulded. Being very sticky, cooked glutinous rice has to be covered with something to keep the pieces of rice cake separate from each other. The famous Japanese dessert called mochi which is made with cooked glutinous rice pounded to a soft dough is covered with toasted soy bean flour (*kinako*). The Indonesian-Malay rice cake called *kuih lopes* is covered with grated coconut and syrup.

RICE DESSERTS AND RICE SNACKS

Today, many rice-based desserts are made with readily-available rice flour whereas in the past, hard-working cooks had to grind their own rice flour in a domestic-size stone mill. Naturally, many desserts came to be made with cooked rice rather than rice flour. In some desserts, they start as rice grains but are prepared in such a way that the rice becomes a cream such as *muhallabia* or a smooth rice dough such as mochi.

Traditional rice cake-making starts with cooking and controlling the texture of the white glutinous rice by adjusting the amount of water in it.

The consistency of cooked glutinous rice varies from very firm and sticky to very soft and very sticky. For cakes, a consistency that allows easy shaping of the rice is what to aim for although even here, cooks can have their own preferences. The marvellous thing is that white glutinous rice can be steamed to exactly the consistency that you enjoy or through a combination of "boiling and then steaming" (page 25). Steaming is the easier way to prepare white glutinous rice for making a rice cake because you can check how the rice is doing and vary the length of steaming and the amount of water or coconut milk sprinkled on the rice to get your preferred texture. However, note that glutinous rice stiffens when it cools—and that some rice cakes need to be re-steamed or boiled again after they are wrapped, so the original semi-cooked texture may not matter in some preparations. Although the recipes for these rice cakes and dumplings suggest boiling the rice or boiling and steaming the rice or just boiling, the rice can also be just steamed using the generic directions for steaming rice (page 24). (By the way, the same steps can be followed for steaming long- or short-grain rice.)

Only in the recipes for puddings is the rice just boiled till creamy. One thing to note is that sugar should never be added to the rice before it is your preferred consistency. Rice must also not be boiled with milk alone, as it will not soften nicely into porridge. Boil the rice with water first till it is near or at the consistency you want before adding milk or sugar. Coconut cream should also not be boiled for too long or the porridge will taste oily.

RICE DESSERTS AND RICE SNACKS

KHEER (INDIAN RICE PUDDING)

Recently, I came across a website <http://www.indianzone.com> that claimed that *kheer* or Indian rice pudding originated in Orissa, a state on the east coast of the Indian subcontinent. Whatever its origins in India, *kheer* is one of the best known of Indian desserts. The pudding can be served warm or cold.

Long-grain rice *100 g (3¹/₂ oz / ¹/₂ cup), soaked 1 hour*
Milk *625 ml (20 fl oz / 2¹/₂ cups)*
Water *250 ml (8 fl oz 1 cup)*
Sugar *65 g (2¹/₂ oz / ¹/₃ cup)*
Cream *60 ml (2 fl oz / ¹/₄ cup)*
Raisins (optional) *¹/₄ cup*
Rose water *¹/₂ Tbsp*

GARNISHING

Pistachios, chopped or thinly sliced

1. Cook rice, 125 ml (4 fl oz / ¹/₂ cup) milk and water to a thick porridge in a pot, taking care not to burn the bottom. Add remainder of milk only when rice is soft and broken up and consistency is what you like.

2. Stir in sugar and return to the boil to dissolve sugar. Turn off heat and add cream and raisins, if using. Add rose water last and mix well.

3. Serve *kheer* warm or cold. Rice pudding thickens when cold. If so, thin with some warm milk. Before serving, garnish with pistachios.

CHEPI KHEER (INDIAN RICE PUDDING WITH TURMERIC LEAF)

This *kheer* is very different from the usual Indian rice puddings because it has coconut cream rather than milk and palm sugar instead of white sugar. If you have a turmeric plant, you can vary Indian-style rice puddings with a couple of fresh turmeric leaves cooked with the rice. If not, flavour and also colour it with some ground fresh turmeric or a pinch of ground turmeric powder. In Southeast and South Asia, fresh turmeric leaves are sold in wet markets as a herb.

Palm sugar *150 g (5¹/₃ oz), grated*
Water *875 ml (28 fl oz / 3¹/₂ cups)*
Long-/short-grain rice *100 g (3¹/₂ oz / ¹/₂ cup), soaked 1 hour*
Turmeric leaves *2, crushed*
Coconut cream *125 ml (4 fl oz / ¹/₂ cup)*

1. Boil palm sugar in 125 ml (4 fl oz / ¹/₂ cup) water and sieve it. Discard any solids. Set aside.

2. Cook rice and crushed turmeric leaves in remaining water to a thick porridge in a pot, taking care not to burn the bottom. Remove turmeric leaves and stir in coconut cream and palm sugar syrup to taste.

3. Return to the boil and turn off heat.

4. Serve *kheer* warm.

Zard Pulao (sweet pilaf)

This sweet rice that a Pakistani friend makes is quite unlike the more usual pudding-like *kheer*. This one is more like a soft rice with syrup and fruit and nuts in it. There is a somewhat similar recipe in *Nuskha-e-Shahjahani: Pulaos From the Royal Kitchens of Shah Jahan*.

Sugar 65 g (2¹/₂ oz / ¹/₃ cup)

Water 625 ml (20 fl oz / 2¹/₂ cups)

Saffron ¹/₂ tsp

Ghee 1 Tbsp

Long-grain rice 100 g (3¹/₂ oz / ¹/₂ cup), soaked 1 hour

Raisins ¹/₄ cup

Almonds ¹/₄ cup, chopped

Pistachios ¹/₄ cup, chopped

1. Boil sugar with 125 ml (4 fl oz / ¹/₂ cup) water. Dissolve saffron in the syrup and stir in ghee.

2. Cook rice with remaining water using your preferred method to get a very soft rice.

3. When rice is done, pour syrup on rice and stir in raisins, almonds and pistachios.

4. Serve warm.

Sweet Kheeri Bhaat (sri lankan coconut rice pudding)

This sweet rice can be cooked into a soft rice or into a thick porridge depending on preference. It can also be made with short-grain rice if a more sticky pudding is preferred. This amount of water will produce a thick porridge. Do not add the sugar before the rice is soft or the rice may not soften properly. If using packaged coconut cream, dilute it with water to get coconut milk.

Long-grain rice 100 g (3¹/₂ oz / ¹/₂ cup), soaked 1 hour

Cinnamon stick 6-cm (2¹/₂-in)

Water 500 ml (16 fl oz / 2 cups)

Salt ¹/₄ tsp

Grated palm sugar ¹/₂ cup

Coconut milk 250 ml (8 fl oz / 1 cup)

GARNISHING

Fresh shredded coconut 1 Tbsp

1. Combine rice, cinnamon stick and water and cook rice to a thick porridge using your preferred method.

2. Stir in salt and palm sugar and cook till the sugar dissolves. Stir in coconut milk last and simmer for 2 minutes.

3. Pour into a large bowl and garnish with some shredded coconut. Serve warm.

MUHALLABIA (LEBANESE/SYRIAN RICE PUDDING)

In Al-Hamidiyeh Souk in Old Damascus at the famous Bakdash ice cream shop (the ice cream was fantastic!), I came across *muhallabia* being made: one of the staff was busy pouring a large pot of the very liquid mixture into little plastic bowls. Although *muhallabia* was once made with rice or ground rice, these days, there are gelling ingredients added. The texture of the Bakdash *muhallabia* did not feel like it was just rice flour, milk and sugar. My *muhallabia* is made with rice but once the rice is porridge, it is ground with a stick blender till smooth. Flavour with rose or orange flower water or a combination for that very West Asian flavour. Substitute with a few drops of rose essence if orange flower water or rose water is not available. Stir in the flavouring only when the cooking is done.

Long-grain rice *100 g (3¹/₂ oz / ¹/₂ cup), soaked 1 hour*

Water *250 ml (8 fl oz / 1 cup)*

Milk *250 ml (8 fl oz / 1 cup)*

Sugar *65 g (2¹/₂ oz / 1/³ cup) or more to taste*

Cream (optional) *60 ml (2 fl oz / ¹/₄ cup)*

Rose water/orange flower water *1 Tbsp*

GARNISHING

Toasted chopped pistachios/ almond slivers

1. Cook rice with water either in a pot on a stove top or in your rice cooker using the porridge setting. When porridge is thick, blend it with a stick blender to a smooth cream.

2. Stir in milk and sugar and return to the boil. Simmer for 5 minutes. Turn off heat when sugar has dissolved. Stir in cream, if using, and flower water.

3. The hot pudding can be divided into individual bowls or into one large bowl to cool down. Refrigerate if possible.

4. Before serving, garnish with a sprinkling of toasted chopped nuts.

Note:

To do a chunky muhallabia, *use the same quantities as above, but omit the blending of the porridge. Add some thinly sliced figs when the rice is a thick porridge and cook for another 5 minutes before you add the milk. Stir in ¹/₄ cup ground almonds with the milk and sugar.*

WEST ASIAN SWEET RICE WITH DATES

This sweet rice is eaten as a snack or to break the fast during the month of Ramadan when it is traditional to break the fast at sunset with some dates and very light food such as a porridge. Breaking the fast with dates is considered especially holy because the Prophet Muhammad did the same. To introduce some tang to this sweet rice, you might want to add some pomegranate molasses too. Look for bottled date syrup in Middle Eastern and South Asian stores.

Long-grain rice *200 g (7 oz / 1 cup)*

Salt *¹/₂ tsp*

Water *1.5 litres (48 fl oz / 6 cups)*

Date syrup *2 Tbsp*

Pomegranate molasses (optional) *2 tsp*

Ghee *2 Tbsp*

Almond slivers *¹/₂ cup*

Raisins *¹/₄ cup*

Dates *¹/₂–1 cup, chopped*

Ground cinnamon *¹/₄ tsp*

Ground cloves *a pinch*

Ground cardamom *a large pinch*

1. Bring rice, salt and water to the boil in a large covered pot. Once it reaches a rapid boil, uncover pot and start timing the boiling. Keep it at a rapid boil for 5 minutes.

2. Turn off heat, pour rice into a large sieve and rinse rice thoroughly in cold water. Drain rice well and stir date syrup and pomegranate molasses, if using, into the rice.

3. Heat ghee in a frying pan and brown almond slivers. Add dried fruit and spices, mix well and turn off heat.

4. Pre-heat oven to 160°C (325°F).

5. Divide rice and fruit-nut mixture into 2 or 3 equal portions and layer in a small casserole. Layer rice and fruit-nut mixture starting with rice and ending with a top layer of fruit-nut mixture. (The number of layers will depend on the size and depth of your casserole.) Cover top with a layer of several sheets of paper towels and put the lid on.

6. Bake in the oven for 20 minutes till rice is tender. Serve warm.

VIETNAMESE GLUTINOUS RICE CAKES WITH SWEET BEAN PASTE

Makes 12–16 pieces

The Vietnamese pair glutinous rice with sweet bean paste to make this dessert. This rice cake can be served in a number of pretty ways if you have the time for it. Blanched banana leaves and even large pandan (screwpine) leaves can be cut and formed into small cases to hold the cakes. Large pandan leaves can also be formed into cones and the rice and bean paste stuffed into the cone. Or do it the modern way and use mini paper cupcake cases to hold the cakes. The quickest way, of course, is to press the rice into a 13 x 18-cm (5 x 7-in) glass or metal tray, smooth the filling on top and cut the rice cake into pieces. This dessert can also be made with sweet red bean paste made with adzuki beans.

White glutinous rice 200 g (7 oz /
    1 cup), soaked overnight

Salt $^1/_4$ tsp

Cooking oil 2 tsp

SWEET MUNG BEAN PASTE

Mung dhal 120 g (4$^1/_2$ oz / 1 cup),
    soaked overnight

Pandan (screwpine) leaves
    (optional) 2, knotted together

Water 750 ml (24 fl oz / 3 cups)

Palm sugar/sugar 65 g (2$^1/_2$ oz /
    $^1/_3$ cup)

Coconut cream (optional) 60 ml
    (2 fl oz / $^1/_4$ cup)

TOPPING

Fresh grated coconut $^1/_4$ cup

Toasted white sesame seeds
    $^1/_4$ cup

Toasted peanuts $^1/_4$ cup, ground

1. To make bean paste, boil soaked mung dhal with knotted pandan leaves in water till it begins to disintegrate or about 20 minutes. To help the process, blend dhal into the water if you have a stick blender or mash with a potato masher. Take out pandan leaves before you do that.

2. Stir bean paste constantly, keeping a close eye on it as it starts to thicken. Add sugar only when beans have disintegrated. If using palm sugar, it is preferable to dissolve the sugar in some water and strain the syrup first before adding it to the bean paste. Palm sugar sometimes has unwanted bits such as dead insects hardened into it. If using coconut cream, add it last and continue cooking till bean paste is thick again. Palm sugar and coconut cream make a particularly flavourful combination.

3. Cook rice using your preferred method. Put salt to boil with rice if boiling and stir in oil when rice is done. If steaming, dissolve salt in a little water and stir into rice together with oil after 10 minutes of steaming. Continue steaming till rice is done.

4. Either shape hot rice into balls or ovals (like for sushi) or press rice into an oiled 13 x 18-cm (5 x 7-in) glass or metal tray and smooth sweet bean paste on top. Mix topping and sprinkle on bean paste or keep topping ingredients separate so cakes have different toppings. Serve.

Note:

An alternative way to serve these rice cakes is to form the rice into small flattened balls using a small square of dampened muslin. Place the rice balls in a small banana leaf, pandan leaf or paper cupcake casing. Top cakes with some sweet bean paste and sprinkle with topping.

Instead of sweet mung bean paste, try making these rice cakes with sweet red bean paste, a coarse paste made of adzuki beans. Soak 1 cup adzuki beans overnight, then boil until beans are soft. Stir in $^3/_4$ cup sugar and stir over low heat till sugar melts and paste is thick. Mash as you stir to get a coarse paste.

STRAITS CHINESE PULOT HITAM
(STRAITS CHINESE BLACK GLUTINOUS RICE PORRIDGE)

Although the instructions here are for stove top cooking, this rice dessert is best done in a slow cooker overnight: you don't have to soak overnight; you don't have to keep a constant eye on it; you don't have to stir it every once in a while; and all the grains come out nicely soft and still a little chewy with minimum attention. If the rice is cooked on the stove top, you have to stir it occasionally to prevent the bottom from catching and you have to keep the flame very low. A heat diffuser helps tremendously. It reduces the need to keep stirring the rice as it cooks. The flavour of the rice porridge is improved with the addition of the second coconut milk (the thinner milk extracted after the cream) to the boiling porridge. To keep coconut cream fresh, add a little salt to it and refrigerate until needed.

Black glutinous rice 200 g (7 oz / 1 cup), soaked overnight

Pandan (screwpine) leaves 4, knotted

Water 1.5 litres (48 fl oz / 6 cups)

Second coconut milk 500 ml (16 fl oz / 2 cups)

Salt a pinch

Sugar 150 g (5^1/$_3$ oz / ^{3}/$_4$ cup)

Fresh coconut cream 375 ml (12 fl oz / 1^1/$_2$ cups)

ON THE STOVE TOP:

1. Put soaked rice, knotted pandan leaves and water into a large pot to allow room for bubbling up and bring to the boil. Skim off scum, if any. Turn down heat and simmer for at least 2 hours or till rice is broken up and soft. *Pulot hitam* is notorious for the length of time that it takes to soften. Stir occasionally to check that the rice is not sticking to the bottom of the pot even when you are using a heat diffuser. Add some second milk during the boiling for added flavour. If more liquid is needed to get the right consistency, add second milk.

2. Add salt and sugar to taste only when rice is soft enough. Bring to the boil to melt sugar. Adjust sugar to taste.

3. To serve *pulot hitam*, ladle into individual serving bowls and drizzle with a generous serving of fresh coconut cream.

USING A SLOW COOKER:

1. To cook *pulot hitam* in a slow cooker, rinse rice clean, then put rice, pandan leaves and 1 litre (32 fl oz / 4 cups) water in a slow cooker. Leave rice to cook overnight.

2. When rice is a thick porridge, thin out slightly with second coconut milk and return to the boil. Add salt and sugar.

3. To serve *pulot hitam*, ladle into individual serving bowls and drizzle with a generous serving of fresh coconut cream.

Note:

In Indonesia, pulot hitam may also be served with durian and fresh coconut cream. The dessert is known as nasi kentan. The black glutinous rice is kept more whole and less porridge-like. Nasi kentan is similar to Straits Chinese durian with rice (page 210).

CHINESE WINTER SOLSTICE RICE BALLS

Nowadays, this particular rice dessert is made with ubiquitous white glutinous rice flour, but in the 1950s and 1960s, the coming of the winter solstice on 21st December was marked by the sight of my mother busy in the backyard grinding rice into rice flour or me being pressed into service to turn the stone mill for her. (I have this mill still as a souvenir of the times.) Enterprising wet market stallholders in Singapore and Malaysia would sell freshly-ground glutinous rice a day or so before for preparing these rice balls. On that day, everyone at home was supposed to eat a bowl of rice balls in syrup to sweeten our passage through winter so that we could turn a year older when Chinese New Year also known as the Spring Festival came around. Such rice balls were also—and are still—prepared as part of certain conservative Chinese wedding rituals. This is a recipe for making rice flour at home the modern way. I have included it for the record! No one makes rice flour when you can buy perfectly good Thai white glutinous flour cheaply. The method could also prove useful for someone without access to glutinous rice flour but with plenty of white glutinous rice.

White glutinous rice *200 g (7 oz / 1 cup), soak 24 hours in cold water*

Pandan (screwpine) leaves *12 leaves*

Sugar *150 g (5¹/₃ oz / ³/₄ cup)*

Water *as needed*

Red food colouring *a few drops*

1. If preparing rice flour from rice, start preparations at least a day ahead of making rice balls and keep wet flour refrigerated until ready to use.

2. To prepare rice flour, blend soaked rice with plenty of water to get a very fine flour. The longer the blending, the finer will be the flour.

3. Spread 2 layers of muslin in a large sieve and pour the rice flour and water into the sieve. Drain rice flour well till you get a dough that is dry enough to roll neatly into balls. At the same time, it should not be too dry or the rice balls will be hard.

4. Prepare pandan juice. Chop 10 pandan leaves and divide into three lots. Place one lot into a food processor with 125 ml (4 fl oz / ¹/₂ cup) water, then strain the juice using a piece of muslin cloth to remove any solids. Use this juice to blend the second lot of chopped pandan leaves. Repeat to strain the juice, then use the juice to blend the final lot of chopped pandan leaves. This step keeps the juice thick. Any leftover pandan juice can be frozen for another day.

5. Divide rice flour into 3 balls. Keep one ball white. Colour one ball pink with red food colouring and the other ball green with enough pandan juice to get a nice green colour, making sure that the dough does not get too wet. If it does, tie up the dough in a piece of muslin and hang up to dry out a little.

6. In the meantime, knot the 2 remaining pandan leaves. Make a syrup by boiling sugar, knotted pandan leaves and 750 ml (24 fl oz / 3 cups) water in a pot large enough to contain the rice balls as well.

7. To make the balls, bring a large pot of water to the boil. When the water is boiling, roll pieces of the dough into small balls and drop them into the boiling water. Try to make even-size balls for better presentation and a more even cooking time.

8. When the balls float up, they are cooked. Scoop out with a perforated ladle and put them into the syrup.

9. Serve warm or cold.

KOREAN PINE NUT PORRIDGE

The porridge can be left with some bite or blended to a smooth soup with a stick blender if preferred. If so, blend the porridge before the red dates are added. The ground pine nuts give this dessert a rich nutty flavour.

White short-grain rice 50 g (1²/₃ oz / ¹/₄ cup)

White glutinous rice 50 g (1²/₃ oz / ¹/₄ cup)

Water 875 ml (29 fl oz / 3¹/₂ cups)

Pine nuts ¹/₂ cup

Chinese dried red dates (jujubes) a handful, seeded and thinly sliced

Sugar 150 g (5¹/₃ oz / ³/₄ cup)

GARNISHING

Black sesame seeds 1 Tbsp, coarsely pounded

1. Using your preferred method, cook the two types of rice with 750 ml (24 fl oz / 3 cups) water to a thick smooth porridge. Blend with a stick blender if a smoother porridge is preferred or to speed up the boiling.

2. Blend pine nuts to a fine paste with 2 Tbsp water. Stir ground pine nuts and sliced dates into porridge and mix well. Bring to the boil, turn down heat and simmer for 2 minutes.

3. Melt sugar with remaining water to get a syrup.

4. Serve porridge hot, sprinkled with some black sesame seeds and syrup on the side for sweetening to taste.

VIETNAMESE SWEET RICE PORRIDGE

This rice porridge can be flavoured with sweet potato, yam (taro), tapioca, red, green or black dried beans, fresh corn niblets or even black glutinous rice. Choose the ingredients with the aim of getting a colourful combination—or based on what you have in the larder. The harder ingredients such as red beans or black glutinous rice must be pre-cooked before being added to other ingredients such as sweet potato which cooks quickly. A combination of sweet potato and yam gives a porridge that looks rather like Straits Chinese bubor cha cha which, however, does not have rice in it. Vary the flavour by substituting palm sugar with brown or white sugar. If you can't obtain fresh coconut cream, use packaged coconut cream.

White glutinous rice 100 g (3¹/₂ oz / ¹/₂ cup)

Pandan (screwpine) leaves 4, knotted

Water 750 ml (24 fl oz / 3 cups)

Yam (taro) 250 g (9 oz), peeled and cubed

Sweet potatoes 250 g (9 oz), peeled and cubed

Palm sugar 100 g (3¹/₂ oz), grated

Salt a pinch

Coconut cream 125 ml (4 fl oz / ¹/₂ cup)

1. Boil rice, knotted pandan leaves and water together till rice is a soft porridge.

2. While rice is boiling, steam yam and sweet potato cubes till soft and add to porridge. Alternatively, boil yam and sweet potato cubes in the porridge till soft but still whole. The sweet potatoes and yam should not be cooked to pulp.

3. Add sugar, salt and more water if porridge is too thick.

4. Stir coconut cream into porridge and bring to the boil. Turn off heat. Do not over boil coconut cream.

Mochi (japanese glutinous rice cakes)

Once, making and eating mochi was a communal activity in Japan and a part of the Japanese New Year celebrations. Family and friends would gather to help with the pounding of the sticky rice to a smooth dough. The chatter and gossip made the pounding more fun besides giving friends and family something to talk about. Nowadays, mochi is found year-round and even outside Japan. It is also made with rice flour and sometimes with other flours added to make the sticky rice dough easier to handle. Still, there are mochi speciality shops in Japan that do it the traditional way and you can see it being done. Pounding glutinous rice the traditional way as described here is hard work because cooked glutinous rice is stiff and hard to pound (especially if you don't have the right mortar and pestle!) Smaller quantities are easier to handle. Although better known to non-Japanese as sweetened rice desserts with assorted fillings such as adzuki bean paste, black sesame seed paste or chestnut purée, mochi is also made with savoury fillings and eaten in various savoury soups as part of the Japanese New Year celebrations. As a sweet, the sticky pieces of mochi are traditionally coated with toasted soy bean flour known as *kinako* (available in Japanese supermarkets). If you can't find *kinako*, the mochi can also be rolled in ground peanuts, sesame seeds and toasted coconut, but never in corn flour which tastes horrible raw. If the mochi is for soup, the larger pieces of mochi can be lightly oiled and kept individually wrapped in foil or a plastic bag until ready to use. It can also be wrapped with perilla leaves (shiso) or strips of seaweed. Mochi freezes well. Defrost frozen mochi to room temperature, then prepare as usual. Eat mochi with care and in small bites. Stories of old folks especially choking on mochi are all too common in Japan.

   The recipe below gives varying quantities of water for cooking the rice. Cook the rice with less water if making the mochi for soup. Firm rice is harder to pound than softer rice but mochi made with firm rice is easier to grill should you want to try this method of softening the mochi. Firm mochi is also tastier in soup. Use the larger quantity of water if making sweet mochi. Sweet mochi needs to be pounded for longer and softer rice is easier to pound. If making mochi for soup, the mochi does not have to be very smooth, unlike for sweet mochi when the smoother it is, the tastier it is.

Traditional Mochi and Sweet Mochi   Makes 8 pieces

TRADITIONAL MOCHI

White glutinous rice 400 g (14¹/₃ oz / 2 cups)

Water 375–500 ml (12–16 fl oz / 1½–2 cups)

Bowl of cold water

Cooking oil for bagging mochi

SWEET MOCHI

Icing (confectioner's) sugar 100 g (3¹/₂ oz / ¹/₂ cup)

Soy bean powder (kinako) 1 cup

1. Cook glutinous rice with water in a rice cooker with a glutinous (sticky) rice setting. If you are making sweet mochi, do not be tempted to cook the sugar with the rice. If you do so, the rice won't soften. Alternatively, steam the white glutinous rice till tender.

2. While rice is still hot and soft, place it in a deep mortar and pound till fairly smooth if making mochi for savoury soups, and very smooth if making sweet mochi. If making sweet mochi, add 1–2 Tbsp icing sugar to the hot rice as you pound.

3. To make mochi into rice cakes for soups, have a bowl of cold water and a small bowl of oil at hand, and aluminium foil or small plastic bags ready. Dampen your hands and form sticky rice dough into a rectangle, square or flattened balls. Oil each piece of mochi and place in a small plastic bag or wrap in aluminium foil. Refrigerate or freeze till you are ready to make the soup.

4. If making sweet mochi, sift the remaining icing sugar and *kinako* together and set aside till sweet mochi is ready for cutting into pieces. If amount is too much, keep some for another day by bagging and freezing the extra after pounding.

5. Sprinkle a dry clean cutting board liberally with sweetened *kinako* powder and place sweet mochi on the powder. Cut into bite-size pieces, rolling each piece in *kinako* powder as you cut.

6. Serve sweet mochi within the same day but box them and refrigerate if not finished. Bring it back to room temperature to soften mochi.

SEE ALSO

- Shiruko (page 208)

- Sekihan (page 126)

- Ebi Zoni (page 182)

SHIRUKO (MOCHI IN SWEET BEAN SOUP)

Red is considered an auspicious colour throughout East Asia and foods that appear at celebrations are often coloured red such as red-dyed boiled eggs at Chinese birthdays. Red beans or adzuki beans come into their own in Japanese New Year celebrations. The beans can be cooked into a soup or if preferred, into a thick granular bean paste on which the piece of mochi sits. If serving mochi on red bean paste, grill the mochi first before putting each piece on a serving of beans. If mochi is very soft, grill it by placing it in a lightly-oiled frying pan.

Adzuki beans *1 cup, soaked overnight*

Sugar *100 g (3¹/₂ oz / ³/₄ cup)*

Orange/lemon zest (optional) *1–2 pieces*

Mochi (page 206) *1 recipe*

1. Boil soaked adzuki beans till beans are soft, adding more water if necessary to get a soup. When beans are soft, stir in sugar and orange/lemon zest. Discard zest after 5 minutes of boiling.

2. If mochi is to be served in soup, put the pieces to boil in the hot soup to soften the mochi. Ladle out and serve.

3. If mochi is to be served on a bed of red bean paste make the boiled adzuki beans into a paste first (see Note on page 199).

Note:

Only mochi that is dried and firm can be grilled the traditional way. The mochi is skewered and the skewer held upright over a coal fire. It is easier to soften cold mochi by heating in the microwave oven for 30 seconds depending on size.

KOREAN SWEET RICE CAKES   Makes 20 small cakes

This is an unusual rice cake in being semi-sweet. The dark soy sauce not only colours the rice but also gives the rice cakes a more complex flavour than just sweetness. There is also a little bit of salt added. The mould I use to make the rice cake is a cupcake tin. The rice cake is then unmoulded into a paper cupcake case.

White glutinous rice *400 g (14¹/₃ oz / 2 cups), soaked 1 hour*

Salt *¹/₄ tsp*

Sugar *65 g (2¹/₂ oz / ¹/₃ cup)*

Dark soy sauce *1 tsp*

Cooking oil *1 tsp*

Sesame oil *¹/₂ Tbsp*

Dried Chinese red dates (jujubes) *50 g (1²/₃ oz / ¹/₂ cup), seeded and cut into strips*

Toasted pine nuts *30 g (1 oz)*

1. Cook glutinous rice using your preferred method until rice is tender. If using a rice cooker, it has to have a glutinous (sticky) rice setting. Add salt to rice at the start of cooking. If the rice is being steamed, stir salt into some water and sprinkle on rice during steaming.

2. When rice is done, stir sugar, dark soy sauce, oils and dates into hot rice. Cool rice till it can be handled.

3. To make rice cakes, have ready a small mould or cupcake tin. Sprinkle a few pine nuts into the bottom of the tin and press some rice on top of the pine nuts, levelling the top. Unmould into a cupcake case. Tap the bottom of the tin sharply and the cake should drop out.

4. Alternatively, grease hands a little and roll the rice into balls with some pine nuts. Place the balls in mini cupcake cases.

LEMPER (INDONESIAN RICE ROLLS)

This Indonesian treat is often made with young coconut palm leaves that have been woven neatly into a tube or a narrow cone. Coconut palm leaves not being so easily available outside island and coastal Southeast Asia, the rolls can also be wrapped in banana leaves and even corn husks, both dried and fresh. Basically, the same recipe is used for a Javanese wedding feast speciality called *jadah manten*. These are rectangles of filled rice wrapped in thin omelette skins. The rectangle of filled rice is clamped between two pairs of large flat bamboo skewers tied together to hold the rectangle. Rather than the thin round bamboo skewers now common, these flat bamboo skewers are the kind commonly used for making *sate* in Indonesia. The rolls are then brushed with coconut cream and browned over a charcoal grill. Talk about fiddly but it does look very pretty! And yes, you can also make your *lemper* this way especially if getting hold of leaves that you can use as wrapping is not easy.

White glutinous rice 600 g
  (1 lb 5¹/₃ oz / 3 cups), soaked
  overnight
Alkali salts (see Glossary) 2 tsp
Coconut cream 125 ml (4 fl oz /
  ¹/₂ cup)
Salt 1¹/₂ tsp

FILLING
Cooking oil 3 Tbsp
Minced beef/chicken 500 g
  (1 lb 1¹/₂ oz)
Sugar 2 Tbsp
Salt 1 tsp
Coconut cream 60 ml (2 fl oz /
  ¹/₄ cup)
Lime juice ¹/₂ Tbsp
Kaffir lime leaves 3, crushed

SPICE PASTE
Shallots 50 g (1²/₃ oz), peeled
Garlic 3 cloves, peeled
Galangal 1 slice
Turmeric 2 thick slices
Dried prawn (shrimp) paste
  (belacan) ¹/₄ tsp
Ground coriander 1 tsp
Ground white pepper 1 tsp
Chilli powder 1 tsp
Water 2 Tbsp

WRAPPING
Palm leaves/banana leaves/dried
  or fresh corn husks
Bamboo skewers 4-cm (¹/₂-in) long
  with sharp ends
Bowl of cold water
Cooking oil for greasing leaves/
  husks

1. Start preparations a day ahead. First, grind together ingredients for spice paste to a fine paste.

2. Prepare filling. Heat oil in a pot and fry spice paste till fragrant. Add minced meat, sugar and salt and coconut cream and simmer till filling is just slightly moist. Stir in lime juice and lime leaves and simmer till filling is fairly dry. Turn off heat.

3. To soften banana leaves, boil water in a wok and blanch leaves a few at a time. Dried corn husks can be softened by soaking in cold water and wiped dry. Fresh corn husks do not need softening but should be well rinsed to get rid of any residual pesticide or dirt.

4. Soak rice with alkali salts overnight. Steam rice for 10 minutes. Stir coconut cream and salt into it and continue steaming till rice is the texture you prefer. Cover rice and leave to cool.

5. To wrap rice rolls, divide rice and filling into 12–14 portions depending on size of wrappers. Spread out a wrapper and grease well with oil. Using wet hands, flatten rice on wrapper, put filling in the centre and roll up in the wrapper. The shape will depend on the kind of wrapper being used. Whatever the shape of the wrapper, try to keep the filling inside the rice roll. Close openings with bamboo skewers.

6. Before serving, place rolls in a flat baking tin and grill at 200°C (400°F) for 10 minutes, turning once to grill the other side.

7. Serve *lemper* warm if the filling is beef. *Lemper* with chicken filling can be served at room temperature.

Cambodian Black Sticky Rice with Fruit

While the Cambodians like their black glutinous rice to be a thick porridge, in parts of Indonesia, *nasi kentan* is black glutinous rice steamed till tender, sweetened with palm sugar syrup, moistened with fresh coconut cream or fresh grated coconut and served with pieces of fresh fruit such as durian, much like the Thai glutinous rice with mango or Straits Chinese glutinous rice with durian (below). The Indonesians also turn black glutinous rice into a savoury rice cake by covering the steamed rice with a savoury-sweet-spicy topping made with ground soy beans or peanuts, chilli, garlic, lime leaves and galangal.

Black/white glutinous rice 200 g
 (7 oz / 1 cup), soaked overnight
Salt 3/4 tsp
Fresh grated coconut 200 g (7 oz)
Sugar/palm sugar syrup to taste
Jackfruit/durian/mango to taste

1. Cook black/white glutinous rice or half-and-half using your preferred method. The rice can be cooked to a thick porridge or kept as a granular rice. Add 1/4 tsp salt to porridge or dissolve the salt in 60 ml (2 fl oz / 1/4 cup water and sprinkle on the rice during steaming. Cool before serving.

2. Mix remaining 1/2 tsp salt into fresh grated coconut. The salt keeps the coconut fresh for longer. Refrigerate until needed.

3. To serve, spoon room temperature porridge or rice into a small dessert bowl. Pour some syrup over, then top with fresh grated coconut and pieces of fruit.

Thai-style Mango with Rice/ Straits Chinese Durian with Rice

The preparation and serving of these two desserts are identical, the only differences being the fruit and the way it is eaten. In Thailand, the usual mango served with white glutinous rice is the very sweet juicy soft mango called honey mango (at least in Singapore). Mango with white glutinous rice is eaten with a fork and spoon. On the other hand, ripe durian is like custard wrapped round a seed and is much harder to serve or eat tidily unlike mango. Durian is usually eaten with your fingers which explains why durian and rice is essentially a treat served at home. When I was a child, durian and rice for dinner was a very special treat at the height of the durian season when the durians would be cheap. Such a dinner is not as strange as it sounds, as durian is a protein-rich fruit.

White glutinous rice 200 g (7 oz /
 1 cup), soaked 1 hour
Water 180 ml (6 fl oz / 3/4 cup)
Salt 1/2 tsp
Fresh coconut cream 250 ml
 (8 fl oz / 1 cup)
Sweet ripe mango 1 per person

1. Cook rice with water using your preferred method until rice is tender. Leave rice to cool.

2. Mix salt and fresh coconut cream together.

3. To serve Thai-style mango with rice, slice mango into 2 halves, slicing each half close to the seed. Score flesh of mango halves and arrange with some rice on a plate. Drizzle a tablespoon of coconut cream on rice before serving.

4. To serve Straits Chinese durian with rice, seed durian and arrange with some rice on a plate. Drizzle a tablespoon of coconut cream on rice before serving.

KUIH SALAT Makes a 22 x 22-cm (8 x 8-in) cake

This Straits Chinese, Indonesian and Malay *kuih* is known as *kuih salat* or *kuih serimuka*. Whatever its name, it is basically steamed white glutinous rice flavoured with coconut cream, with a layer of pandan (screwpine) leaf-flavoured custard steamed on top. Instead of flavouring it with pandan juice, the egg custard can also be flavoured with finely mashed fresh durian pulp. Both ways, *kuih salat* is delicious. The reason the weight of eggs has been given is that eggs are not the same everywhere.

RICE LAYER

White glutinous rice *300 g (11 oz / 1¹/₂ cups)*

Water *250 ml (8 fl oz / 1 cup)*

Salt *¹/₂ tsp*

Dried butterfly pea flower (*Clitoria ternatea*) *2 Tbsp or a few drops of blue food colouring*

Thick coconut milk *125 ml (4 fl oz / ¹/₂ cup)*

CUSTARD TOPPING

Sugar *150 g (5¹/₃ oz / ³/₄ cup)*

Plain (all-purpose) flour *2 Tbsp*

Eggs *6 or 300 g (11 oz) without shells*

Coconut cream *150 ml (5 fl oz / ²/₃ cup)*

Pandan (screwpine) juice (page 202) *150 ml (5 fl oz / ²/₃ cup)*

1. Prepare rice layer. Cook rice with water and salt in a rice cooker with a glutinous (sticky) rice setting or steam until tender.

2. If using butterfly pea flower to colour the rice, soak flowers in 60 ml (2 fl oz / ¹/₄ cup) water to extract colouring.

3. When rice is done, remove to a bowl and stir in thick coconut cream and blue colouring. Streak colour through the rice rather than have the rice a solid colour.

4. Line a 22 x 22-cm (8 x 8-in) cake tin or glass dish with banana leaves, then pack in hot rice. Press rice down with a spoon to get a level surface.

5. Prepare custard topping. In a bowl, mix sugar and flour to dissolve any lumps of flour.

6. Beat in eggs lightly, then stir in coconut cream and pandan juice.

7. Put mixture into a small saucepan and place over low heat, stirring till sugar is dissolved. The mixture should be smooth. Be careful not to allow lumps to form.

8. Pour hot mixture over hot rice.

9. Place cake tin or dish in a steamer filled with water. Steam for about 30 minutes or till custard is cooked.

10. To prevent drops of water falling on the custard and making pock-marks in the custard while steaming, tie a large piece of cloth around the lid to soak up the water vapour.

11. Cool *kuih* thoroughly to allow custard to firm up before cutting to serve.

Kuih Lopes *Makes 12 triangles*

This is a common Indonesian, Malay or Straits Chinese glutinous rice snack which is made fabulous because it is sweetened with palm sugar for which there is no substitute. Fresh grated white coconut may be substituted with unflavoured desiccated coconut, in which case the desiccated coconut should be cooked in some palm sugar syrup for 5 minutes. Fresh grated coconut does not need to be cooked. Instead pour some syrup over the rice cake and spread the fresh grated coconut on top. To keep the fresh coconut from going off, do this Indonesian trick: mix in $1/2$ tsp salt and steam the coconut for 5 minutes.

White glutinous rice 600 g
   (1 lb 5^1/$_3$ oz / 3 cups), soaked
   overnight
Alkali salts (see Glossary) 1 tsp
Fresh grated coconut without skin
   300 g (11 oz)

PALM SUGAR SYRUP
Palm sugar 150 g (5^1/$_3$ oz)
Water 125 ml (4 fl oz / ^{1}/$_2$ cup)
Pandan (screwpine) leaves 3,
   knotted
Banana leaves for wrapping

1. Make palm sugar syrup a day ahead. It keeps well in the refrigerator. Put palm sugar and water with knotted pandan leaves into a pot and bring to the boil. Simmer gently to melt sugar. Strain syrup and discard any solids. Bottle syrup and keep refrigerated until needed.

2. Soak rice overnight with alkali salts.

3. Drain rice and steam for 10 minutes, taking care to turn rice over halfway through so rice cooks evenly.

4. Prepare banana leaves by softening them. Either hold banana leaves one by one over a gas flame or blanch them in a wok of hot water. Cut leaves into 20 x 16-cm (8 x 6-in) pieces.

5. Divide steamed rice into 12 equal portions. Wrap each portion with a piece of banana leaf, shaping it into a triangle. Secure with rubber bands. Repeat till rice is all wrapped up.

6. Steam wrapped cakes for at least an hour. Press the centre to see how firm it is. The rice cake should be very firm.

7. To serve *kuih lopes*, unwrap parcels and garnish rice cakes with palm sugar syrup and grated coconut.

Pulot Inti (Glutinous rice with coconut topping)

It is almost impossible to go wrong with this dessert. What's more, unlike many Southeast Asian rice desserts, it can be made with canned desiccated coconut. What you do need is palm sugar. Look for this in Asian stores patronised by Southeast Asians. The rice is sometimes streaked with blue colouring from the dried butterfly pea flower (*Clitoria ternatea*). The cake can be made into a large piece, then cut up or shaped into small pieces and neatly packed into banana leaf cases Thai-style.

White glutinous rice 400 g (14^1/$_3$ oz
   / 2 cups), soaked overnight
Coconut cream 60 ml (2 fl oz /
   ^{1}/$_4$ cup)
Salt ^{1}/$_4$ tsp
Dried butterfly pea flower (*Clitoria
   ternatea*) (optional) 2 Tbsp
   or a few drops of blue food
   colouring

TOPPING
Palm sugar 150 g (5^1/$_3$ oz)
Water 85 ml (2^1/$_2$ fl oz / ^{1}/$_3$ cup)
Fresh grated coconut without skin
   300 g (11 oz)
Pandan (screwpine) leaves 2,
   knotted

1. Steam glutinous rice for 10 minutes. Mix coconut cream and salt together and stir into rice. Steam rice for another 30 minutes or till rice is your preferred texture.

2. Prepare topping. Put palm sugar and water into a small pot and simmer to melt sugar. Strain and discard any solids.

3. Return syrup to the pot, add grated coconut and pandan leaves and boil up briefly. The mixture should be thick. If it is too liquid, simmer till it thickens. Discard pandan leaves and cool topping.

4. If using dried flowers for the colouring, soak flowers in 60 ml (2 fl oz / ^{1}/$_4$ cup) water to extract colour, or use blue food colouring.

5. To assemble cake, streak rice with some blue colouring if using and pack rice into an 20 x 20-cm (8 x8-in) cake tin. Press rice down and spoon topping over. Cool thoroughly before cutting to serve.

Note:

Pulot inti can also be shaped in bite-size pieces rather like sushi. Take a tablespoonful of rice and press lightly into a ball inside a paper cupcake case or banana leaf case. Make an indentation in the centre and fill with some topping pressed on the rice. Repeat till rice and coconut are used up.

TAPEH (FERMENTED GLUTINOUS RICE)

This fermented rice is very popular in the Straits Chinese, Indonesian, Malay and Indian Muslim communities in Southeast Asia. In Singapore, cafés and restaurants in the Arab Street-North Bridge Road area will sometimes offer freshly-made *tapeh* for sale. The yeast or *ragi* for making *tapeh* is also sold only in Geylang Serai Market by the little old ladies who sell flowers. Once upon a time, I used to buy my *ragi* from this untidy grocery store in Arab Street. When buying *ragi*, specify that you want sweet *ragi*. *Tapeh* can be made with white or black glutinous rice as well as tapioca. White glutinous rice must be thoroughly picked through for every bit of long-grain rice for the *tapeh* to be smooth. Long-grain rice becomes gritty in *tapeh* and is unpleasant. If making *tapeh* with black glutinous rice, make sure that the rice is well-boiled or steamed till really tender.

White/black glutinous rice 600 g
   (1 lb 5¹/₃ oz / 3 cups)
Ragi 1 Tbsp
Water 750 ml (24 fl oz / 3 cups)

1. If using black glutinous rice, soak rice overnight before boiling.
2. Pound *ragi* to powder and sift. Measure out 1 Tbsp.
3. Prepare a glass jar large enough to hold *tapeh*. Rinse jar in hot water and dry with a clean towel. Prepare an old clean sweater and several clean dishcloths to wrap the jar.
4. Cook rice with water using a rice cooker with a glutinous (sticky) rice setting. When rice is done, open the lid and let the rice cool till a lump on the inside of your wrist feels warm but not uncomfortably hot. Sprinkle powdered *ragi* into rice and mix well using a clean spoon.
5. Scoop rice into prepared glass jar. Cover rice of jar loosely with a clean tea towel. Wrap jar in tea towels and swaddle it in the old sweater.
6. Place glass jar in a draught-free and warm spot in the kitchen. (I find the space near the back of a refrigerator perfect.) Leave rice to ferment for 48 hours at room temperature. Refrigerate after that to slow down fermentation. It will keep for several weeks in the refrigerator and gets sweeter with time.
7. Serve *tapeh* chilled.

KUIH WAJEK

Where there are coconut palms aplenty, there you will find palm sugar and coconut milk. Combine the two with white glutinous rice and you get this easy snack. Whatever its name, *kuih wajek* is found all over Southeast Asia as well as in Sri Lanka which produces lots of excellent palm sugar called jaggery. There are several ways of making *kuih wajek*. Here are two methods. The first yields a more al dente rice, the second a softer one. Very similar to *kuih wajek* is Filipino *biko*, the only difference is that toasted grated coconut is sprinkled on top of the rice cake before serving.

White glutinous rice 200 g (7 oz /
   1 cup), soaked 1 hour
Grated palm sugar 100 g (3¹/₂ oz)
Coconut cream 60 ml (2 fl oz /
   ¹/₄ cup)
Salt ¹/₄ tsp

METHOD 1

1. Drain rice and steam for 10 minutes, taking care to turn rice over halfway through so rice cooks evenly.
2. Put palm sugar, coconut cream, salt and steamed rice into a frying pan and stir together over low heat till sugar has melted and coconut cream and sugar are well mixed into rice.
3. The hot rice can be formed into balls and put into cupcake cases or pressed into a cake tin and left to cool before gently prising out using a flat-bladed knife onto a serving plate. Cut to serve.

METHOD 2

1. Prepare rice with 250 ml (8 fl oz / 1 cup) water using your preferred method until rice is tender. If using a rice cooker, it should have a glutinous (sticky) rice setting.
2. Mix together grated palm sugar, coconut cream and salt and stir into cooked rice when done. Continue stirring till sugar has melted.
3. Complete with Step 3 above.

Pulot Rempah Udang
(Glutinous rice rolls with prawns and spices) Makes 12 large or 24 small rolls

The Indonesians call this *pulot panggang*, while the Straits Chinese and Malays in Singapore and Malaysia call it *pulot rempah udang*. If you're unable to find fresh grated coconut, use dried desiccated coconut available all over the world in tins. Have extra banana leaves on hand because fresh banana leaves tear easily and you may need to layer to fix a tear. In the US, frozen banana leaves are sometimes found in large Asian stores. The filling and leaves can be prepared a day ahead. If you are making this for a party, you might want them in 24 small rolls rather than 12 large rolls. Divide the filling and rice accordingly.

White glutinous rice 600 g
(1 lb 5¹/₃ oz / 3 cups), soaked
30 minutes
Salt 1¹/₂ tsp
Water 500 ml (16 fl oz / 2 cups)
Coconut cream 60 ml (2 fl oz /
¹/₂ cup)

FILLING
Fresh grated coconut without skin
200 g (7 oz / 2 cups)
Ground coriander 1 Tbsp
Ground white pepper 1¹/₂ tsp
Cooking oil 2 Tbsp
Shelled prawns 200 g (7 oz),
peeled and chopped
Salt ³/₄ tsp
Sugar 3 tsp
Water 125 ml (4 fl oz / ¹/₂ cup)

FOR WRAPPING
Banana leaves 12, each
20 x 30-cm (8 x 12-in) or 24,
each 10 x 30-cm (4 x 12-in)
Bamboo skewers with sharp ends
24 or 48, each 3-cm (1-in) long
Cooking oil for greasing leaves
Bowl of cold water

1. Prepare rice. Cook rice with salt and water in a rice cooker with a glutinous rice (sticky rice) setting. When rice is done, stir in coconut cream. Cover rice and leave to cool.

2. Divide rice into the number of rolls you want to make. (One quick way to do this and to get even-sized rolls is to weigh the cooked rice and divide accordingly.)

3. Prepare filling. In a dry wok, dry-fry grated coconut over low heat till a golden colour and very fragrant. Alternatively, toast grated coconut in a microwave oven. The grated coconut should be reduced by half to about 100 g (3¹/₂ oz).

4. Blend toasted coconut in a food processor or pound in a mortar and pestle till fine.

5. Mix ground coriander and pepper with a bit of water to a thick paste.

6. Heat oil in a pan and fry spice paste till fragrant taking care not to burn it. Add chopped prawns, salt and sugar and fry till prawns change colour. Add pounded toasted coconut and 125 ml (4 fl oz / ¹/₂ cup) water and cook for 5 minutes, stirring constantly. The filling should be moist.

7. You should get about 350 g (12 oz) filling. Divide filling into the number of rolls you want to make.

8. To wrap parcels, the banana leaves need to be softened by blanching in boiling water or held briefly over a gas burner. Rinse softened leaves and wipe dry. Cut leaves to size with kitchen scissors.

9. Have nearby a large bowl of cold water and a small bowl of oil for greasing leaves.

10. Dampen hands in bowl of cold water, then press a portion of rice into a rectangle on a greased piece of leaf along its shorter side.

11. Put one portion of filling on rice, then roll filling up in rice, wetting your hands again if need be to prevent rice from sticking to your hands.

12. Roll leaf round the rice and fasten both ends with a bamboo skewer. The roll should be covered by at least 2 layers of leaf. Trim off excess leaf from ends.

13. Repeat till all rolls are done.

14. Before rolls are served, grill them under a 220°C (428°F) grill or on a wire rack placed over a gas burner for 5 minutes to warm through. The rolls can be kept refrigerated and toasted just before eating.

KEE CHANG (CHINESE SODA DUMPLINGS) Makes 12

Although these rice dumplings are traditionally wrapped in fresh bamboo leaves that used to appear in quantity for the celebration of the Dragonboat Festival in Singapore, these days, they are harder to find as more households give up making these dumplings and buy them ready-made. What is available year-round from Chinese dried goods stores are dried bamboo leaves. These stores often also sell alkali salts (see Glossary). If using lump salts, break and pound till fine and measure out. Soda dumplings are almost always eaten with a dip of sugar. The Straits Chinese way is to eat it with palm sugar and if available, a generous helping of fresh grated white coconut. Note that traditionally, a chemical (I don't know what) was added to the boiling water. This now-banned chemical kept the rice from sticking to the leaves. These days, whether the dumpling sticks to the leaves is hit-and-miss. (It didn't stick when we did the picture!)

White glutinous rice *600 g*
  (1 lb 5¹/₃ oz / 3 cups)
Alkali salts *3¹/₄ tsp*
Bamboo leaves *40 leaves*
Straw twine/raffia string

1. Soak glutinous rice with 2 tsp alkali salts in a basin of cold water overnight. The rice will turn a pale yellow. Drain rice and spread rice on a steamer lined with muslin. Steam for 20 minutes. The rice does not have to be cooked through.

2. Soften bamboo leaves before using either by soaking in cold water overnight or boiling the leaves in a large pot of water with ¹/₄ tsp alkali salts for 10 minutes. Wipe the leaves clean as they can be somewhat dusty.

3. If using straw twine, soak in cold water till pliable. Straw twine is brittle when dry. Cut straw twine/raffia into 60-cm (23¹/₂-in) lengths and bundle twine/raffia together neatly and knot one end into a loop. Hook up the bundle such that you can reach it easily for tying up the dumplings.

4. With a bowl of cool water at hand, wrap dumplings (page 223).

5. When dumplings are done, bring a large pot of water to the boil together with 1 tsp alkali salts. Lower in dumplings and boil for 2 hours.

6. Take dumplings out and hang them up to cool before serving.

7. Soda dumplings can be kept for several days without refrigeration in a cool spot. If refrigerated, softened by boiling again for 15 minutes.

Note:

Wrapping rice dumplings is a skill acquired with practice. If you doubt your ability to get your dumplings wrapped tightly enough to withstand boiling for 2 hours, steam the dumplings instead. If steaming dumplings, soak the rice with 3 tsp alkali salts and don't add any to the boiling water.

STRAITS CHINESE RICE DUMPLINGS   Makes 12–16 dumplings

Once upon a time, in the weeks before the Chinese fifth lunar month, straw twine and bamboo leaves appeared in Singapore markets for the making of rice dumplings. They still do and some households still make rice dumplings. However, most don't as rice dumplings are now so popular as fast food that rice dumpling franchises are everywhere and rice dumplings are sold year-round in Singapore. Rice dumplings may come with traditional Chinese-style fillings (page 222) or with this very tasty Straits Chinese-style filling flavoured with spices. The experts make Chinese rice dumplings from scratch with uncooked rice but it takes experience to gauge how much rice and how tight the wrapping should be. If it is too tight, the rice might not cook right through. If it is too loose, the filling might get diluted with water during the boiling. Make it easier by steaming the rice for 10 minutes first. The filling should be made a day ahead.

White glutinous rice 600 g
(1 lb 5^1/$_3$ oz / 3 cups), soaked
overnight

Salt 2 tsp

Water 125 ml (4 fl oz / ^{1}/$_2$ cup)

Cooking oil 2 Tbsp

Dried butterfly pea flower (Clitoria
ternatea) 3 Tbsp

FILLING

Lean pork 300 g (11 oz)

Dried shiitake mushrooms 30 g
(1 oz), soaked 30 minutes in
250 ml (8 fl oz / 1 cup) water

Ground coriander 1^1/$_2$ Tbsp

Ground white pepper 1 tsp

Cooking oil 2 Tbsp

Shallots ^{1}/$_2$ cup, peeled and thinly
sliced

Sugared winter melon 100 g
(3^1/$_2$ oz), finely chopped

Dark soy sauce 1 Tbsp

FOR WRAPPING

Dried bamboo leaves 40 leaves

Alkali salts ^{1}/$_2$ tsp

Straw twine/raffia string

A small bowl of oil for greasing
leaves

A bowl of cold water for
dampening hands

1. Prepare filling and bamboo leaves a day ahead. When buying bamboo leaves, try to get the larger leaves which make for easier wrappings. If small, estimate 2 leaves per dumpling with some extras in case of tears.

2. To prepare bamboo leaves, heat a wok of water with ^{1}/$_2$ tsp alkali salts and boil leaves for 10 minutes. Wipe dry as leaves are sometimes dusty, then keep the leaves soaking in cold water to prevent them drying out overnight. The dried leaves can also be softened by soaking in cold water for several hours but such leaves are less pliable than boiled ones.

3. Cut straw twine/raffia into 16 pieces of 60-cm (23^1/$_2$-in) each and soak straw twine in some cold water for 10 minutes. Straw twine is brittle when dry. Bundle twine/raffia together neatly and knot one end into a loop.

4. To prepare filling, boil pork in a pot of water. Drain and cool, then cut into very small pieces.

5. Trim tough stems off mushrooms and slice caps into small pieces. Keep soaking water for cooking filling.

6. Mix together ground coriander and pepper with 1 Tbsp water.

7. Heat oil in a pot and fry sliced shallots till golden brown, taking care not to burn it. Scoop out and set aside. Fry coriander and pepper paste till fragrant, then add pork, mushrooms, winter melon, dark soy sauce and mushroom water. Fry till filling is only slightly moist. Stir in fried shallots.

8. When ready to make dumplings, start by preparing rice. Steam soaked rice for 10 minutes. Mix salt, water and oil together and mix well into steamed rice. Leave rice covered until it is cool enough to handle. If colouring rice, soak dried butterfly pea flowers in 1–2 Tbsp water for 30 minutes. Use the liquid to streak the rice blue.

9. Divide rice and filling into 12–16 portions. The size of the dumplings depends on the size of the leaves. Wrap dumplings (page 223).

10. The wrapped dumplings can either be boiled or steamed. The latter reduces the risk of soggy corners or lost dumplings if they haven't been well-wrapped. (For steaming, see step 11 on page 222.)

11. Fill a large pot with cold water and bring to the boil. Put in dumplings and return to the boil. Keep it on the boil for an hour. Remove dumplings and hang them up to drain well. Trim any protruding ends neatly.

12. Rice dumplings should be kept well-aired by hanging them up in a cool spot, never packed inside a plastic bag. Kept well-aired, they keep for several days without refrigeration. If not consumed after 3 days, boil them up again for 30 minutes.

CHESTNUT AND CHICKEN RICE DUMPLINGS, CHINESE-STYLE

One of the traditional fillings for Chinese rice dumplings that are made during the fifth lunar month celebrations is fatty pork with salted chestnuts. Sometimes called "salty dumplings" unlike the sweeter Straits Chinese dumplings, the fatty pork gives the dumplings combined with the sticky rice a really good mouth-feel. The salted chestnuts add that salty touch. These days, the filling is as likely to be made with lean pork as with even leaner chicken breast meat. Quantities for rice and all steps other than for the filling are identical with Straits Chinese rice dumplings (page 220). Note that unlike *kee chang,* these meat-filled dumplings do not stick to the leaves because of the oil.

White glutinous rice *600 g*
(1 lb 5¹/₃ oz / 3 cups), soaked overnight
Salt *2 tsp*
Water *125 ml (4 fl oz / ¹/₂ cup)*
Cooking oil *2 Tbsp*

FILLING

Dried shiitake mushrooms *25 g*
(1 oz / ¹/₂ cup), softened in 250 ml (8 fl oz / 1 cup) water
Belly pork *100 g (3¹/₂ oz)*
Cooking oil *2 Tbsp*
Chopped shallots *2 Tbsp*
Skinless chicken breast meat *100 g (3¹/₂ oz), cubed small*
Fresh/salted chestnuts (see note) *150 g (5¹/₃ oz)*
Ground white pepper *¹/₄ tsp*
Dark soy sauce *1 Tbsp*
Salt *1¹/₂ tsp*

FOR WRAPPING

Dried bamboo leaves *40 leaves*
Alkali salts *¹/₂ tsp*
Straw twine/raffia string
A small bowl of oil for greasing leaves
A bowl of cold water for dampening hands

1. Prepare filling and bamboo leaves a day ahead. When buying bamboo leaves, try to get the larger leaves which make for easier wrappings. If small, estimate 2 leaves per dumpling with some extras in case of tears.

2. To prepare bamboo leaves, heat a wok of water with ¹/₂ tsp alkali salts and boil leaves for 10 minutes. Wipe dry as leaves are sometimes dusty, then keep the leaves soaking in cold water to prevent them drying out overnight. The dried leaves can also be softened by soaking in cold water for several hours but such leaves are less pliable than boiled ones.

3. Cut straw twine/raffia into 16 pieces of 60-cm (23¹/₂-in) each and soak straw twine in some cold water for 10 minutes. Straw twine is brittle when dry. Bundle twine/raffia together neatly and knot one end into a loop.

4. Prepare filling. Trim off and discard mushroom stems and slice or cube mushroom caps. Keep soaking water for cooking filling.

5. Boil belly pork and cut into small thin strips.

6. Heat oil in a pot and fry chopped shallots till golden brown, then add pork, chicken, mushrooms, chestnuts and seasoning together with mushroom water. Stir-fry till meat is cooked and filling is still slightly moist. Adjust saltiness with a taste test.

7. When ready to make dumplings, start by preparing rice. Steam soaked rice for 10 minutes. Mix salt, water and oil together and mix well into steamed rice. Leave rice covered until it is cool enough to handle.

8. Divide rice and filling into 12–16 portions. The size of the dumplings depends on the size of the leaves. Wrap dumplings (page 223).

9. The wrapped dumplings can either be boiled or steamed. The latter reduces the risk of soggy corners or lost dumplings if they haven't been well-wrapped. (For boiling, see step 11 on page 220.)

10. Place a Chinese steamer with at least 2 layers on a large wok filled with water. Arrange the dumplings loosely on the trays if possible. Steam for 1 hour, adding water to wok when needed. When done, remove dumplings and hang them up to drain well. Trim any protruding ends neatly.

11. Rice dumplings should be kept well-aired by hanging them up in a cool spot, never packed inside a plastic bag. Kept well-aired, they keep for several days without refrigeration. If not consumed after 3 days, boil them up again for 30 minutes.

HOW TO WRAP CHINESE RICE DUMPLINGS

1. Assemble the rice, filling and leaves near you. Have a large bowl of water nearby for wetting your hands and a bowl of oil with a brush for greasing the leaves.

2. Grease 2 leaves and layer them such that you get a larger surface area to work with. Fold the leaves in half, then fold one-third from the edge near you up. Lift leaves up and open into a cone.

3. With dampened hands, put a portion of rice into the cone. Press the rice upwards as a thin layer round the cone and a little higher than the dumpling will be for covering up the filling. Keep the centre hollow for the filing.

4. Spoon some filling into the hollow, pressing it to pack tightly. Turn the excess rice near the top over to cover filling.

5. Fold the ends of the leaves to cover the opening and shape the ends to form a neat four-cornered pyramid-shaped dumpling. Tie with twine in such a way that the ends are held tightly round the dumpling.

BANH CHUNG (VIETNAMESE RICE DUMPLINGS) Makes 6 bundles

The Vietnamese make these rice dumplings to celebrate *Tet*, the Vietnamese Lunar New Year. *Tet* celebrations mean several days of enjoyment and feasting and these dumplings are perfect because they are made ahead and once cooked, can be kept over several days, and be eaten on their own or with other dishes. The dumplings can be made from scratch with raw rice, but I always find wrapping steamed rice easier. Mung dhal is skinned split mung beans which also comes split with the green skins still on or whole with the green skins. The beans with skin have more texture while mung dhal dissolves into the rice and gives the glutinous rice more mouth-feel. If you can get your hands on Vietnamese green glutinous rice (see picture on page opposite Dedication) called *com*, it would be very festive as *com* in grain form is very rare. (And there I was with a bagful of *com* in my fridge that I forgot about when doing this picture!)

White glutinous rice 600 g
(1 lb 5^1/$_3$ oz / 3 cups), soaked overnight
Salt 2 tsp
Water 375 ml (12 fl oz / 1^1/$_2$ cups)

FILLING

Mung dhal/mung beans 200 g
(7 oz / 1 cup), soaked 1 hour
Cooking oil 2 Tbsp
Shallots 25 g (1 oz), peeled and chopped
Fish sauce 3 Tbsp
Ground black pepper 1 tsp
Sugar 2 tsp
Salt ^{1}/$_2$ tsp
Belly pork/pork shoulder 500 g
(1 lb 1^1/$_2$ oz), cut into small strips
Water 125 ml (4 fl oz / ^{1}/$_2$ cup)

FOR WRAPPING

Banana leaves 6–10, each
50 x 30-cm (15^1/$_2$ x 12-in)
Straw twine/raffia string
Cooking oil for greasing banana leaves

CONDIMENT

Nuoc cham (page 181)

GARNISHING SUGGESTIONS

• *Daun kadok*
• *Laksa* leaves
• Mint leaves
• Coriander leaves
• Spring onion

1. Cook rice with salt and water in a rice cooker with a glutinous (sticky rice) setting. Leave rice in covered pot to cool. Divide rice into 6 equal portions.

2. Prepare filling. Boil mung dhal/mung beans with plenty of water till beans are tender but still whole. Alternatively, cook mung dhal/mung beans in a slow cooker overnight. Drain and divide into 6 equal portions.

3. Heat oil in a wok and fry chopped shallots till fragrant and brown. Stir in all other ingredients for filling and simmer over low heat till pork is tender and filling only slightly moist. About 15 minutes should do it although it does depend on the size of the strips of meat and how tender it is. Divide filling into 6 equal portions.

4. Prepare banana leaves by blanching in hot water in a wok or singeing over a gas burner or a hot plate. If leaves have been blanched, wipe dry and clean with a wad of dry paper towels. If leaves have been singed, wipe clean with a wad of damp paper towels.

5. To wrap dumplings, have on hand a bowl of cold water and a small bowl of oil for greasing leaves.

6. Lay a banana leaf on a flat surface. Brush liberally with oil. Using wet hands, flatten a portion of rice to a rectangle about 25 x 15 cm (10 x 6-in). Spread one portion of dhal on the rice, topped by a portion of meat filling in the centre. Cover the filling with rice.

7. Fold long sides of banana leaf over rice, then fold the short ends towards the middle, compressing the rice as you wrap up the bundle. Secure the parcel with straw twine/raffia string. Repeat until ingredients are used up.

8. Steam wrapped dumplings for 30 minutes.

9. To serve rice dumplings, unwrap, then cut each roll into 6–8 pieces. The dumplings can be served cold or warm, on its own or with a salad or pickles. It can also be served with pepper leaf wraps and a choice of fresh herbs. Serve nuoc cham as the condiment.

Note:

If the banana leaves are not large enough, overlap pieces of banana leaf to make up the required size.

KUBBAT HALAB (ALEPPO RICE ROLLS) Makes 18 rolls

Halab is the Arabic name for Aleppo, one of the ancient world's trading hubs and today the second largest city in Syria, which has given its name to this traditional Iraqi favourite. When I was in Aleppo, I looked out for it but never saw *kubbat Halab* on the restaurant menus that I looked at. This is probably another one of those dishes named for a place that does not have such a dish, just as there is no Hong Kong noodles in Hong Kong or Singapore noodles in Singapore! Don't make these rice rolls with basmati rice but rather with a long-grain rice that gets a little tacky when a little more water than usual is added to it. The slightly tacky rice is more easily shaped into a roll to be stuffed with minced meat. The amount of water necessary to get the right texture depends on your long-grain rice. Some recipes suggest adding corn flour to make the cooked rice more tacky but this is unnecessary. Cooked long-grain rice has enough starch to hold the shaped roll together if you cook your rice with enough water. The rolls can be made ahead of time and fried in plenty of hot oil to get a crisp shell just before serving.

Long-grain rice 600 g (1 lb 5^1/$_3$ oz / 3 cups)

Salt 1^1/$_2$ tsp

Ground turmeric ^{1}/$_2$ tsp

Water 1.625 litres (54 fl oz / 6^1/$_2$ cups)

A bowl of cold water with a few drops of rose water

Cooking oil for deep-frying

FILLING

Cooking oil 1 Tbsp

Onion 50 g (1^2/$_3$ oz), peeled and finely chopped

Minced lamb/chicken/beef 200 g (7 oz)

Salt 1^1/$_2$ tsp

Any *baharat* (pages 32–33) 2 tsp

Almonds 50 g (1^2/$_3$ oz), skinned and chopped

Dates 100 g (3^1/$_2$ oz), chopped

Parsley/coriander leaves ^{1}/$_4$ cup, chopped

1. The filling can be made a day ahead. To make filling, heat oil in a pot and fry onion till transparent and some bits are browning. Add minced meat, salt and *baharat* and stir-fry till meat is cooked and dry. Stir in chopped almonds, dates and parsley/coriander leaves. Mix well, then turn off heat.

2. When ready to make rice rolls, cook rice with salt and ground turmeric using your preferred method until rice is tender. Cool rice before making *kubbat*.

3. To get even-sized rolls, divide rice and filling into 18 roughly equal portions. A quick way is to weigh the cooked rice and filling and divide accordingly.

4. To make rolls, have on hand the bowl of cold water sweetened with a few drops of rose water. Wet your hands with some of the water and press a portion of rice into an egg-shaped ball. Press a thumb into the centre at one of the narrow ends to form a deep hollow. Fill the hollow and close the opening by pressing the rice ball together, wetting hands if necessary. Repeat till all the filling and rice are used up. Place rolls on a large flat dish, not on top of each other to prevent them from sticking. Rest rolls for some 15 minutes to allow water to evaporate and to dry the outside of rolls before deep-frying.

5. Deep-fry rolls to a golden brown. The rolls should have room to float freely in the hot oil. Serve rolls as a snack or part of a meal with yoghurt sauce (page 47).

QUICK KUBBAT HALAB Makes 15 patties

The patties have to be thin enough so that the raw minced meat will cook properly. You can also make them as balls. This makes a good party snack because the patties can be made bite-size more easily than proper *kubbat halab*.

Any *baharat* (pages 32–33) 1 tsp

Salt 1 tsp

Minced lamb/chicken/beef 150 g (5^1/$_3$ oz)

Chopped onion 1 Tbsp

Chopped parsley/mint/coriander leaves ^{1}/$_4$ cup

Cooked long-grain rice 500 g (1 lb 1^1/$_2$ oz / 3 cups)

Cooking oil for frying

1. Mix *baharat* and salt into minced meat, then stir in chopped onion and herb of choice. Lastly add rice and mix gently together without mashing rice excessively. Divide into 15 portions.

2. Pressing each lump of rice firmly, shape into flat patties about 1-cm (^{1}/$_2$-in) thick. Alternatively, roll mixture into small ovals or balls.

3. Heat a small pot of oil and deep-fry patties till brown and there is a nice crisp crust.

PEARL BALLS, CHINESE OR THAI-STYLE Makes 20 meat balls

This is a very attractive party dish or snack because it is small and easy to eat. Pearl balls can be made with any favourite minced meat mixture. They are so-called because of the covering of glistening grains of white glutinous rice. However, mixing black and white glutinous rice will give an interesting speckled effect. Pearl balls are Thai or Chinese, depending on the seasoning in the meat balls as well as the condiments served with the pearl balls. Hot Chinese tea goes well with pearl balls.

White/black glutinous rice 300 g
 (11 oz / 1 1/2 cups), soaked
 overnight
Coriander leaves

CONDIMENTS
Light soy sauce
Chilli sauce
Thai-style chilli dip

CHINESE-STYLE MEAT BALLS
Minced pork/chicken 200 g (7 oz)
Salt 1/2 tsp
Sesame oil 1 tsp
Fresh prawns 200 g (7 oz), shelled
 and chopped
Water chestnuts 2, peeled and
 chopped
Ginger 2 thin slices, finely chopped
Finely chopped spring onion 1 Tbsp
Corn flour 1 Tbsp

THAI-STYLE MEAT BALLS
Minced pork/chicken 200 g (7 oz)
Fish sauce 1 Tbsp
Cooking oil 1 tsp
Prawns 200 g (7 oz), shelled and
 chopped
Coriander leaves 1 small bunch,
 finely chopped
Bird's eye chilli 1, seeded and finely
 chopped
Corn flour 1 Tbsp

PICKLED CARROT SLICES (OPTIONAL)
Carrots 250 g (9 oz)
Boiling water 500 ml (16 fl oz /
 2 cups)
Rice vinegar 125 ml (4 fl oz / 1/2 cup)
Sugar 1/4 cup
Salt 1 tsp

1. These pearl balls can be served with pickled carrot slices, if desired. The pickled carrot slices have to be prepared a day ahead.

2. Peel carrots and slice thinly. Pour boiling water over carrots placed in a sieve. Let carrots cool. Shake off any excess moisture by thumping sieve hard against the side of sink. Mix together vinegar, sugar and salt in a bottle. When carrots are cool, put them into the pickling mix. Pickle overnight before serving.

3. Mix together ingredients for meat balls of choice and divide into 20 portions. Roll each portion into a smooth rounded ball.

4. Drain rice well on paper towels to dry the grains a little. Mix black and white glutinous rice together if using both types. Alternatively, make all-white, all-black and white-black pearl balls.

5. Roll each meat ball in the rice, making sure that grains are pressed into the meat. Arrange meat balls in a steamer and steam for 45 minutes or till rice fluffs up and meat ball is cooked.

6. Serve pearl balls garnished with coriander leaves or place each pearl ball on a thin slice of pickled carrot and top with a coriander leaf. The three items can also be skewered together with a toothpick. Serve with light soy or fish sauce and one of the chilli sauces on the side.

GLOSSARY

Akali salts

Asafoetida

Bay leaves, Indian (left)

Cardamons, black (left) and green (right)

Cassia, Chinese (left), Ceylon (middle), Indonesian (right)

Chinese celery

Cloves

Coriander

Cumin, black (right)

Dates, West Asian

Daun salam (Indonesian bay leaf)

Fennel seeds

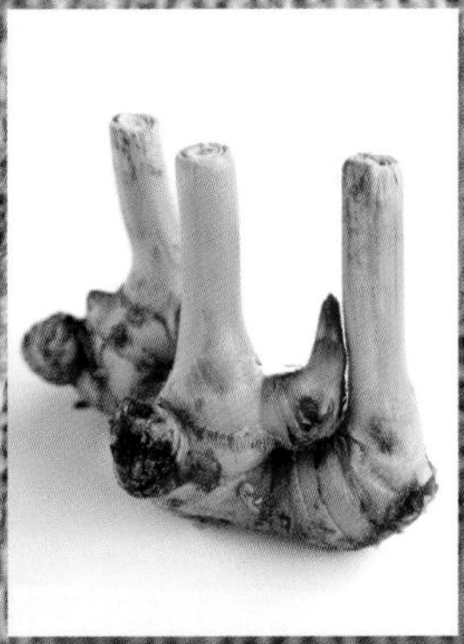

Galangal, greater

Katsuoboshi

Maldive fish

Nigella

Noomi Basra

Palm sugar

Pomegranate molasses

Pomegranate powder

Pandan leaves

Prawn paste, dried

Rose, dried

Safflower

Saffron

Sesame seeds, black (left), white (right), unhulled (centre)

Soy bean powder

Sweet potatoes

Tamarind paste

Taro (yam)

Turmeric, fresh (left), dried (right)

231

Advieh see Spice mixes

Alkali salts

Used only with glutinous rice to give it a springy texture in certain preparations and in the case of Chinese soda dumplings, to give it that characteristic soda flavour and yellow colour. Different kinds of alkali salts may be used from sodium carbonate to sodium bicarbonate to potassium bicarbonate. Lye water or alkali water sold as a food additive in Asian stores can contain a combination of various alkali salts. Sometimes alkali water may also be labelled "potassium water". Lye or alkali water sometimes goes by the Cantonese term *kan sui* or Hokkien term *kee chui*. Handling the alkali salts dissolved in water is easier in one sense but getting the quantities right is harder because it is not easy to gauge the strength of the salts. Be very careful with alkali salts as some types can cause severe burns. Another form of soda used in the preparation of glutinous rice cakes is sometimes called betel lime liquid or lime water.

Allspice (Pimenta dioica [L.] Mer.)

Also called Jamaica pepper, allspice came to be so-called because it smells of a combination of cinnamon, cloves and nutmeg. This spice is often used in West Asian cooking as well as in the spice mixes called *baharat*.

Alya

Fat rendered from the tail-fat of fat-tailed sheep, a breed of sheep common in West Asia, northern South Asia, western China and Mongolia, was once one of the two important types of oil in West Asia. The other was olive oil. *Alya* was the fat of choice in medieval Persia and West Asia particularly in pilafs which were always prepared for guests. While still used, *alya* has been increasingly replaced by other oils and in the case of pilafs, by ghee. *See also* Ghee

Anchovies, dried (Fam. Engraulidae Stolephorus indicus (Van Hasselt)

Known also as Indian anchovy but better known as *ikan bilis* in Malay, this little dried fish is sometimes seen fresh in wet markets in Southeast Asia but is more often found dried. There is also dried Japanese anchovies which are bigger and more expensive than the Southeast Asian variety. Dried anchovies are common in sambals eaten with rice. The dried fish is also fried with peanuts to make a snack and a side dish eaten with Southeast Asian coconut rice.

Anise, Aniseed see Fennel

Asafoetida (Ferula asafoetida)

This ancient spice once used by the Romans and Greeks is a resin from several species of ferula, a perennial herb plant grown in Iran, Afghanistan and India which are still the main sources and users of asafoetida. Its name combines the Persian word *asa* which means *mastic* or *resin* and the Latin word *foetida* which means *stinking*. In ancient times it was an expensive resin used in tiny amounts—as it still is—to flavour stews and rice dishes, pickles and chutneys. Sometimes called devil's dung because of its strong smell, it is known as *hing* in Hindi and *perungayam* in Tamil. *Hing* comes either as pure resin or compounded asafoetida which means it has been mixed with other ingredients. It is sold either as a solid cake or powdered. Compounded asafoetida smells less strongly than pure asafoetida. It is believed to have medicinal and antibiotic properties.

Attar see Roses

Aubergines (Solanum melongena)

Believed to be native to South Asia, aubergine cultivars come in colours that range from white to dark purple to bright purple to green. They can be round, ovoid, long and pendulous, fat and pendulous, or be tiny berries. Aubergines have a reputation for bitterness but with the exception of the tiny ones popular in Indochina, the green or purple aubergines found in Southeast Asia are so mild that they are also eaten raw. Aubergines are said to have been introduced to the Mediterranean region by Arab traders. Aubergines are especially popular in West Asia and common in rice dishes, stews and bread dips.

Baharat see Spice mixes

Bay leaves (Laurus nobilis; Cinnamomum tejpata; Eugenia polyantha Wight)

There are several kinds of bay leaves although the packaged bay leaves sold in western supermarkets is *laurus nobilis*, also called Turkish bay leaf. Indian bay leaf (*Cinnamomum tejpata*) was known to Roman cooks as *malabathrum* or *malobathrum*. The long three-veined leaves which look nothing like *laurus nobilis* come from a tree related to the cinnamon tree and native in the Himalayan region. They are sold loose in Indian grocery stores and today used mainly in South Asian cooking. Indonesian bay leaf (*Eugenia polyantha Wight*) or *daun salam* is not well known outside of Indonesia and Malaysia. The leaves of a large tropical tree, *daun salam* is sold as fresh leaves in wet markets and used both dried as well as fresh. It is milder than Turkish or Indian bay leaf. *Daun salam* is sometimes mistakenly called Indian bay leaf.

Belacan see Prawn paste, dried

Bhar see Spice mixes

Black cumin see Cumin, black

Bean curd *see* Soy bean

Bhar *see* Spice mixes

Brinjals *see* Aubergines

Cardamom *(Elettaria cardamomum White et Mason)*

Green or beige cardamoms are usually at least half the size of brown or black cardamoms or even smaller, have ridged skins and are more strongly flavoured. The green colour indicates that the cardamoms are freshly harvested, and the colour lightens to white or beige with age. Some green cardamoms are also bleached to get white cardamoms. If kept in an airtight container stored in the fridge, cardamoms remain fragrant for a number of years. Although cardamoms are usually used in their pods, the seeds can also be removed and pounded finely to make a little go a longer way. In West Asia, cardamom in coffee is popular and there is a belief that cardamoms are an aphrodisiac. In India, cardamom seeds are sometimes used in *paan* and in the dish of after-dinner spices that are chewed for sweetening the breath. *See also* Cardamoms, black

Cardamoms, black *(Amomum subulatum Roxb.)*

Also called Nepali cardamoms, these black or rather dark brown cardamoms are larger than green cardamoms, have somewhat thick ridged skins. The plant which is a member of the ginger family is native to the Himalayan mountain region. The spice has a somewhat smoky flavour because it is traditionally dried by smoking.

Cassia, Chinese *(Cinnamomum cassia (L.) Presl)*

A fragrant bark often called Chinese cinnamon, Chinese cassia is known as *gui pi* or *mu gui* in Mandarin and *gwai sam* or *yuk gwai* in Cantonese. Cassia comes in pieces of thick grey-brown bark with patches of pale grey, not neatly curled into quills unlike Ceylon or Indonesian cinnamon. Cassia is also vaguely bitter, unlike Ceylon cinnamon. It is one of the key ingredients in Chinese five-spice powders as well as in the spice mixes of parts of West and Central Asia both of which regions have centuries-old trade ties with China. Related to Chinese cassia is Vietnamese cinnamon which is a thinner bark that looks like its Chinese cousin.

Chinese celery *(Apium graveolens)*

Chinese celery is a relative of western celery but with a much stronger flavour. Sometimes called Chinese parsley, Chinese celery is used as a herb and so commonly used in soups and for making stock that its Malay name is *daun sop* (soup leaves). Chinese celery make a good base for vegetable stock as well as chicken stock. Substitute with western celery or parsley.

Cinnamon *see* Cinnamon, Ceylon; Cinnamon, Indonesian; Cassia, Chinese

Cinnamon, Ceylon *(Cinnamomum zeylanicum Blume)*

Coloured a reddish-brown and made up of very thin layers of bark curled into slender quills, Ceylon cinnamon is easily broken into smaller pieces as well as toasted and ground into powder, unlike the much thicker Indonesian cinnamon.

Cinnamon, Chinese *see* Cassia

Cinnamon, Vietnamese *see* Cassia

Cinnamon, Indonesian *(Cinnamomum burmannii [Nees & T. Nees] Blume)*

Compared to Ceylon cinnamon, Indonesian cinnamon is very thick and very hard to break apart into smaller pieces. So the cinnamon is used as you find it which is usually in 6 to 8 cm (2 1/2–3-in) lengths and in varying quill sizes. It is the commonest of cinnamons in Singapore. The colour of the cinnamon is like Ceylon cinnamon although it can sometimes be darker. The fragrance is also similar to Ceylon cinnamon but not as sweet as Ceylon cinnamon.

Chillies *(Capsicum frutescens)*

Sometimes called chilli peppers or red peppers to distinguish them from pepper (*Piper nigrum*), the distribution of this Mexican and Central American native is now worldwide with an equally wide variation of flavours from sweet to explosive. Sweet pepper as a spice is paprika and one of the common ingredients in West Asia spice mixes. Red chilli powder is more common in South Asian cooking along with fresh green chillies. Spicy chillies both fresh and dried are also key ingredients in many Southeast Asian spice pastes together with the root herbs like lemon grass and galangal.

Cloves *(Syzygium aromaticum, syn. Eugenia aromaticum or Eugenia caryophyllata)*

The aromatic dried flower buds of a tree in the Myrtaceae family, cloves are native to the Moluccas Islands (now called Maluku) in Indonesia but is now commercially grown in many parts of the world. Cloves are used in many Asian rice dishes especially West Asian pilafs. It was Arab traders who brought spices to Europe. The European desire to cut out the Arab middleman set the European explorers on their voyages of discovery that resulted in European colonies in Asia and South America.

Coconut *(Cocos nucifera)*

This very important member of the palm family contributes several key ingredients to Southeast Asian cuisines. The flesh of the nut is grated and two kinds of milk extracted. The first is the thick cream also known as first milk or *santan* which is squeezed out from grated coconut without or with just a tiny amount of water added. The second is called coconut milk and this is squeezed out from grated coconut mixed with some water. Grated coconut that has been squeezed for santan can be mixed with some water and squeezed to get second milk. This is thinner and not as rich as coconut milk from grated coconut squeezed for the first time. Another essential ingredient from coconut palms is palm sugar without which Southeast Asian desserts won't be what they are. Packaged coconut cream is widely available but some brands are too heavily boiled and have an oily flavour that makes it unsuitable for desserts flavoured with fresh coconut cream. However, this kind of coconut milk is fine for cooking with rice or enriching curries.

Coriander *(Coriandrum sativum)*
Both the seeds and the leaves are used worldwide. The seeds are an essential ingredient in South Asian and Southeast Asian curry powders as well as used on its own in various iconic dishes. The leaves are also known as cilantro and as a herb, coriander leaves are common in rice cooking.

Cumin *(Cuminum cyminum)*
Used as whole seeds and as powder, this spice is an important ingredient in West, South and Southeast Asian cooking. It is one of the basic ingredients in almost all curry powders as well the spice mixes of West and South Asia that are sprinkled on rice and all kinds of dishes. The powdered spice is also commonly used by itself when it really packs quite a flavour despite the small amount. *See also* Black cumin; Nigella

Cumin, Black *(Bunium persicum [Boiss.] B. Fedtsch.)*
In India, black cumin is also called Kashmiri cumin and sometimes mistaken for nigella. This particular cumin is not well known outside of Iran, Central Asia and northern South Asia in Kashmir, Pakistan and Afghanistan. Black cumin is used in meat and rice dishes such as biryani. If unavailable, substitute with cumin. *See also* Nigella

Curry leaves *(Murraya koenigii)*
The fresh leaves are used in South Asian, Sri Lankan and Burmese chutneys and curries. Known as *karupillay* in Tamil, the plant which grows into a small tree with bright red berries that attract birds is found in many an Indian home in Singapore, Malaysia, South India and Sri Lanka. Fresh and dried leaves may be available in Asian stores that carry Indian foodstuffs. If fresh leaves are found, freezing for later use is better than drying them.

Date palm *(Phoenix dactylifera)*
The date palm may be the oldest food plant in the world. Date seeds have been found in a cave dwelling in northern Iraq dating back 50,000 years with human cultivation of date palms starting circa 5,000 BCE. Believed to have originated from the region around the Persian Gulf, the date palm has significance in Judaism, Christianity and Islam, the three major religions that arose from West Asia. Dates remain an essential item in West Asian diets not only during religious occasions such as Ramadan. The fruit is eaten fresh and dried as well as used in cooking both savouries and sweets. A syrup is made from dates that is used as a sweetener and flavouring. There are different varieties of dates with varying flavours and textures.

Eggplant *(Solanum melongena) see* Aubergines

Fennel seeds *(Foeniculum vulgare)*
Originating from the Mediterranean region, the seeds are essential in Asian cooking from West to Southeast Asia but the leaves and fleshy stalks are not usually eaten, unlike in Europe. Called *jintan manis* in Malay (which translates into sweet cumin), *shamir* in Arabic, *saunf* in Hindi, there is some confusion between fennel and anise (*Pimpinella anisum L.*), with the same word referring to both spices. Anise or aniseed is sometimes sold as fennel although the two seed spices do not look alike apart from the pale brown colour. Fennel seeds are larger, straight with pointed ends; aniseed is smaller, rounder and with ends that curl slightly towards each other.

Fenugreek *(Trigonella foenum-graceum)*
Known as *hulba* in Arabic, *halba* in Malay, *methi* in Hindi and *venthiyam* in Tamil, the seeds are used in vegetable, dhal and fish curries in South and Southeast Asia where the leaves are also used as a herb. Fenugreek is also popular in West Asia in stews and the fresh leaves are used in Iran.

Galangal, greater *(Languas galanga or Alpinia galanga (greater))*
Known also as *khaa* in Thailand, *lengkuas* in Singapore and Malaysia, *laos* in Indonesia, greater galangal is an essential ingredient in Southeast Asian cooking and the one used in most Southeast Asian spice pastes. It is a large, tough, fibrous rhizome with an orange-red skin. Young rhizomes are paler, more tender but also less strongly flavoured.

Galangal, lesser *(Languas officinarum/ Alpinia officinarum (lesser))*
Known as *kencur* in Indonesia and *chekok* in Malaysia, both the roots and the leaves of this small herb-like plant which is a member of the ginger family can be used. The finely sliced leaves are used to dress rice salads while the root is ground into spice pastes. *Kencur* is hard to find outside of Southeast Asia but the roots do grow easily into an attractive houseplant with delicate white flowers.

Garam masala see Spice mixes

Ghee

Sometimes spelt *ghi* and called *samn* in Arabic, ghee is clarified butter with all the milk solids removed, thus yielding a fat that does not burn so easily, unlike butter. This is the oil of choice for preparing pilafs and festive dishes in South and West Asia but being more expensive than ordinary oils it is less common in home-cooking. The flavour of the ghee will affect the final flavour of the biryani. So if you buy tinned ghee instead of making your own, pick your brand of ghee with this in mind. Indian ghee and Australian ghee do not taste the same.

Ginger *(Zingiber officinale)*

This best known member of the ginger family is now found all over the world in mainstream supermarkets. It is an essential ingredient in many South Asian spice pastes and spice mixes. Ginger is sold as old or young ginger, the latter being a pale yellow-pink rhizome with very thin skin, milder flavour and less fibre than old ginger which is more common in spice pastes. Ginger comes as fresh roots as well as dried and ground. Old ginger is also pounded and the juice extracted for flavouring.

Indian bay leaves *see* Bay leaves

Kaffir lime *(Citrus hystric D.C.)*

Known also as *makrut* lime or *limau perut* in Malay, the peel of its fruit and leaves are used for their incredible fragrance. Found and used all over Southeast Asia, the leaves are usually used crushed in curries and stews and added at the last minute to retain the fragrance. The fruit itself has almost no juice and only the peel is used. Lime or lemon leaves or zest are poor substitutes.

Katsuoboshi see also Maldive fish

This is dried, smoked and mould-cured skipjack tuna or bonito *(Katsuwonus pelamis)* that resembles hard chunks of wood. Usually used thinly shaved, it is one of the basic flavourings in Japanese soup stock or dashi and is typically sprinkled into stews and soups. Shaved *katsuobushi* is sold in Japanese supermarkets. It can also be used like Sri Lankan Maldive fish for making *seeni sambol* (page 56).

Kimchi

The Korean national dish, kimchi is a fermented vegetable relish traditionally made with Tientsin cabbage but also with other vegetables. Instead of vinegar, fermentation gives kimchi its sourness and chillies, garlic and ginger add zing. The strongly-flavoured, spicy red kimchi exported all over the world is winter kimchi and traditionally pickled at the start of autumn in September for consumption during the winter months. Winter kimchi is very tasty as a side dish with Korean or Japanese rice dishes.

Kinako *see* Soy bean powder

Lemon *(Citrus limon [L.] Burm.)*

The English word *lemon* is derived from the Arabic *limun* which may not be surprising as it is believed that Arab traders were responsible for the spread of the wild varieties of citrus fruit. Lemon juice is often added to stews in West Asia and lemon wedges served with rice dishes and kebabs. Lemons may also be dried and dried lemon powder also used as flavouring. Citric acid sold as lemon crystals is a substitute for lemon juice.

Lemon grass *(Cymbopogon citratus)*

Lemon grass is a tropical grass that is an essential root herb in Southeast Asian cuisines. The most fragrant and edible part of lemon grass is the thick bulbous base near the woody root. If used whole, this bulbous part is bruised first. It is also one of the essential ingredients in many Southeast Asian spice pastes. Called *serai* in Malay or *sereh* in Indonesian, lemon grass is increasingly available fresh in Western supermarkets as well as Asian stores in areas where there are large communities of Southeast Asians.

Lime leaves *see* Kaffir lime

Lime water *see* Alkali salts

Limes, dried *see* Noomi Basra

Limu Omani *see* Noomi Basra

Lye water *see* Alkali salts

Makrut lime *see* Kaffir lime

Maldive fish

Made from tuna that is dried and smoked like Japanese *katsuobushi*, Maldive fish is also called Maldive fish chips. Traded from the Maldives in the Indian Ocean long ago, Maldive fish is today an integral part of Sri Lankan cuisine and used to flavour curries much like dried prawn paste *(belacan)* in Southeast Asian cooking or dried prawns in Chinese cooking. Like *katsuobushi*, Maldive fish has to be shaved thinly or chipped and pounded before cooking. *See also Katsuobushi*

Mint *(Mentha piperita)*

There are several varieties of mint, of which the most popular are spearmint and peppermint. Fresh mint is widely used in West and South Asian cooking with rice and lamb. Mint dries well and any extra can be dried for later use.

Nigella (Nigella sativa L.)

It looks a little like black sesame seeds but with very sharp pointed ends and has sometimes been confused with black sesame seeds. Nigella has also been called black cumin, black caraway and even simply black grains or black seeds. In India, nigella is called *kalunji* (black onion seeds) or *kalo jeera* (black cumin) in Bengali. In Malay, it is *jintan hitam* or black cumin. Nigella is, however, a very ancient West Asian spice whose flavour is released only when the seeds are chewed on. It is not commonly used outside of West and South Asia. Amongst Indians interested in ayurvedic medicine, nigella is considered a medicine and supposed to be used sparingly. Nigella is not to be confused with black cumin (*Bunium persicum [Boiss.] B. Fedtsch.*) *See also* Cumin, black

Noomi Basra

Also known as *limu Omani, limoo Amani, Basra* limes and *loomi Basra*, these dried limes came originally from the Persian Gulf region with Oman and Basra, Iraq, being the common sources although Iran produces dried limes too. Freshly dried limes are lighter in colour than older ones. The dried limes are used either whole in stews or ground up in spice mixes and seasonings. Dried limes are cooked with strong-tasting meat such as mutton to tone it down. The flavour of dried limes is not the same as fresh limes. A possible substitute for *noomi Basra* is the preserved limes made in Penang, Malaysia, as a snack. The fragrance is more like *noomi Basra* than fresh limes. These preserved limes sold in small boxes are not dry and hard like *noomi Basra* but damp and chewy as it is considered a dried fruit. They can be added to stews but not spice mixes. Look for *noomi Basra* in grocery stores patronised by West Asians. Here is a recipe for drying your own limes but I must add that I have never tried it: Boil the limes in salted water for 5 minutes, drain and spread on a wire-rack, then sun-dry till the limes are dry and light. Or spread the limes out in a food dehydrator if you have one.

Mustard seeds (Brassica nigra [L.] Koch)

There are also brown mustard seeds but black is more common in South Asian vegetarian cooking. The seeds can be used whole or ground to a paste.

Oils

Using the right oil gives you the authentic flavour: ghee gives pilaf its special flavour; sesame oil gives many Korean and Chinese dishes its special character. Try to use the oil specified in the recipe. Where not specified, use any bland oil such as corn, soy or sunflower.

Olives (Olea europaea; Heb. zayith, Gk, elaia)

Known in Hebrew as *zayith* and in Greek as *elaia*, the olive tree is believed to be a native of the area bordering the Mediterranean Sea now known as Palestine. The olive tree is believed to have been domesticated in this region more than 6,000 years ago. Olive trees are amongst the oldest cultivated trees in the world and were grown even before the invention of the alphabet, the basis of modern European languages, in 4000 BCE. The Phoenicians who invented the alphabet traded in olive oil with the ancient world and also spread the olive to the Greeks who adopted both the alphabet and the cultivation of olive trees. The word for oil comes from the Latin word for olive—*olea*. Olives and olive oil are common in West Asian salads, dips and pickles. It is also used in stews.

Onion (Allium cepa)

Believed to have originated from the region around Iran, onions have been grown and eaten for more than 5,000 years. Today it is among the top 10 vegetables eaten worldwide. The main types are white, red and yellow onions. They have different characteristics when cooked. Red and yellow to a lesser extent are the common varieties in Asia. Onions are common in many rice dishes as well as the stews eaten with rice, with fried onions flavouring many pilafs. Onions are said to have medical properties, one of which is as bacteriacide. *See also* Shallots

Palm sugar

This is sugar from the sap of a variety of palm trees. The sap is boiled down to a moist heavy sugar whose colour can be a rich dark brown or a pale off-white. Dark brown palm sugar is more likely to be from Sri Lanka, Malaysia and Indonesia, while the off-white variety is from Indochina. The dark brown palm sugar is more fragrant than the off-white variety. Palm sugar used in Southeast Asian rice desserts gives them their special flavour. There is no substitute for this flavour. Thai palm sugar may come as a thick pale beige paste packed into bottles or as beige cakes while the dark brown kind usually comes in cakes. In Malaysia and Singapore, palm sugar is known as *gula Melaka* because the best was said to come from this ancient west coast port. In Myanmar and Sri Lanka, it is called jaggery. The sweetness of palm sugar varies. Look for it in stores with Southeast Asian patronage. *See also* Dates

Pandan (Screwpine) leaf (Pandanus amaryllifolius Roxb.)

Although there are commercial attempts to reproduce the flavour of pandan as a food flavouring, these are not particularly successful if you are familiar with the unique fragrance of pandan leaves. Malay and Straits Chinese coconut rice or *nasi lemak* must be flavoured with *pandan* leaves. The fragrance of pandan leaves resemble that of good jasmine rice but lasts longer than that from hot jasmine rice whose smell dissipates when the rice cools. Pandan leaves are also an important leaf herb used in numerous Southeast Asian rice desserts whether these are boiled rice puddings or wrapped and toasted. The flavour of pandan combines well with that of banana leaves and palm sugar.

Parsley (Petroselinum crispum [Mill.] Nyman ex A. W. Hill)

This is a common herb in West Asia and often chopped and sprinkled in West Asian dishes. There is the curly leaf and flat leaf variety with the flat leaf being the more usual variety in West Asia.

Pomegranate (Punica granatum L.)

The juice and dried pomegranate "seeds" which also include the juicy fruit are used in Persian and North Indian cooking to give a sweet-sour flavour. Dried pomegranate seeds are to be found in West Asian grocery stores and used as a thickener for stew. There is also pomegranate syrup or molasses as well as pomegranate juice. Grenadine syrup is a more refined product made from boiled down pomegranate juice for cocktail mixes. Pomegranate juice has in recent years become trendy as a healthy fruit juice and the unsweetened juice may be found in the organic food sections of supermarkets. Because the tartness varies from molasses to juice, the only way to get a taste that suits you is to do the taste test during the cooking and to add the juice or molasses according to taste.

Prawns, dried

There are two types of dried prawns common in Southeast Asian markets, one consisting of small prawns with their shells removed, salted and dried and called *hae bee* in Chinese. The other type consists of very tiny whole prawns salted and dried in their shells. These tiny prawns are called *grago* in Malay. The larger *hae bee* is usually soaked in some cold water first to soften them and then pounded or chopped and fried to flavour certain rice dishes. It may be omitted if not available.

Prawn paste, dried

This is a thick flavouring made with tiny prawns and salt and usually dried into a block. It is called *belacan* in Singapore and Malaysia, *belacan* or *terasi* in Indonesia, *kapi* in Thailand, *mam tom* in Cambodia, *bagoong* in the Philippines and *pazon-nga-pi* in Myanmar. *Belacan* is an essential ingredient in many Southeast Asian spice pastes and should not be confused with sambal *belacan* which is a condiment made with *belacan* and fresh red chillies and sometimes with lime juice added. Sambal *belacan* is essential in Malay salads such as *nasi ulam* or fried rice. Outside of Southeast Asia, dried prawn paste can be found in most Asian stores and the best known is probably by Lee Kum Kee (a Hong Kong brand) in which the *belacan* has been blended with water into a thick pinkish-grey sauce. It is an acceptable substitute for Southeast Asian prawn paste when making spice pastes but is not suitable for toasting.

Rose (Rosa damascena Miller)

Rose water and rose oil called *attar* in India are used to flavour pilafs and biryanis in India and West Asia particularly Iran where flowery, fruity flavours are enjoyed and flowery scented rice not uncommon. Rose water and *attar* are more commonly used in various famous Indian desserts such as *gulam jamun* and *rasgulla*. In Singapore and Malaysia, red rose syrup is mixed with milk to make pink *susu Bandung* (Bandung milk). Why it is called *susu Bandung* is unclear as it does not seem to have originated from Bandung, Indonesia. With fruit and flower teas becoming fashionable, rose petal tea is a substitute for rose water or *attar*.

Safflower (Carthamus tinctorius L.)

The flowers of this plant which is grown for its oil seeds produce red and yellow dyes for food preparation. It is a cheap substitute for saffron and widely sold in West Asia as such.

Saffron (Crocus sativus L.)

Considered the most expensive spice in the world, saffron is regarded as the "king of spices" by pilaf cooks in West and South Asia. Believed to have originated from Persia (perhaps appropriately enough as it is believed that Persian cooks gave the world pilafs) the best saffron has a characteristic iodine-like flavour with a hint of bitterness if used in excess, and a rich orange-red colour. Hence the word "saffron" also means this rich orange-red colour. Saffron the spice is the stigmata harvested from the crocus flower and hundreds of thousands of flowers are needed to yield 1 kg (2 lb 3 oz) of saffron threads. The high cost of saffron comes also from the laborious hand-harvesting of the stigmata. A very ancient spice going back thousands of years, saffron is one of the ingredients of advieh or Iranian spice mix. Cheap ground turmeric is sometimes packaged as "saffron powder" which it is not. Saffron is always sold in tiny boxes and in very small amounts of stigmata threads. The threads are always soaked in some water or milk and mixed into the pilaf after the rice is cooked but before the infusion stage.

Saffron powder *see* Turmeric

Sesame (Sesamum indicum L.) *See also* Nigella

These come black or white with the white sesame seeds varying in colour from white to a pale brown. One of the oldest oil seeds, sesame seeds are used in many parts of Asia but in different ways. White sesame seeds are an important part of West Asian *za'atar*, Japanese and Korean sesame salts, as well as in various rice dishes. Sesame oil is more important in East Asia, the dark very fragrant oil being the result of heat treatment. Frying white sesame seeds bring out the fragrant oils. White sesame paste made from untoasted sesame seeds and known as tahini is important in West Asian cooking and is used to flavour stews as well as bread dips such as hummus. While sesame oil is used in East Asian savoury cooking, the seeds are more common in pastries and desserts. A famous Chinese dessert made with ground sesame seeds is sesame cream. Powdered sesame seeds both black and white are exported from China. South Asian cooking uses sesame seeds mainly in pickles and Indian sesame oil called gingelly oil is used in ritual cleansing. Indian gingelly oil does not smell as strong as Chinese sesame oil and is very pale in comparison.

Seaweed see Konbu

Shallots (Allium ascalonicum)
Believed to have originated from Palestine—Ascalon was an ancient Palestinian city—shallots, like onions, have been eaten for thousands of years. Similar in flavour to onions, shallots are smaller and ovoid rather than round like onions and may come in small clusters. Like onions in West Asian cooking, shallots are basic ingredients in Southeast Asian spice pastes. Flavourful fried shallots are used in porridges and rice soups and other rice dishes. Small shallots may be sprouted into spring onions.

Soy bean powder
Known as kinako in Japanese, toasted soy bean powder is sold in packets in Japanese supermarkets for coating mochi, a popular very sticky glutinous rice dessert.

Soy beans (Glycine max)
Cultivated in China for thousands of years, soy beans are made into numerous ingredients that feature prominently in the cooking of Asia. Chief among these are soy sauces, dark or light, tofu or bean curd, soft or firm, as well as soy bean sprouts which is not to be confused with mung bean sprouts. Soy bean sprouts have very large heads and are longer than mung bean sprouts. Cooked soy beans are also fermented to make different kinds of fermented beans used in East and Southeast Asian cooking. Chinese fermented soy beans is taucheo or doujiang which comes as whole beans. Japanese fermented soy beans is miso which comes in different stages of fermentation from pale blonde to dark brown and mashed to a smooth paste. The darker the colour, the stronger the flavour. Medium-brown miso is practically identical in flavour with Chinese taucheo and one can substitute for the other. Northern Chinese hot bean sauce is also made with broad beans and not necessarily with soy beans. It resembles Korean toenjang, a thick bean paste usually spiced with chilli used in Korean cooking.

Spice mixes see also Za'atar
In West and South Asian cooking, spice blends are used to season food during as well as after cooking with a small amount sprinkled on top of the cooked food. The blends called garam masala in South Asia, advieh in Iran and baharat in Iraq and other parts of West Asia and bhar in Lebanon differ from cook to cook and spice shop to spice shop. Where it was once traditional to prepare the spice mix

fresh from scratch, buying a packet of spice mix is becoming the norm. One way to get maximum freshness but without the bother of toasting and grinding seeds is to mix your own blend from various powdered spices or restrict the toasting and grinding to just one or two of the harder to find ground spices. All spice mixes should be refrigerated to extend shelf life. See pages 30–34 for various spice blends.

Spring onions (Allium fistulosum)
Sometimes called scallions, green onions or Welsh onions, this is probably the commonest of herbs all over Asia and invaluable as a quick garnish for rice. Sold in bunches, spring onions are almost always eaten raw although the Vietnamese make a delicate onion oil using fried green onions. Thai fried rice traditionally came with stalks of spring onion to be munched on with the fried rice. Spring onions are more commonly thinly sliced and sprinkled on dressed rice and porridges.

Star anise (Illicium verum Hooker fil.)
Its name in Chinese means "eight corners", a perfect description of this spice that is one of the ingredients of Chinese five-spice powder as well as commonly used whole in various stews and braised meats. The strong anise-citrus-clove fragrances make star anise great with strong-tasting meats like beef, mutton and duck in Chinese cooking. It is sometimes used whole in rice dishes.

Sumac (Rhus coriaria L.)
Sometimes spelt as sumach or shoomak, this souring agent is the ground leaves and berries of a plant native to West and Central Asia. It is used in West Asian food like tamarind is in Southeast Asia. The dried fruit is boiled to yield a sour liquid for cooking and the ground fruit is sold as a spice. The reddish-purple powder may be sold as pure sumac or mixed with other herbs such as thyme and sold as za'atar, a spice mix sprinkled on food, eaten with bread and used in cooking. Note that there are related ornamental plants found in the West that are also called sumac but which are poisonous. The original Aramaic word for this ancient spice was sumaqa and in Arabic, sumaq. See also Za'atar

Sweet potato (Ipomea Batatas)
A tropical American native, sweet potatoes are now found all over East and Southeast Asia. There are many varieties with the colour of the starchy flesh varying from white to bright orange to pale yellow to purple-white. Called yams in parts of the US, sweet potatoes are used in desserts as well as cooked with rice to pad out the rice in parts of Asia.

Taro (Colocasia Esculenta Schott)
Although commonly called yam in Singapore and Malaysia, taro must not be confused with sweet potatoes which are also called yams in the US. Taro is also called cocoyam or

dasheen. Found all over Southeast and East Asia, there are some 200 varieties with the cooked tubers varying in quality from fluffy to firm, the fluffy kind being considered the best variety. In Southeast Asian cooking, a firm taro is considered a dud and no amount of steaming or boiling will turn it fluffy. This starchy tuber has poisonous calcium oxalate crystals that irritate bare skin but which are destroyed with cooking. There are quite a number of iconic Southeast Asian and East Asian savouries and sweets made with taro or with taro as one of its main ingredients.

Terasi see Prawn paste, dried

Turmeric (Curcuma longa)
A member of the ginger family, it is a common root herb in South and Southeast Asia and the Himalayan regions. Ground turmeric, sometimes sold misleadingly as saffron powder, is important in rice cooking as a colouring to stain the rice yellow which is considered an auspicious colour. Turmeric comes whole as fresh or dried, as well as in powder form.

Thyme (Thymus vulgaris L.)
One of the ingredients of za'atar, one of several West Asian spice mixes, thyme is more common in Western cooking than Asian. The Arabic word for thyme is zatr or zhatar which explains why za'atar is so-called. Thyme, both dried and fresh, is an important European and American spice but almost never used in Asia outside of the West Asian countries such as Jordan. There are several varieties of thyme and thyme-like plants.

Vegetable oil see Oils

Wasabi (Wasabia japonica, (Miq.) Matsum., Eutrema japonica)
Wasabi is a rhizome with a brown-yellow skin, green-yellow flesh and a fragrance and heat that combines well with sushi. It is an expensive root herb because the plant is difficult to grow and the root must be served freshly grated. What is sold as wasabi whether in tubes and ready-to-serve wasabi or in powder form is actually not true wasabi but rather horseradish that has been coloured to mimic true wasabi's greenish tint. Mustard is sometimes added to reproduce wasabi's complex spiciness. Wasabi is one of the essential condiments with sushi.

Yam see Taro

Yoghurt
Yoghurt is a Turkish word for a fermented milk product that has been eaten in Central, West and South Asia for thousands of years. It is produced from milk fermented by lactic cultures.

The two main groups of cultures are *Lactobacillus bulgaricus* and *Streptococcus thermophilus*. Any kind of milk can be cultured and turned into yoghurt but the most common is yoghurt made from cow's milk. In India, yoghurt is called *dahi* in Hindi and *tyroo* in Tamil. Yoghurt is called *mast* in Farsi and *laban* in Arabic.

Za'atar
Originally *za'atar* referred to a wild herb that grew in the more verdant parts of West Asia as well as a family of herbs in the thyme, oregano and marjoram family. *Za'atar* today refers to a variety of spice blends made up of ground sumac, sesame seeds and green herbs. Its colour can range from reddish-brown to green, depending on the blend and what it is to be used for. The *za'atar* for sprinkling on food, to be eaten with bread or as a pizza bread topping differs from the ones used for stews and cooking. *See also* Spice mixes, Thyme.

BIBLIOGRAPHY

Andoh, Elizabeth. *At Home with Japanese Cooking*. New York, Alfred A. Knopf, 1980.

Ariff, Mervet, Azad Itrat, Benkhelifar, Aiicha, and Driscoll, Nadia. *Authentic Etiquette of Eating and Hosting from the Qur'aan and Sunnah with 150 recipes from around the world*. Qur'aan and Hadeeth text and meanings reviewed by Muhammad Al-Jibaly. 1st edition. [Birmingham, UK], Path to Knowledge Publishing, 1999.

Banarjee, Satarupa. *Cooking with Yoghurt*. New Delhi, UBS Publishers' Distributors Ltd, 1994.

Basan, Ghillie. *The Middle Eastern Kitchen*. London, Kylie Cathie Ltd, 2001.

Besa, Amy, and Dorotan, Romy. *Memories of Philippine Kitchens*. New York, Stewart, Tabori and Chang, 2006.

Boga, Yasa. *The Best of Indonesian Desserts*. Singapore, Times Editions, 1998.

Der Haroutunian, Arto. *The Whole Grain Cookbook*. London, Pan Books, 1987.

Gumus, Dogan. *The Art of Turkish Cooking*. English translation by Claudia Kutt and Gulgun Ercumen. Istanbul, Do-gu Yayinlari, 1988.

Hensperger, Beth, and Kaufmann, Julie. *The Ultimate Rice Cooker Cookbook*. Boston, Mass., The Harvard Common Press, 2002.

Homma, Gaku. *The Folk Art of Japanese Country Cooking: A Traditional Diet For Today's World*. Berkley, Calif., North Atlantic Books, 1991.

Ibrahim, Lamees. *The Iraqi Cookbook*. Northampton, Mass., Interlink Books, 2009.

Iny, Daisy. *The Best of Bagdad Cooking With Treats from Teheran*. New York, Saturday Review Press, 1976.

Kritakara, M.L. Taw, and Amranand, M.R. Pimsai. *Modern Thai Cooking*. Bangkok, Editions Duang Kamol, 1977.

Mallos, Tess. *The Complete Middle East Cookbook*. Boston, Charles Tuttle, 1993.

Mattoo, Neerja. *The Best of Kashmiri Cooking*. New Delhi, UBS Publishers' Distributors Ltd, 1995.

Mazda, Maideh. *In a Persian Kitchen*. Rutland, Vermont, Charles E. Tuttle, 1960.

Mi Mi Khaing. *Cook and Entertain the Burmese Way*. [Yangon, ?, ?]

Nakano, Yoshiko. *Where There Are Asians, There Are Rice Cookers: How National Went Global Via Hong Kong*. Hong Kong, Hong Kong University Press, 2009.

The National Indian Association of Women Cookbook. 10th edition. Calcutta, 2001.

Noh Chin-hwa. *Practical Korean Cooking*. Elizabeth, NJ, Hollym International Corp., 1985.

Noh Chin-hwa. *Traditional Korean Cooking*. Elizabeth, NJ, Hollym International Corp., 1985.

Noriega, Violeta A. *Philippine Recipes Made Easy*. Bellevue, WA, Paperworks Press, 1993.

Nuskha-e-Shahjahani: Pulaos from the Royal Kitchen of Shah Jahan. Translated [from the Persian manuscript] by Salma Husain. New Delhi, Rupa & Co., 2004.

Owen, Sri. *Indonesian Regional Cooking*. New York, St Martin's Press, 1995. First published in Great Britain by Doubleday.

Owen, Sri. *The Rice Book*. New York, St Martin's Press, 1993. First published in England by Doubleday.

Pham, Mai. *Pleasures of the Vietnamese Table; recipes and reminiscences from Vietnam's best market kitchens, street cafes, and home cooks*. New York, Harper Collins, 2001.

Ramazani, Nesta. *Persian Cooking: A Table of Exotic Delights*. Bethesda, Maryland, Iranbooks, 1997. Originally published by Quadrangle Books, New York, 1974.

Rice Almanac: Source Book of the Most Important Economic Activity in the World. Eds:
J.L. Mcclean, D.C. Dawe, and G.P. Hettel. 3rd ed. Wallingford, UK, CABI Publishing,
Published in association with International Rice Research Institute, International
Centre for Tropical Agriculture, West Africa Rice Development Association, Food and
Agriculture Organisation, 2002.

Roden, Claudia. *A New Book of Middle Eastern Food*. London, Penguin, 1986. First
published as *A Book of Middle Eastern Food* by Thomas Nelson 1968. New and enlarged
edition.

Salloum, Habeeb, and Peters, James. *From The Land Of Figs And Olives*. New York, Interlink
Books, 1997.

Scarre, Chris, Dr. Ed.-in-chief. *Timelines of the Ancient World*. Smithsonian Institution Review
Panel: Dr J. Daniel Rogers and Dr Jane MacLaren Walsh. London, Dorling Kindersley,
1993.

Shaida, Margaret. *The Legendary Cuisine of Persia*. New York, Interlink Books, 2002.
Originally published by Grub Street, London, 2000.

Tannahill, Reay. *Food in History*. New York, Stein and Day, 1973.

Veerasawmy, E.P. *Indian Cookery*. Bombay, Jaico Publishing House, 1956.

Zaouali, Lilia. *Medieval Cuisine of the Islamic World: A Concise History With 174 Recipes*.
Translated by M.B. De Bevoise. Foreword by Charles Perry. Translated from the original
French and the published Italian edition of the book. Berkeley, University of California
Press, 2007.

Zschock, Day. *The Little Black Book of Sushi*. White Plains, NY, Peter Pauper Press, 2005.

Websites

International Rice Research Institute <IRRI Home Page>
Gernot Katzer's Spice Pages <http://www.uni-graz.at/~katzer/engl/>
Asian Recipes Online <http://www.asianonlinerecipes.com/>
Numerous food blog sites where bloggers talk about their favourite family dishes

INDEX BY COUNTRY

This index groups recipes according to region and country, with the listing within these categories by one of the significant ingredients and not necessarily the rice. The index uses the English terms with the native name, if given, in brackets to aid identification. The entries may differ a little from the recipe titles which may be in non-English. Certain entries are also repeated where relevant.

Rice Pudding with Turmeric Leaf (Chepi Kheer) 195
Rice with Lime Dressing 144
Salmon Kedgeree 142
Sesame Rice 143
Shah Jehan-style Fish Pilaf (Mahi Pulao) 113
Shah Jehan-style Pineapple Pilaf (Ananas Pulao) 100
South Indian Tamarind Rice (Puliyodarai) 146
Spiced Rice (Masala Bhaat) 96
Tomato Rice 1–2 (Tamatar Pulao 1–2) 98
Vegetarian Pilaf 106
Yoghurt Rice 103

NEPAL
Dhal Curry 43
South Asian-style Chicken Biryani, Quick 83
Green Coriander Rice with Eggs 107

PAKISTAN
Green Biryani 108
Sweet Pilaf (Zard Pulao) 196

SRI LANKA
Milk Rice (Kheeri Bhaat) 68
Onion Sambal (Seeni Sambol) 56
Sweet Kheeri Bhaat (Coconut Rice Pudding) 196
Yellow Rice (Kaha Bhaat) 66

SOUTHEAST ASIA
(INDONESIA, MALAYSIA, MYANMAR, PHILIPPINES, SINGAPORE, STRAITS CHINESE)

INDONESIA
Chicken Porridge (Bubur Ayam) 185
Chicken Rice (Nasi Ayam) 79
Clove Rice 69
Coconut Rice (Nasi Uduk) 70
Fried Rice (Nasi Goreng) 154
Nasi Gurih 70
Nasi Kanten 200
Nasi Rawon 188
Pandan Rice 69
Rice Rolls (Lemper) 209
Wedding Rice Rolls (Jadah Manten) 209
Yellow Rice 64

MALAYSIA
Fried Rice (Malay/Straits Chinese Nasi Goreng) 131
Rice Cakes with Vegetable Curry (Lontong) 158
Nasi Ulam 156
Penang Oyster Porridge 180

MYANMAR
Burmese Coconut Rice 68
Onion Chutney 130
Salted Fish Fried Rice 130

PHILIPPINES
Arroz Caldo (Filipino Rice Soup) 174
Glutinous Rice Cake (Biko) 215

SINGAPORE
Beef Fried Rice 136
Chicken Rice 80
Chicken Rice with Pandan 82
Eurasian Corned Beef Fried Rice 134
Garlic Rice 82
Ginger Rice 81
Lobster Rice Soup 186
Millionaires' Fried Rice 136
Oyster Sauce Fried Rice 138
Porridge Side Dishes 172
Prawn Biryani 110
Rice Porridge Three Ways (Teochew Muay, Taiwan and Thai Porridge) 170
Rice Salad 156
Salted Fish Fried Rice 130

STRAITS CHINESE
Black Glutinous Rice Porridge (Pulot Hitam) 200
Chicken Curry 42
Durian with Rice 210
Fermented Glutinous Rice (Tapeh) 215
Fish in Four Flavours, Straits Chinese Fried 40
Fried Rice (Malay/Straits Chinese Nasi Goreng) 131
Glutinous Rice Rolls with Prawns and Spices (Pulot Rempah Udang) 216
Glutinous Rice with Coconut Topping (Pulot Inti) 215
Kuih Lopes 214
Kuih Salat 212
Kuih Wajek 215

Meat Curry Powder, Straits Chinese 35
Nasi Lemak 68
Nasi Lemak Chilli Sambal 41
Nasi Ulam 156
Peanuts and Anchovies 40
Rice Dumplings 220
Sambal Belacan 41
Vegetable Curry, Malay/Straits Chinese (Sayur Lodeh) 158
Yellow Rice (Nasi Kunyit) 64

WEST ASIA
(IRAN, IRAQ, JORDAN, GULF ARAB STATES, LEBANON, PALESTINE, SYRIA, TURKEY)

IRAN
Advieh 1–3 31
Cherry Rice 84
Chicken Pilaf (Shirini Polo) 86
Chicken Pilaf with Apricots 78
Grilled Lamb and Rice (Chelo Kebab) 152
Herb Rice (Sabzi Polo) 72
Rice and Lentils (Ada Polo) 74
Rice Cake (Kateh) 23
Rice Crust (Tah-Deeg) 22
Rice with Ghee 70
Parboiled Rice 23
Lamb Stew with Lime (Khoresht Ghaimeh) 149
Chicken Peach Stew (Khoresht-e-Hulu) 150
Meat Stew in Pomegranate-Walnut Sauce (Khoresht Fesenjaan) 150

IRAQ
Aleppo Rice Rolls (Kubbat Halab) 226
Baharat 1–4 32
Chicken with Red Rice (Dajaj Wa Timman Ahmer) 88
Jewish Slow-cooked Chicken with Rice (Tabyeet) 118
Kubbat Halab, Quick 226
Ladies' Finger Stew, Iraqi (Margat Bamia) 50
Lentil Porridge (Mujadara) 190
Minced Meat Stew with Rice (Timman Queemah) 166
Saffron Rice (Timman Z'affaran) 76

JORDAN
Baked Kofta in Yoghurt Sauce, Jerash-style, 48

INDEX OF BASIC RECIPES